Art of Leadership

Art of Leadership

C.H. Sharma

RANDOM

RANDOM PUBLICATIONS
NEW DELHI (INDIA)

Art of Leadership

ISBN 978-93-5111-917-3

Published in 2016 in India by

RANDOM PUBLICATIONS

4376-A/4B, Gali Murari Lal, Ansari Road
New Delhi-110 002
Phone : +9111-43580356, 011-23289044, 011-43142548
e-mail: sales@randompublications.com,
info@randompublications.com, randomexports@gmail.com

Reprinted 2023

Type Setting by : Friends Media, Delhi-110089
Printed at : Replika Press Pvt. Ltd.

Preface

The concepts of leadership, related elements, styles and characteristics are described. Attempts have been made towards understanding major dimensions of leaders and leadership with focus on team leadership.

Leaders help themselves and others to do the right things. They set direction, build an inspiring vision, and create something new. Leadership is about mapping out where you need to go to "win" as a team or an organization; and it is dynamic, exciting, and inspiring.

A leadership style is a leader's style of providing direction, implementing plans, and motivating people. It is the result of the philosophy, personality, and experience of the leader. Rhetoric specialists have also developed models for understanding leadership.

Leadership, although largely talked about, has been described as one of the least understood concepts across all cultures and civilizations. Over the years, many researchers have stressed the prevalence of this misunderstanding, stating that the existence of several flawed assumptions, or myths, concerning leadership often interferes with individuals' conception of what leadership is all about.

The book "Art of Leadership" provide important background on leadership and management development programs, defining the parameters of a typical organizational program.

– Author

Contents

1

Leadership

INTRODUCTION

During the early nineteenth century, Wellington's and Napoleon's observations made sense. With the onset of battle, communications became muddled, artillery was immobilised, and a commander's ability to control his forces was limited. Consequently, the leadership of a single general could prove decisive in battle by maintaining clarity of command and control. We are now at a totally different stage of warfare. This not to say that the fog of war has completely lifted, but visibility and synchronised actions, and the speed, precision, and lethality of response is beyond comparison to anything that has preceded it.

The battlefield success of the doctrine and technology of Network Centric Warfare was not based upon a single brilliant plan, or a single individual or group, but rather was a property of the network, both technologically and organisationally. As Operation Iraqi Freedom so vividly illustrated, battle plans can now be changed very rapidly, affecting all aspects of operations—strategy, tactics, logistics and PSYOPs, operations, kinetics, and all types of forces.

The competencies that make NCW a success are network properties; they are no longer solely the province of charismatic leaders or chance, but the result of diverse competencies and a new understanding of the role and growth of network leadership, and how it is learned and rewarded.

GOOD LEADERS

Good leaders are made not born. If you have the desire and willpower, you can become an effective leader. Good leaders develop through a never ending process of self-study, education, training, and experience (Jago, 1982). This guide will help you through that process.

To inspire your workers into higher levels of teamwork, there are certain things you must **be**, know, and, do. These do not come naturally, but are acquired through continual work and study. Good leaders are continually working and studying to improve their leadership skills; they are NOT resting on their laurels.

Before we get started, lets define leadership. Leadership is a process by which a person influences others to accomplish an objective and directs the organisation in a way that makes it more cohesive and coherent. This definition is similar to Northouse's (2007, p3) definition — Leadership is a process whereby an individual influences a group of individuals to achieve a common goal.

Leaders carry out this process by applying their leadership knowledge and skills. This is called Process Leadership (Jago, 1982). However, we know that we have traits that can influence our actions. This is called Trait Leadership (Jago, 1982), in that it was once common to believe that leaders were born rather than made.

Roles and Relationships

Roles are the positions that are defined by a set of expectations about behaviour of any job incumbent. Each role has a set of tasks and responsibilities that may or may not be spelled out. Roles have a powerful effect on behaviour for several reasons, to include money being paid for the performance of the role, there is prestige attached to a role, and a sense of accomplishment or challenge.

Relationships are determined by a role's tasks. While some tasks are performed alone, most are carried out in relationship with others. The tasks will determine who the role-holder is required to interact with, how often, and towards what end. Also, normally the greater the interaction, the greater the liking. This in turn leads to more frequent interaction. In human behaviour, its hard to like someone whom we have no contact with, and we tend to seek out those we like. People tend to do what they are rewarded for, and friendship is a powerful reward. Many tasks and behaviours that are associated with a role are brought about by these relationships. That is, new task and behaviours are expected of the present role-holder because a strong relationship was developed in the past, either by that role-holder or a prior role-holder.

Culture and Climate

There are two distinct forces that dictate how to act within an organisation: culture and climate.

Each organisation has its own distinctive culture. It is a combination of the founders, past leadership, current leadership, crises, events, history, and size. This results in rites: the routines, rituals, and the "way we do things." These rites impact individual behaviour on what it takes to be in good standing (the norm) and directs the appropriate behaviour for each circumstance.

The climate is the feel of the organisation, the individual and shared perceptions and attitudes of the organisation's members. While the culture is the deeply rooted nature of the organisation that is a result of long-held formal and informal systems, rules, traditions, and customs; climate is a short-term phenomenon created by the current leadership. Climate represents the beliefs about the "feel of the organisation" by its members. This individual perception of the "feel of the organisation" comes from what the people believe about the activities that occur in the organisation. These activities influence both individual and team motivation and satisfaction, such as:

- How well does the leader clarify the priorities and goals of the organisation? What is expected of us?
- What is the system of recognition, rewards, and punishments in the organisation?
- How competent are the leaders?
- Are leaders free to make decisions?
- What will happen if I make a mistake?

Organisational climate is directly related to the leadership and management style of the leader, based on the values, attributes, skills, and actions, as well as the priorities of the leader. Compare this to "ethical climate" — the feel of the organisation about the activities that have ethical content or those aspects of the work environment that constitute ethical behaviour. The ethical climate is the feel about whether we do things right; or the feel of whether we behave the way we ought to behave. The behaviour (character) of the leader is the most important factor that impacts the climate.

On the other hand, culture is a long-term, complex phenomenon. Culture represents the shared expectations and self-image of the organisation. The mature values that create tradition or the "way we do things here." Things are done differently in every organisation. The collective vision and common folklore that define the institution are a reflection of culture. Individual leaders, cannot easily create or change culture because culture is a part of the organisation. Culture influences the characteristics of the climate by its effect on the actions and thought processes of the leader. But, everything you do as a leader will affect the climate of the organisation.

EARLY LEADERSHIP

Leadership among Greek warriors was based upon "a first among equals" principle. Such leadership was a product of a culture of equality and mutual accountability. In a very tangible sense, cultures are networks of social relationships. Military cultures, especially in battlefield situations, have highly articulated roles and codes of conduct and mutual accountability.

Although an individual may gain prominence and status apart from a group, it is often not the result of individual achievement, but how the individual exemplifies certain traits that represent the best traits of that group, such as sacrifice, decisiveness, courage, initiative, and prowess. In fact, to attribute successes to the individual that derive from the group undermines a core principle of true leadership: the group comes before the individual.

In the following stanzas taken from Alfred Lord Tennyson's ode to Wellington, many of the qualities that continue to make leaders great are captured:

- ...Mourn for the man of amplest influence, Yet clearest of ambitious crime, *our greatest yet with least pretence,* Great in council and great in war, Foremost captain of his time, *rich in saving common-sence* And, as the greatest only are, In his *simp licity sublime...*
- ... *Who never sold the truth to serve the hour,* Nor palter'd with Eternal God for power; Who let the turbid streams of rumor flow Thro' either babbling world of high and low; Whose life was work, whose language rife *with rugged maximus hewn from life;* Who never spoke against a foe; Whose eighty winters freeze with one rebuke All great self-seekers trampling on the right. *Truth-teller was our England's Alfred named;* Truth-lover was our English Duke; Whatever record leap to light He never shall be shamed...

By embodying the best qualities of a group, a military leader does not try to elevate himself above his peers, but brings Honour and distinction to them, be they his company, brigade, division, or service. These qualities of "simplicity sublime" and "truth-teller" are parts of the best of military culture. They are hard to transfer from the field of battle into bureaucratic and administrative assignments, where often different kinds of codes of conduct are rewarded. As noted earlier, small networks of 150-200 individuals can still be coordinated by face-to-face relationships and personal codes of Honour and accountability.

At such a scale, combat relationships are more transparent and accountable, and hence, not so easily "gamed" and "politicised" as in hierarchical, formal organisations. It is not surprising that many who succeed on the battlefield fail to adjust to the rules of a bureaucratic organisation, whose codes of success are often at variance with those of the battlefield group.

In bureaucratic organisations, successful leadership can entail the subordination of the interests of the group to the promotion of the individual, as visibility to outside parties is associated with an individual leader who is *personally* credited with a certain policy or success. Under such circumstances, the leader in bureaucratic groups becomes a marker, a kind of shorthand, for the success or failure of an issue, policy, or campaign—not the exemplar of the group.

This kind of leadership can entail taking much of the credit and little of the blame, thereby undermining the very principles of transparency and accountability upon which effective peer networks depend. The systemic failure of corporate leadership and governance in the United States over the last 10 years can be partly attributed to a bureaucratic culture wherein a company's success was almost totally attributed to the skills of the CEO and senior management.

This was reflected in senior executive compensation packages that ballooned to 301 times the average worker's pay package. Yet when the downturn came, and even widespread fraudulent practices were revealed, very few corporate leaders were held accountable, and shareholders and employees assumed the bulk of the losses. These failures were neither personality - nor individually-based, but were systemic in terms of how leaders were selected, cultivated, rewarded, and held accountable. The systemic subversion of governance leadership roles needed to achieve independence, truth telling, and transparency has been its own kind of perverse "network effect." This chapter's treatment of leadership is not founded upon any "great man" leadership model.

This is not to say that individual qualities are not important, but rather that sustainable and replicable qualities of leadership are treated here as a network property, made possible by the combination of the character of the social network and the individuals themselves. Moreover, it will be argued that there are several different types of leadership roles and the relative importance and combination of these roles depends upon the circumstances and structure of the organisational networks involved.

THE CORE OF LEADERSHIP

Leadership is the art of engaging the hearts and minds of ordinary people to achieve extraordinary results. This Isn't the Company I Joined, I've been interviewing gifted leaders from a wide range of industries. Each has his or her unique corporate responsibilities to carry out. Each has to deal with widely different competitive pressures, customer demands, marketing strategies, stockholder expectations, and Workforce requirements.

Each represents an organisation that is affected in specific ways by the new global economy, the IT revolution, the disappearance of stable currency values worldwide, and the collapse of the old Industrial business paradigm as an organising model for their companies. But all share one thing in common: an apparently innate set of emotional and intellectual qualities that make up what I call the Core of Leadership.

The components of that core are:

- Vision.
- Integrity.
- Trust.
- Values.
- Vulnerability.
- Motivation.

Together they produce what we all instantly recognise as leaders. How they do it is easier to note in practice than it is to define in principle. Because we aren't just talking about special skills or strategies these people exercise, we're talking about individual character. Like the force of gravity or the lump of uranium in a nuclear generator, the leadership core works invisibly. And like any living system, it sometimes works intuitively and mysteriously. But its positive effects upon others can be readily observed, and those observations, in turn, can be put to immediate use by anyone charged with leading fellow employees at any level of an organisation.

LEADERSHIP AS VISION

In contrast to control-minded authority of the past, today's leaders must exercise power through a shared purpose and vision. An organisational vision is not the same as long-range or even strategic planning. Planning is a linear process; progression Towards a goal. Vision is more holistic — a sense of direction that combines a good business strategy with a comprehensive organisational purpose that declares its own importance.

A vision describes a business as it could become over the long term and outlines a feasible way of achieving this goal. To transform an organisation, leaders must adopt and communicate a vision of the future that impels people beyond the boundaries and limits of the past. Leaders who articulate such visions aren't mystics, but broad-based thinkers who are willing to take risks. Visionary leaders don't have to be brilliant, highly innovative, or incredibly charismatic. But they do have to be intently focused on what it is they are trying to achieve. Fred Smith, ounder and Chief Executive Officer of Federal Express, put it in these very practical terms: "If there is any indication that the leader is not totally committed to achieving the vision, then all the sweet talk in the world will not get people to support it."

LEADERSHIP AS INTEGRITY

A leader must be seen to stand for something, must act from deep-seated principles, and must rely on strong personal beliefs. Leading with integrity implies a willingness to embody the attitudes and Behaviours you want to see in employees. Steve Wikstrom is the Co-Chief Executive Officer of Reell Precision Manufacturing Corporation, a $35 million company that produces wrap spring clutches and constant torque hinges for foreign and domestic customers. "In our company we try to create relationships that allows us to 'call' one another on Behaviour that doesn't represent our values.

A recent example occurred during the development of our latest strategic plan. Every year we get the top dozen leaders together once a week, for six to eight weeks. At the end of each of the weekly sessions, we have 'homework' assignments to prepare for the next meeting. At the beginning of one session, a participant told us that at the last meeting he had offered to send us information that we had agreed to review and return with our comments. He went on to say that of the twelve messages he sent out, only three responses had been received. He then asked all of us what we were going to do about this issue of 'irresponsibility.' The meeting stopped and we discussed how to better Honour our commitments. Right at the top of the organisation's leadership, we are aware of the need to mirror whatever Behaviour we expect to receive in kind."

LEADERSHIP AS TRUST

Until recently, managers' primary function has been supervision — telling employees what to do and measuring how well they did it. But the new breed of knowledge workers increasingly don't want or need to be micro-managed. They need to be set free in the sphere of their own authority. They need to be trusted. Trust is an attitude of confidence in another person, a positive set of expectations about that person's competencies and character. The powerful influence of one person's expectation on another's Behaviour is known as the "Pygmalion Effect." Eliza Doolittle explains it in George Bernard Shaw's play Pygmalion: "You see, really and truly, apart from the things anyone can pick up, the difference between a lady and a flower girl is not how she behaves but how she's treated. I shall always be a flower girl to Professor Higgins because he always treats me as a flower girl and always will; but I know I can be a lady to you because you always treat me as a lady and always will." The difference between leaders who complain about the lack of responsibility in today's employees and those who speak with pride of the creative contribution and dedication of their staff may lie in the realm of management's expectation.

LEADERSHIP AS VULNERABILITY

Recognition of the potential of the Workforce for contributing solutions to organisational problems has increased while the infallibility of leaders and the certainty of management tasks have declined. The unquestioned authority of leaders in the corporation of the past has been replaced by the need to acknowledge the expertise of those below, and to enlist employees as true partners. Moving from a model in which leadership made all the decisions and knew all the answers to an organisational environment of openness, candor, and empowerment takes a willingness by leaders to become and remain highly vulnerable.

There has never been a time in which our organisations have experienced more uncertainty and chaos. It may sound ironic, but the corporate leader who can say to his or her employees, "Sure, I'm scared too," will have done more for company morale with that single admission than a dozen phony pep talks ever could. Why? Because, as Sue Swenson, president of Leap Wireless, observes: "When leaders are perceived as human and vulnerable, employees identify with those attributes and begin to see the potential for success and leadership in themselves."

LEADERSHIP AS VALUES

Webster defines value as "a principle, standard or quality considered inherently worthwhile or desirable." The root is the Latin valor, which means strength. Values are a source of strength for an enterprise or an individual. As leadership strategy moves from coercion to cooperation, the key to bonding people to the goals of the organisation automatically becomes the intangibles — relationships, commitments and shared values.

Founding President and Chief Operating Officer of Ritz-Carlton Hotels, "Values are the heart and soul of our organisation. It is not enough for people just to fill functions. They have to know what we are all about." Leaders must stay focused on values and keep them energised — which is the hardest part.

For that, you need to find processes that renew and revitalise values. One process that Ritz-Carlton uses is called the "Line Up." Fifteen minutes before shift begins every day, the leader of the line up goes through the basics of that day. Employees of R-C all over the world are reminded of the same "value of the day," as prepared by the corporate office. Added to that is a "teaching" — an issue brought to our awareness, based on customer-service input, and then some comments about the daily value that are customised to the individual hotel.

LEADERSHIP AS MOTIVATION

The secret to being a great motivator is realising that motivation isn't something that can be forced or ordered. Motivation is an intrinsic capacity of human beings that can be tapped, nurtured, and developed — but never coerced. In essence, all motivation is self-motivation.

It manifests when leaders hold a compelling vision of the future, have a strong personal desire to realise the vision, and possess the ability to engage people's individual motivation in the common cause of that vision so that a true interconnection emerges. Motivational leaders inspire exceptional levels of commitment and performance. Prior to forming his own public relations firm, Bob Dilenschneider served as president and CEO of Hill and Knowlton.

He talked with me about his most memorable boss: "Barney Clarke, the CEO of Columbia Gas Systems, was brilliant — a genius who thought way outside the box. Although I suspect he had the answers all the time, he spent hours talking with us, involving us and making us feel as if we were an integral part of a huge change — as if we were making history.

And he got so much out of all of us. We'd work 'round the clock. Working with Barney was exciting, exhausting, incredibly intense, and absolutely thrilling!"

THE RELATIONSHIP BETWEEN LEADERSHIP AND INFLUENCE

What is the relationship between leadership and influence? Is leadership always influence and is influence always leadership? To say that leadership always entails influence is like saying that all snow is white. It's true but the inference doesn't work the other way. That is, not all white things are snow. Similarly, although all leadership is influence, there are lots of types of influence that don't count as leadership.

Here are a few examples:

- Intimidating or forcing someone to do something.
- Bribing someone to do your bidding.
- Paying for things you want someone to do for you.
- Teaching a student to behave better in a classroom.
- Encouraging your children to eat their vegetables.

The last two examples are not leadership because they have nothing to do with a group striving to achieve a goal. Teaching students and encouraging children to eat vegetables is for their own interest, not for the good of a larger group. Similarly, salespeople may be very influential but their influence is self-interested. The salesperson and the customer do not constitute a group.

FORMAL AUTHORITY AND LEADERSHIP INFLUENCE

Suppose you are the boss and you decide to ramp up production by 50 per cent, requiring everyone to work faster and longer hours without overtime. Is this leadership? No, it may be influence but it is not leadership because the employees had no choice.

To say that leadership is informal influence means that followers have a free choice to follow or not. What are some prime examples of true leadership influence? One of the most familiar is Martin Luther King's demonstrations against segregation on buses which led the U.S., Supreme Court to outlaw this practice. King had no formal authority or other power to move the U.S., government.

This is the real meaning of leadership. Another example of genuine leadership influence was the Sony employee who influenced management to adopt his idea for PlayStation despite their feeling that Sony wasn't into making toys. Whenever you convince your colleagues or your boss to adopt a new idea, you have shown them leadership. Or, you might simply set a good example for others and, if they follow, you have shown leadership. Market leading businesses influence their competitors to change course, another example of real leadership. When executives make decisions that take their teams in new directions, they are taking managerial actions, NOT showing leadership because employees have no choice. To count as leadership, influence must be informal and followers must get on board completely of their own free will. Leadership is also a group phenomenon and is aimed at serving some unselfish purpose, something to improve the group's effectiveness. For this reason, even if your children willingly follow your plea to eat their vegetables, you haven't shown leadership because you and your kids are not a group working Towards a common goal.

INFORMAL LEADERSHIP AND INFLUENCE

We often distinguish between formal and informal leadership. The only difference between these concepts is that the informal leader takes charge informally. The formal leader has been given formal authority to govern the group while the informal leader is granted this role by the group itself. The informal leader has personal power - charisma, knowledge or some form of expertise that the group values. It is vital to recognise that the conventional concept of informal leadership is not the same thing as saying that all leadership influence is informal. The conventional concept, formal or informal, is all about being in charge of the group. The claim made here is that real leadership is independent of position, as it was in the case of Martin Luther King. He was not an informal leader in the conventional sense - the Supreme Court didn't recognise him as their informal leader.

As another example, a technical geek might influence his peers to adopt a new piece of software. He has influenced them informally. However, this geek might be so disinclined to manage the group that they might never view him as their informal leader - someone who they would turn to for help in organising their day to day work, who they would look to for advice and the resolution of conflict. The geek's informal leadership is a one-off act, not an ongoing role. His influence is informal but he is not what we normally call an informal leader because he has no interest or ability to take charge of the group in a managerial sense. So what? By reformulating the meaning of leadership, I am saying that the old distinction between formal and informal leadership is outdated. There is really only formal and informal management because all leadership is informal where this term refers to willingly following someone's lead NOT to informally taking charge of the group.

LEADERSHIP DEVELOPMENT

Leadership development refers to any activity that enhances the quality of leadership within an individual or organisation. These activities have ranged from MBA style Programmes offered at university business schools to action learning, high-ropes courses and executive retreats.

DEVELOPING INDIVIDUAL LEADERS

Traditionally, leadership development has focused on developing the leadership abilities and attitudes of individuals. Just like people aren't all born with the ability to, say, play football like Zinedine Zidane or sing like Luciano

Pavarotti, people aren't all born with the ability to lead. Different personal characteristics can help or hinder a person's leadership effectiveness and require formalised programmes for developing leadership competencies. Yet, everyone can develop their leadership effectiveness. Achieving such development takes focus, practice and persistence more akin to learning a musical instrument than reading a book. Classroom-style training and associated reading is effective in helping leaders to know more about what is involved in leading well.

However, knowing what to do and doing what you know are two very different outcomes; management expert Henry Mintzberg is one person to highlight this dilemma. It is estimated that as little as 15 per cent of learning from traditional classroom style training results in sustained Behavioural change within the workplace.

The success of leadership development efforts has been linked to three variables:

- Individual learner characteristics.
- The quality and nature of the leadership development Programme.
- Genuine support for behavioural change from the leader's supervisor.

Military officer training academies, such as the Royal Military Academy Sandhurst, go to great lengths to only accept candidates who show the highest potential to lead well. Personal characteristics that associated with successful leadership development include leader motivation to learn, a high achievement drive and personality traits such as openness to experience, an internal focus of control, and self-monitoring.

Development is also more likely to occur when the design of the development programme:

- Integrates a range of developmental experiences over a set period of time. These experiences may include 360 degree feedback, experiential classroom style Programmes, business school style coursework, executive coaching, reflective journaling, mentoring and more.
- Involve goal setting, following an assessment of key developmental needs and then evaluate the achievement of goals after a given time period.

DEVELOPING LEADERSHIP AT A COLLECTIVE LEVEL

More recently, organisations have come to understand that leadership can also be developed by strengthening the connection between, and alignment of, the efforts of individual leaders and the systems through which they influence organisational operations. This has led to a differentiation between leader development and leadership development. Leader development focuses on the development of the leader, such as the personal attributes desired in a leader, desired ways of behaving, ways of thinking or feeling. In contrast, leadership development focuses on the development of leadership as a process. This will include the interpersonal relationships, social influence process, and the team dynamics between the leader and his/her team at the dyad level, the contextual factors surrounding the team such as the perception of the organisational climate and the social network linkages between the team and other groups in the organisation. One practical example of developing leadership specifically so as to influence an organisation's safety culture is described by Burman and Evans. Both forms of development may mutually influence each other, as exemplified in the concept of "Deep Change" in Robert E. Quinn 's 1996 book of the same title.

Leadership development can build on the development of individuals to become leaders. In addition, it also needs to focus on the interpersonal linkages between the individuals in the team. In the belief that the most important resource that an organisation possesses is the people that comprise the organisation, some organisations address the development of these resources. In contrast, the concept of "Employeeship" recognises that what it takes to be a good leader is not too dissimilar to what it takes to be a good employee. Therefore, bringing the notional leader together with the team to explore these similarities brings positive results. This approach has been particularly successful in Sweden where the power distance between manager and team is small.

SUCCESSION PLANNING

The development of "high potentials" to effectively take over the current leadership when their time comes to exit their positions is known. This type of leadership development usually requires the extensive transfer of an individual between departments. In many multinationals, it usually requires international transfer and experience to build a future leader. Succession planning requires a sharp focus on organisation's future and vision, in order to align leadership development with the future the firm aspires to create. Thus successive leadership development is based not only on knowledge and history but also on a dream. For such a plan to be successful, a screening of future leadership should be based not only on "what we know and have" but also on "what we aspire to become". Persons involved in succession planning should be current leadership representing the vision and HR executives having to translate it all into a Programme.

Meir Jacob and Amit Cohen three critical dimensions should be considered:

1. Skills and knowledge.
2. Role perception and degree of acceptance of leading role.
3. Self-efficacy.

These three dimensions should be a basis of any leadership succession programme.

TYPES OF NETWORK LEADERSHIP ROLES

There are at least eight different kinds of leadership roles in a networked organisation. Each of these can be associated with specific network *signatures* consisting of patterns of links and nodes and the social rules governing their interactions. For example, some network leaders, such as visionaries, primarily generate new information and typically do not directly request others to perform tasks for them.

They generally work in conjunction with connector and facilitator leaders who help them get their information out. Connectors, unlike visionaries, may have many symmetric dyadic interactions and act as gateways for a variety of sub-networks, whereas truth-teller leaders may only interact weakly with other members, having strong ties with a relatively small number of peers. Many of these roles can coexist in the same person.

However, as networks grow in scale and complexity, these roles often become highly differentiated and expressed as Searle's *institutional* facts.

The Exemplar or "Alpha Member"

Most peer networks, whether they are military, technological, recreational, adolescent, criminal, terrorist, artistic, professional, or athletic, are founded by individuals who exemplify the standards and qualities that characterise the best competencies of the peer network. These are the role models that others imitate. Sometimes their role can be simply symbolic, even ceremonial, but they are non-etheless important in setting the tone and culture of the organisation. Successful and charismatic founders of new organisations, from Bill Gates, Steve Jobs, and Sam Walton to Osama Bin Laden and Aum Shinrikyo, all embody values and personalities that become the values of their organisation. These leaders also exemplify the assessment criteria and set the standards for becoming a member of a network. In the military, each Service has its own types of exemplars: pilots and Seals for the Navy; Green Berets, and Rangers for the Army; and fighter pilots for the Air Force. These exemplars embody what is considered the most difficult and admired professional qualities that set that Service apart.

The Gatekeeper

For every network there are membership rules—criteria for being included, retained, elevated, and excluded. The gatekeeper decides who is in and who is out. In Congressional politics, the party leadership plays this role by deciding who gets what committee assignments and whose bills take precedence in a legislative agenda. This is a role that President Johnson as the former majority leader of the Senate understood brilliantly, while President Carter—an outsider, visionary, truth-teller, and moralist—never fully appreciated. In many military organisations, the drill sergeant often plays multiple leadership roles, acting as exemplars, enforcers, and gatekeepers. He weeds out recruits whom he believes fail to meet the standards of his unit. The gatekeeper role is especially important for elite units that seek to achieve a high degree of exclusivity based upon exceptional standards of excellence. Like the doorman to exclusive clubs, the gatekeeper role is a combination of truth-teller, applying the standard for admittance, and enforcer, denying admittance to those parties that fail the test.

The Visionary

The role of the visionary leader is to imagine futures, determine what is limiting about the present, and show what is possible in the future. Visionary leaders such as Steve Jobs, Winston Churchill, Walt Disney, Craig Venter, Billy Mitchell, and Thomas Edison are a constant fount of new ideas and are "at war with the present." Many high technology startups have been founded by visionaries, but eventually end up being run by operatives or fixers.

The visionary leader imagines new possibilities, creating new institutional facts and realities, and therefore plays a critical role in moving networked organisations in new directions. This is an absolutely critical role in the start-up or crisis phase of an organisation. However, it can also be disruptive in circumstances where continuity and execution are critical to success.

Visionaries play a vital and sometimes contentious role within the military. They are often the first to see weaknesses in prevalent military doctrine, to espouse new technologies and doctrines, and therefore, to challenge current leadership and entrenched interests. Consequently, unless they are able to prove themselves within wartime, their ideas can languish for decades.

Rare are the individuals such as Lord Nelson or Napoleon, who were both visionaries and the senior commanders. In the case of Billy Mitchell, Col. John Boyd, or even Winston Churchill, it was only later in their careers that their innovations were appreciated. However, as the nature of warfare today is in constant transition with respect both to doctrine and new technologies, the visionary will have increased influence. The visionary role is best coevolved with that of the truth-teller.

The Truth-Teller

In every network organisation, someone has to keep the network honest. This entails the very challenging task of identifying free riders and cheaters. In knowledge-based organisations, it is also about ferreting out half-truths, spin, blunders, and lies. Such a leadership role can become easily compromised.

Like the accounting function in a corporation or the judicial function in the legal system, truth-tellers can lose their independence, and Hence, effectiveness. Since, these are often the first roles to go in times of stress, successful leadership is exemplified here by independence, transparency, accuracy, and candor in the face of enormous pressure. As Tennyson's ode to

Wellington eloquently and astutely expresses, truth telling and resistance to the lure of fame go hand in hand and are a critical and enduring signature of effective leadership.

One of the arguments for modesty in leadership is that the lure of celebrity and its attendant rewards can compromise independence and hence, credibility. Therefore, if a leader is to be an effective truthteller, he or she must also be credible, and even the hint of self-dealing can undermine his effectiveness. The challenges are especially acute and consequential within military organisations. If credibility breaks down, trust soon becomes the next casualty, and then the overall effectiveness of the chain of command.

The admonition "Don't shoot the messenger" is taken from military experience and reflects the high potential cost of reporting unwanted information. In response to such pressures, the military developed the doctrine of "ground truth" after the Vietnam War. The truth telling goal is to provide authenticated and accurate reporting of the outcomes of missions.

It can take enormous courage to resist the inevitable pressures of peers and superiors to report what they want to be known, rather then the truth of the matter. Being a truth-teller can be highly unpopular and a long road to advancement.

Even highly established and previously unchallenged military institutions can come under enormous pressure for truth telling. The armed forces newspaper, *stars and stripes*, undertook its own "ground truth investigation" into morale in Iraq in 2003 and was widely censured by some members of Congress and threatened with a reduced budget for its reporting. Similarly, the success and credibility of the enquiry into the alleged tortures within Abu Ghraib and elsewhere within Iraq and Afghanistan will depend upon individuals assuming very strong truth-teller leadership roles.

The Fixer

This is an individual who knows how to get things done and measures him or herself not just by how many people they might know, but rather how they can get things done that others cannot. Such individuals are results oriented. They "know where the bodies are buried" and what "makes people tick." In politics, they are the operatives, the Mr. Fix-its. They are all about opening and closing loops—getting tasks done. In Tennyson's words, they abide by the "rugged maxims hewn from life."

They are without illusions and are inherently pragmatic. They may interact with a range of other network leaders—visionaries, truth-tellers, and connectors—but always with a concrete outcome in mind. Within the military there is the archetype of the "scrounger," an individual who is highly skilled at finding and assembling "found" materials, people, and resources to solve a variety of human and mission needs, from chocolate and silk stockings during

WWII, to scrap iron as armor platting for Humvees in Iraq. Fixers are gifted improvisers, what the French call "bricolagers," who take common available materials and repurpose them into something useful.

In contrast to those who work through formal channels and depend upon approved procedures, fixers typically are "rule benders" and work through informal networks. Within the British Army during the late Victorian period, the Quartermaster was famous for the orderly but creative acquisition of supplies under the most trying and unpredictable of circumstances.

The Connector

These network leaders participate in multiple social networks, connecting not only with a large number of members, but a highly diverse number of members as well. They are known for having numerous friends, connections, and contacts—for being consummate networkers. Like the visionary leaders, they can introduce variety and options into a network through the diversity of people with whom they interact.

They are critical for identifying and accessing new resources and helping to get a message out. By building links across network boundaries, they can help a networked organisation break out of the "lock ins" of scale-free networks and introduce greater diversity, and Hence, robustness. During WWII, General Eisenhower as the Supreme Allied Commander developed a reputation as a highly accomplished connector leader by virtue of his ability to relate to the different interests and cultural styles of the allied commanders.

He was able to make and sustain connections among contending parties in order to keep the alliance together and on course. He was also able to exercise significant control over those whose primary allegiances were to different military organisations.

The Enforcer

In smaller networks, this role is often combined with that of the gatekeeper and even the truth-teller. However, in larger networks it is an independent role. Enforcement can mean physical coercion, but more often entails psychological or peer pressure.

Like the truth-teller function, independence and transparency are critical for overall network effectiveness. Clearly, force and military means are the enforcement methods of last resort, but are necessary in order to buttress other forms of enforcement, which can vary from guilt and shame to legal redress. Most networks have their own forms of redress and enforcement that entail exclusion.

The power of ostracism in Greek city-states, for example, was extremely effective because it not only removed an individual's right of protection but destroyed their social identity as well. An exceptional example of a senior commander acting to enforce discipline across all levels of command was the Duke of Wellington's order during the Peninsular Campaign in 1807. Wellington issued an order that any breach in military discipline towards the treatment of the Spanish civilians and military would result in an immediate flogging and hanging. Paul Kennedy, this order was enforced with impartiality and force and was instrumental to Wellington's success.

The Facilitator

In order for a network to grow and evolve, it must be able to add new members and reach across network boundaries in order to do so. The facilitator role is pivotal in creating communities or sub-networks that provide the greatest form of network value. By assuming a leadership role in helping others, facilitators create value that benefits an entire network or community, whereas a connector, while playing a similar value creation role, appropriates value to himself and only indirectly benefits the overall group.

The role of facilitator in many respects resembles that of the "community coordinator" in the development of communities of practice, a method developed for helping to create and leverage knowledge. Within the military, this role is filled primarily as a staff function to a commander, and therefore may not appear to have the caché of the connector or visionary leadership roles. However, in networked organisational structures where decisionmaking is be more distributed and less hierarchical, this leadership role is vital to coordinating and enabling other actors and decisionmakers.

In the case of networked organisation, the facilitator role and the associated skills of enabling cooperation and self-organisation will play a more critical role than within current hierarchical organisations. When self-synchronisation depends upon peer-based cooperation, the facilitator role is a prerequisite for effective operations.

THE EXISTING SITUATION OF LEADERSHIP, MANAGEMENT AND COMMAND

Therefore, most Officers hold a basic definition of each component of this trinity and indeed, how they are related to each other.

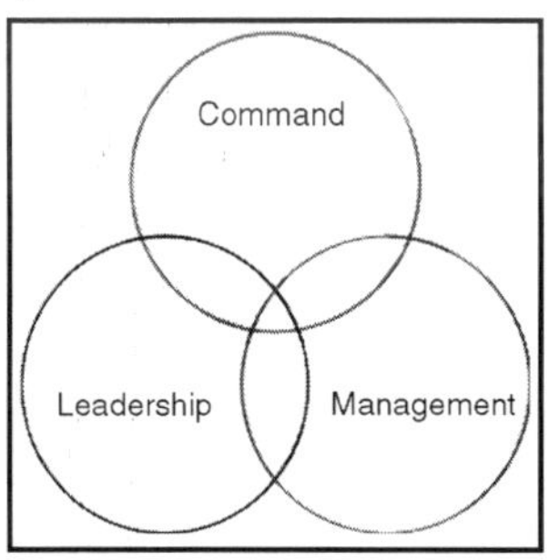

Fig. A Simple Interrelationship Between Command, Leadership and Management

AN ALTERNATIVE MODEL FOR LEADERSHIP, MANAGEMENT AND COMMAND DOCTRINE

A New Approach

The world of work is changing at a rapid pace, greatly influenced by shifting societal trends, technology and globalization. These trends cannot be treated as separate issues; their interdependent effects will continue to exert powerful influences on the RAF, its culture and how leadership, management and command is viewed and practiced. Therefore, proactively adapting leadership, management and command philosophies to meet these challenges of this millennium will enhance the overall effectiveness of the RAF.

To date, however, the military style of leadership, management and command training (and doctrine) has often focused on 'hard' skills such as planning, organising and directing, all within an impersonal hierarchical structure. However, current thinking (from both the corporate world and academia) is now shifting towards an increase in the importance of 'soft' skills such as communication and motivation. In addition, the supply of human capital is undergoing a pervasive and powerful shift: the workforce – in the UK today – is a mosaic of individuals with varied ages, backgrounds, skills, aspirations and styles. Therefore, the definition of diversity will continue to evolve from merely race and gender to include age, disability, family structure, sexual orientation, ethnic culture, language and religious affiliation. Thus, organisations that can lead, manage and command this diversity will have a greater opportunity to thrive in the years ahead.

Indeed, research now shows that 'respect for the differences in people' is now one of the most important qualities in a leader. Further, the Industrial Society has now published research on the 5 weakest areas of the less successful leader:

- Failure to be sensitive to peoples feelings.
- Failure to recognize other peoples' stress.
- Failure to develop and guide staff.
- Failure to encourage feedback on their own (the leader's) performance.
- Failure to consult those affected before making decisions.

Although the above list was generated from Industrial leaders, it has equal applicability to the RAF and serves to reinforce previous arguments about the personal or human side to leadership, management and command: the above failures are all 'soft-skill' orientated.

Therefore, to undergo the necessary transformation in leadership, management and command philosophies and, therefore, to provide the relevant training, Officers will now have to accept the feasibility of working alliances with subordinates who question old practices and propose new solutions and to think of the link between them, as essential as the link between strategy and operations. Furthermore, it will be vital that too much emphasis is not put on leadership traits or leadership doctrine from the past: even successful organisations may undo themselves in the future if they continue to act today in the way they have acted in the past.

Organisational Leadership

Leadership exists at every level of the organisation and it is not a function of rank. From the airmen in the RAF today, to the Air Marshals at the corporate level, everybody has an individual leadership responsibility to those who serve under them. Indeed, given their generational characteristics, the recruits of tomorrow (both Officers and airmen) will likely have little organisational loyalty: they will view themselves as 'free agents' who will only work for a leader who provides the most developmental challenges and opportunities, that focus on promoting commitment, involvement, intellectual stimulation and individual consideration. Therefore, leaders will need to routinely ask for inputs from subordinates and share information freely while focusing on trust, respect and empowerment that will help to strike a balance between the leaders and those that they lead.

Leadership and Strategy

The necessity to make the right decision and then carry it out in the 'right way,' is reflected currently by the Services formal decision-making tool, the Formal Estimate. In essence, this estimate consists of 4 parts:

- Mission Analysis.
- Evaluation of factors.
- Consideration of courses of action.
- Selection of the best course of action.

Whilst the format of the process and the language has a unique military favour, the concept of working out what to do, analysing the relevant factors, and selecting a choice, is the basis for strategy in the civilian world. In this context, it is here that leadership is closely related to strategy. Strategy is the job of projecting into the future: surveying an organisational situation or problem and deciding between alternative courses of action that have many possible consequences. Again, strategic leadership exists at every level in the RAF.

THE CHARISMATIC APPROACH TO LEADERSHIP

The trait approach to leadership began with the premise of the "Great Man Theory of Leadership." This theory claimed that there are certain people who appear to have special leadership skills that have seemed to set them apart from the average person. As discussed there, researchers' attempts to find traits that distinguished "born leaders" from everyone else were unsuccessful.

However, history is full of political and religious leaders such as Mohandas Gandhi and Martin Luther King Jr. who seem to fit the "Great Man" idea. Weber also worked on understanding the process by which some leaders can inspire such devotion and commitment from followers. Weber proposed the idea that some leaders are perceived by their followers to possess a trait he called "charisma." The term "charisma" was originally defined as the ability to perform religious miracles. Weber used the term to refer to leaders who appear to have exceptional, almost superhuman abilities to perform difficult feats and succeed in seemingly impossible situations.

Some theorists have extended the idea of "charismatic" leadership to the context of organisations. There have been well-publicized examples of organisational leaders who seem to arouse the same type of response in their followers as Gandhi and King did in theirs. Examples include Steven Jobs of Apple Computers, Lee Iacocca of Chrysler, and Mary Kay Ash of Mary Kay Cosmetics. Although there are differences among these and other cases, a few similarities are clear. In each case, the leader was able to inspire unusual effort and performance from their subordinates. Because of this inspiration, Jobs and Ash turned their ideas into corporations worth hundreds of millions of dollars, and Iacocca took a large corporation on the bring of insolvency and converted it into a large profit maker.

Many reports have been published listing the strategies and tactics of successful charismatic leaders. Sometimes these reports have implied that charismatic leadership is the key to organisational success. However, it should be clear from everything we have written about leadership that such sweeping generalizations are likely to be wrong. In many if not most cases, the success of charismatic leadership is short-lived. In fact, as we shall describe, the characteristics that can help make a person a charismatic leader often include the seeds of their eventual downfall. Lee Iacocca, for example, eventually became more concerned with improving his public image nationally than with the operations of Chrysler. As a result, Chrysler once again began struggling. Although Iacocca (and Chrysler) eventually righted themselves, there are many cases in which charismatic leaders have led once-successful corporations to ruin.

Having said this, research suggests that charismatic leadership can lead to organisational success. Bryman (1992) reported that measures of charismatic leadership tend to correlate with job performance at about.3. Although this is not a very high correlation, it must be considered that the success of charismatic leadership depends on the situation in which the leader and the members of the leader's group of subordinates are in.

In fact, a number of theorists have proposed very similar theories of charismatic leadership. These theories are comparable to Fiedler's contingency theory of leadership in some ways. They propose that certain traits lead some people to adopt what could be called a "charismatic" style of leadership. There are certain situations in which this style leads to successful performance and some in which it backfires. However, this theory differs from Fiedler's in that communication is specifically described as part of the leadership process. Thus charismatic leadership theory fits the input-process-output model.

A THEORY OF CHARISMATIC LEADERSHIP

Leader characteristics. According to most theorists, charismatic leaders have a number of traits in common. First, they are high in the "Nepo," or "need for power" characteristic. Second, they have great self-confidence. Third, they are unusually willing to take risks. Fourth, they have a strong conviction in the correctness of their beliefs.

Of course, having relevant traits is not enough. Advocates of the trait approach ignored the fact that leaders are most successful when performing tasks they are skilled in or knowledgeable about. Successful charismatic leaders generally have a great deal of experience in the organisational area in which they are managing. Lee Iacocca had many years of experience in the automobile industry before he took charge of Chrysler.

Finally, charismatic leaders have developed a "vision" of what their group or organisation should stand for. This vision is often abstract, but must be simple enough for subordinates to understand. For example, Steven Jobs had a quest to improve education through making computers available to the average person. Mary Kay Ash wanted to help women learn to become independent and empower themselves.

Thus, charismatic leaders have particular traits, relevant experience, and a vision.

Leader style. Charismatic leaders perform a number of characteristic behaviours that we can call a "charismatic" style of leadership. First, they are able to successfully communicate the content of their vision and confidence in their subordinates' ability to attain it. They do this through both verbally and non-verbally. Verbally, charismatic leaders tend to use a number of different strategies when addressing subordinates. Shamir, House, and Arthur (1993) have listed some of the strategies.

- They often refer to shared values and moral justifications. As discussed, Jobs described Apple's goal as bringing computers to schools and the average person. He also referred to Apple as if it were David taking on IBM as an evil Goliath. Thus the competition between the two multimillion dollar corporations was represented as a fight between good and evil.
- They tend to refer to distant goals rather than near ones. For example, Jobs was more likely to discuss what Apple Computer could eventually do rather than what would occur tomorrow.

- They tend to emphasize the collective identity of the subordinates. The needs of the corporation are always more important than the desires of its individual members for the charismatic leader.
- They tend to express high expectations for the subordinates. Their task is described as very difficult, and success as requiring great effort.
- They tend to show great confidence in the ability of their subordinates. No matter how hard the task as they have described, the subordinates have the "right stuff" to succeed.

Second, charismatic leaders deliver this content in an animated non-verbal style. They have great variety and dynamism in their voice, and use gestures, movements and eye gaze actively when talking.

In addition, the charismatic leader must "live" their vision. They must seem to practice exactly what they preach. If a charismatic leader expects their subordinates to put in sixty hour weeks, the leader should put in seventy. If the charismatic leader wants subordinates to look upon the organisation as their family, they must take on the role of maintenance leader. If a charismatic leader wants the subordinates to trust their own abilities and judgements, the leader must trust the decisions and actions that the subordinates take.

Situational factors. This style of communicating and behaving appears to be successful only in the right situations. First, the circumstance should be particularly stressful or uncertain. This would occur either in a newly-formed organisation or in an older organisation that is having problems that threaten its survival. Second, the subordinates need to be creative and dedicated. What can happen is that subordinates of this type who have become apathetic under other leadership styles are inspired when a charismatic leader takes over. Third, the leader must have the power to actually follow through on their vision. For example, if a middle-level manager has certain goals that those higher up in the organisation do not value, then the manager will not be able to see their ideas through. Results. When a charismatic leader is able to communicate their vision and their confidence in their subordinates' ability to attain it, and when the situation is as we have described, the result in subordinates is

- Unusual confidence in and loyalty to leadership
- Strong identification with the organisation and the leader's vision
- High motivation and commitment
- Increased self-confidence.

This can result in tremendous effort on the part of the subordinates and great success for the organisation.

However, when the situation does not meet the requirements we listed above, the charismatic leader will not be successful. Further, although many of the traits of the charismatic leader are important in helping the leader succeed, they can and often do lead to eventual failure. Their high self-confidence and need for power can lead them to be extremely autocratic and self-serving. They can have little tolerance for subordinates disagreeing with them, and often blame others for their own errors. In the long-run, subordinates often tire of the charismatic leader, lose their dedication, and may even work to undermine the leader's authority. Further, if the charismatic leader has superiors in the organisation, they often tire of the leader's style and become unwilling to tolerate any mistakes on the leader's part. There have been many reported examples of charismatic leaders who were not at the top of their organisation being forced to leave the organisation after only three or four years.

Explanation for the Effect

In attempting to explain why charismatic leaders succeed or fail, theorists have been influenced by the contingency view that leader characteristics and situational factors are input variables affecting the outcome of job performance. They also have also considered the process variables of communication and behaviour linking the input and output. In addition, they have described the importance of the subordinates' perception of the charismatic leader in a way reminiscent of the perceptual approach. In fact, they have used the same psychological factors in their explanations as the perceptual theorists.

Salience effects. As we have discussed, perceptual theorists stress the impact of the salience of a group member's behaviour on the odds that they will emerge as a group leader. Analogously, charismatic advocates talk about the importance of salience in the process by which a leader becomes viewed by followers as charismatic. The charismatic leader's animated communication style and inspirational communication content serve to catch the subordinates' attention, as does their attempts to behave consistently with their vision.

Implicit theory effects. We have also described the role of implicit theories in the process by which group member form leadership-relevant impressions of one another. One theorist, Conger (1989), has particularly emphasized the importance of the impression formation process on subordinates' evaluations of their leader as charismatic. After viewing the leader's salient behaviour, subordinates may then use their implicit leadership theories to develop a particularly strong and positive impression of the charismatic leader. Like the "ideal organisational leader," the charismatic leader may be viewed as confident, visionary, trustworthy, and expert. Analogously, if things start going bad, the subordinates might change their impression of the leader to include characteristics the "ideal leader" does not have. The charismatic leader might now be viewed as stubborn, dictatorial, and back-stabbing.

Although there is great agreement among scientists about this theory, much of it is speculative, and little of it has received research examination. A welcome addition to the work on charismatic leadership has come from two experiments testing it. Howell and Frost study. Howell and Frost (1989) gave business students an individual task to perform in which each acted like a business executive making a decision. Two other confederates also "worked" on the same individual task side-by-side with the real participant. The task was described by a "leader" displaying one of the following leadership styles:

- Task-oriented. The leader described the task and told the participants to follow the instructions, show good judgement, and be methodical in their work. The task-oriented leader sat behind a desk to distance themselves from the participants, used a "moderate" tone of voice, intermittent eye gaze, and "neutral" facial expressions (no smiling or nodding).
- Maintenance-oriented. The leader described the task and told the participants to relax, work at their own pace, and not to worry about the outcomes. They sat at the front edge of the desk to lessen interpersonal distance, used a "warm" tone of voice, direct eye gaze, and "friendly" facial expressions (smiling and nodding).
- Charismatic. The leader described the task, emphasized the importance of the results to the future of the students' coursework, encouraged them to be creative, and expressed confidence in their ability. They alternated between sitting at the front edge of the desk and pacing around the room, used a "captivating" tone of voice, direct eye gaze and "animated" facial expressions.

Then the leader left and the task began. At one point, the leader returned and spoke again. The task-oriented leader reminded the participants to focus on the task, the maintenance-oriented leader thanked the participants for performing it, and the charismatic leader reiterated confidence in the participants' abilities to perform the task. At the end of the task, the participants reported their feelings about their experience on a questionnaire.

The findings showed support for the value of charismatic leadership. The charismatic leader condition was highest on task performance, with the maintenance leader condition lowest. Turning to the questionnaire measures, the charismatic and task-oriented leader conditions were highest on participants' satisfaction with their own performance and the charismatic and maintenance-oriented leader were highest on participants' satisfaction with the leader.

Kirkpatrick and Locke study. Kirkpatrick and Locke (1996) noted a weakness with the Howell and Frost study. Howell and Frost had the charismatic leader both exhibit a certain style of non-verbal behaviour and express a particular type of communication content. The results showed that this combination led to more satisfactory results for the charismatic leader conditions than for the task-oriented or maintenance-oriented. However, there is no way of knowing whether it was non-verbal style or verbal content that led to these findings. Kirkpatrick and Locke then performed a study to distinguish between these two possible factors. They asked participants to perform a routine assembly task, in which they inserted pages into notebook binders according to a set of instructions. Before the task began, a leader either expressed a "vision" (commitment to quality) and confidence in the participants' abilities, or merely gave factual information about how paper is made. Half of the "vision" and half of the "factual" leaders used the charismatic non-verbal style as Howell and Frost had defined them. The other half used Howell and Frost's task-oriented non-verbal style. Kirkpatrick and Locke found that of the two possible factors, only the verbal expression of vision had an effect on quality of performance. This effect was indirect, working through changes in participants' goals and self-confidence.

A SEMIOTIC APPROACH TO STUDY CHARISMATIC EFFECTIVENESS

Though Lewin's theory provides a useful framework for integrating the motivational forces underlying charismatic leadership, it offers little guidance about how one might operationalize and test the theory's predictions. Since, Lewin's theory addresses socially-constructed meaning, an appropriate tool for empirical investigation is semiotics - the science of signs.

Semiotics explicitly deals with the interface between individual and social values, the critical issue in effecting social change. As a formal mode of analysis, it identifies the rules that govern the construction and destruction of meaning in a particular social system. Like Lewin's (1951) field theory, it rests on the assumption that all meaning is contextualized and resides in a system of underlying oppositions. Semiotic analysis offers a systematic means of linking multiple surfacelevel expressions of opposition to the system of meaning that underlies them.

The Structure of Meaning

The units of signification in any communicative act express meaning through their differences (Eco, 1979). The social codes that regulate meaning arise from underlying oppositional structures. Two kinds of opposition interact to give meaning to a sign, or a unit of signification. For a given sign, the first opposition, called contradiction, expresses the total absence of the sign. For example, non-love contradicts love; non-conventional contradicts conventional. A sign can express either end of the contradiction, but not a combination (*e.g.*, one cannot express love and non-love at the same time).

For a given sign, the second kind of opposition, called contrariety, includes another sign. The contrary sign, by social construction, also opposes the meaning of the original sign. For example, hate is contrary to love; innovation is contrary to convention. A given sign may have multiple contraries. Hate, loathing, and disgust each opposes love. Innovation, deviance, and spontaneity oppose convention. In contrast to contradictions, a sign may include combinations of contrary meaning or values. For example, one can express love and hate at the same time, though this combination expresses a complex and unstable condition. Based on our theoretical framework, a charismatic leader performs the task of translating innovative ideas into socially conventional ideas, that is, translating a value into its contrary. Semioticians typically employ a visual representation of a value's contradictions and contraries. Figure depicts such a representation for the values of convention and innovation. Convention is contrary to innovation, and non-convention is contrary to non-innovation. Convention contradicts non-convention, and innovation contradicts non-innovation. This framework sets the stage for our subsequent discussion of leaderfollower interactions.

By practice, the dominant positive social value, in this case social convention, occupies the upper left corner of the semiotic square. Conventions represent socialized, institutionalized, and endorsed ideas or values, the frame through which most people experience their world. The contrary, innovation, occupies the upper right corner. The contradictions occupy positions diagonal to the values they oppose. The values depicted in a semiotic square relate hierarchically; the assertion of the dominant value presumes the negation of its contrary (convention presumes non-innovation). However, negation of the contrary only allows the possibility of the dominant value (non-innovation makes convention possible). Understanding the process by which one can effect change in social norms depends on this hierarchy.

Replacing one dominant value with another directly (*e.g.*, replacing convention with innovation), or shifting the balance of one in favour of the other, will lead to increasing tension that is likely to undermine change efforts (Lewin, 1951). According to Lewin, an effective change strategy begins by "unfreezing" the dominant value. Here, this means advocating its contradiction (*e.g.*, replacing convention with non-convention before advocating innovation.

The terms and structural relations defined by a semiotic square can provide a theoretical starting point for identifying the components of meaning of any set of values within a social system. In this study, they depict values concerning leadership, values believed to both motivate leaders and to serve as standards by which society judges leader effectiveness.

The Social Structure of Values

Leaders operate and are judged within a social system whose values define what is "effective." Values associated with charismatic leadership imply rejection of the status quo and reliance on non-conventional solutions to existing social problems. These values oppose the socially-endorsed dominant cultural values represented by conventional leadership. Neither the conventional nor the innovative values contain "objective" content. Conventional leadership may mean one thing in the U.S., and something quite different in Cuba. Yet in a given social context, innovation/ non-convention always opposes convention/ non-innovation.

Within such a meaning system, charismatic leadership, by definition, attempts to persuade society to embrace a contrary of a current social convention, that is, innovation. The logical relations depicted in the semiotic square imply that charismatic leadership is, at its essence, the contrary of conventions. As one adopts more institutionalized conventions, one appears less charismatic. According to this model, negation of existing beliefs is a fundamental characteristic of charismatic leadership.

The social structure of leaders' values identifies value components at a societal level. However, it does not reflect the personal values that motivate or predispose charismatic leaders to promote non-endorsed social values. Nor does it describe the personal value changes required when members of society follow the charismatic leader. Therefore, we need to more closely examine the personal value structure of leaders and of society's members.

The Personal SubStructure of Values

The two sets of motivators define individual human behaviour in relation to social values: desire and fear.

The terms of the personal value system interact with the social value system to generate what one observes in human behaviour. Different value combinations lead to either conflicting or compatible relations. For example, desire that is, aspirations, intentions or a conscious impulse towards something positive interacts with endorsed social values to produce a compatible or balanced relation of personal and social values. Similarly, fear that is, the anticipation of danger or the impulse to avoid or overcome a negative combined with unendorsed social values (innovation), produces compatibility in personal-social values. Both relationships are stable over time, are deemed "effective" and represent "socialized" members of society.

On the other hand, people experiencing fear of society's conventions are unlikely to remain stable over time or to be "effective." Similarly, desire combined with socially unendorsed values (innovation) produces an unstable tension. Charismatic leaders represent this combination of tension – desire for innovation. Their leadership aims at replacing current social convention with their personal values in order to achieve a state of balance for themselves.

The charismatic leaders as having the power to modify the beliefs and preferences of individuals in order to create a new compatibility between personal and social values. Previous theory suggests that charismatic leaders effect such a change through frame re-alignment. Our analysis suggests that before followers will align around a new interpretive frame, they must reverse their previous relationship with the existing socially dominant values. As described below, this occurs through introducing conflict in a compatible convention-based structure and compatibility in a conflictive innovation-based structure.

2

Leadership Change: Tools and Strategies

INTRODUCTION

Bainbridge outlined a five step process of redesign for organisations undergoing planned change.

The five steps included:

- The design stage to determine overall requirements;
- The definition stage where the design is specified and documentation of the design stage requirements occurs;
- The development stage, where new capabilities are cultivated through training, education and restructuring;
- The dismantling stage, where redundant parts of the organisation are removed or converted into new capabilities; and
- The deployment stage, where new capabilities are introduced into the new organisational environment, both internally and externally.

This design process is accomplished within a carefully arranged change process architecture. "This includes the link to strategic objectives, the definition of measures and the production of the high-level design itself". The vision of change must be expressed as clearly as possible and used consistently to spearhead every step of the change design process, including the specification of design principles. Design principles reflect the context and also the content of both internal and external desired change outcomes. Specification and communication of these principles by leaders are necessary to facilitate adoption and adaptation within the organisational culture. Pettigrew pointed out the wisdom of considering the content, the context (inner and outer) and the process of change within organisations. There is a need to "explore content, context and process linkages through time". Strategies of organisational change have become a viable vehicle for business success and the creation of competitive performance.

The ability to handle strategic change is now a defining characteristic of successful post-industrial organisations. "The leitmotiv of modern management theory is that of understanding, creating and coping with change. The essence of the managerial task thus becomes one of establishing some rationality, or some predictability, out of the seeming chaos that characterizes change processes". An open systems approach can facilitate emergent change processes within an organisation. The linkages and interdependencies between the organisation and the external environment can be used to create a pattern for emergent change adaptation. Galpin described a process for implementing planned change at a grassroots level, using the strengths and capabilities of the human resources within an organisation as the central hub for change. This process included stages of:

- Setting goals;
- Measuring performance;
- Providing feedback and coaching and
- Instigating generous rewards and recognition.

Galpin also outlined the strategic steps leaders needed to employ in order to initiate the change process.

These steps were:

- Defining the need to change;
- Developing a vision of the result of change;
- Leveraging teams to design, test, and implement changes;
- Addressing the cultural aspects of the organisation that will help and sustain change; and
- Developing the essential attributes and skills needed to lead the change effort."

Cognitive mapping and computer assistance for group decision support are alternative change strategies that can help to cultivate group support for the planned initiatives. The cognitive maps or strategic belief systems of managers and employees can have a profound effect on how change is planned and implemented. Cognitive maps become a practical tool "by acting as a device for representing that part of a person's construct system they are able and willing to make explicit,". However, the cognitive map is "significantly biased by the necessary social interaction, or social gaze, that is the basis of elicitation through interview". Still, cognitive maps can be a strategic tool for negotiation and decision making in the change planning and implementation process.

Flamholtz and Randle identified strategic transformational planning as a key tool for change in an organisation. This process describes the planning necessary to transform an organisation into what it needs to become to maximize the fit and reduce the gaps between corporate size, environment, business concept and organisational design. Flamholtz and Randle labeled these transformations as First, Second, and Third kinds. A First kind transformation related to professional management transformation. Planning revitalization or second kind transformation related to all layers of the corporate pyramid, while business vision transformations focused on changes needed to address new markets and the firm's role in the existing markets. All three of these transformations were addressed by using the transformational planning process:

- Assessing the environment;
- Reviewing the existing business;
- Resolving core transformational issues and
- Developing the written strategic transformational plan.

Organisational managers at the top must exhibit leadership, commitment, and conviction to the change and transformation process. Incremental change, often the result of a carefully thought out analysis and planning process, has been the most common form of planned change within organisations. A feeling of control is afforded, enough time and commitment are present, and each step of the process can be trialed and adapted to. However, with the advent of technology and globalization, a deep change is necessary. "Deep change differs from incremental change in that it requires new ways of thinking and behaving. It is change that is major in scope, discontinuous with the past and generally irreversible. Deep change means surrendering control". Deep change on any level entails inherent risk. To adapt to the profound changes of our times, leaders must be willing to go out on a limb, to take some big risks by stepping outside of well-established boundaries.

THE PHENOMENON OF CHANGE

Lewin produced the first viable model of change in his force field model. In this model, change was characterized as a state of imbalance between driving forces and restraining forces. If these forces were balanced or in equilibrium, no change could take place. Change is inherent in every context and is a relative concept. "Every phenomenon is subject to change, however apparently stable its nature". That change exists is a predictable notion. "In every industry and business, change ebbs and flows in recurring cycles that to at least some extent can be charted and therefore anticipated and managed". Change is disruptive, messy, and complicated.

Even with the best laid plans, events rarely occur exactly as they were predicted. "Real change in real organisations is intensely personal and enormously political". Change processes entail not only structures and ways of doing tasks, but also the performance, expectations and perceptions of all involved parties. Change has become widespread and unpredictable, but is still manageable.

An inherent characteristic of change is that it is risky, especially when it encompasses many different sectors within an organisation or society. Change can also be planned or emergent. Wilson pointed out that a shift from emergent models of change to planned ones has steadily occurred over the past two decades. A total shift is not advised though, since, the political and economic context of the surrounding environment can not be ignored, and must also be adapted to. Strategies to deal with unplanned change are just as necessary as planned ones.

EFFECTS OF CHANGE ON ORGANISATIONS

To effectively adapt to change, most established organisations have a daunting task ahead of them in a variety of operational and procedural areas. Business processes must be redefined and redesigned and adapted to specific geographical and cultural settings. The workforce needs to be retrained to be ready for changes in how work is done, what skills and knowledge is needed, and how to relate to global collaborators and customers. The very culture of an organisation needs to be reshaped to properly support the new processes introduced. Structures, reward systems, appraisal measurements and roles need redefinition. Leadership styles and management procedures must shift and adapt, and ways of relating with customers, suppliers, and other stakeholders need refining. Technological advances and capabilities must be introduced, and preparation of the workforce to work with the new IT structures is needed. Successful adaptation to change necessitates "an understanding about how to convert and rebuild from the complexities and legacies of the old, as well as generate designs about the new".

Change necessitates that organisations realistically move beyond antiquated processes, empower and retrain employees, and incorporate advances in IT into the everyday work setting. No longer are organisations reacting to sequential or occasional change. New changes now occur as organisations are in the throes of initiating the change process. Change has become perpetual. In order to cope, organisations need a design process with strategies and guidelines for thriving amongst a multitude of changes. "Real change is an integrated process that unfolds over time and touches every aspect of an organisation,".

EXTERNAL TOOLS FOR CHANGE

Noer cautioned leaders to not rely too heavily on external tools for change. "The futile quest for an external, objective tool is a dysfunctional heritage of the old paradigm; the outgrowth of the erroneous attempt to graft the objectivity of the scientific method onto the subjective phenomena of the human spirit. It is a fundamental mismatch". According to Noer, the leader, as a person, is the most important tool for change. The leader's spirit, insight, wisdom, compassion, values, and learning skills are all important facets in the capabilities to lead others to embrace change and redesign. To be lasting, deep change must not only be made amidst organisational layers, but within each of the players themselves. Deep personal change can be uncomfortable, yet the need for each member of an organisation to become empowered, and internally driven is essential for success in this era of change and evolvement. Quinn cautions that if players are not willing or able to make these deep personal changes, then"slow death" is the alternative. Slow death, "a meaningless and frustrating experience enmeshed in fear, anger, and helplessness, while moving surely towards what is most feared" is the consequence of resistance to change. Burnout can occur if this resistance to change persists, resulting in loss of employment or even destruction of the organisation as a whole. The leader who instigates change within a firm is often subject to speculative suspicion. "Because resistance is so common, learning to overcome it is crucial to managing change at every level". The transition stage where the change process is instigated must be handled expertly and with enthusiasm. Leaders must own and align the proposed changes, setting expectations, and modeling and communicating the rationale to all members of the organisation. The processes of engaging and rewarding help to motivate members, smoothing the transition period, and attempting to win the hearts and minds of all involved to the change process.

CHARACTERISTICS OF LEADERS OF CHANGE

Leadership to promote and implement educational change has not been uniform. Knowledge about the qualities of the individuals who have successfully implemented such strategies has been minimal. If the educational community has knowledge of successful strategies and programmes, why is there limited implementation? Did the leader make the difference? What are the characteristics these people possess that enabled them to change their districts and schools?

Although knowledge is limited on what types of leaders are needed, there are a number of assumptions about leadership. In educational organisations there is an assumption that leaders of educational change should be both leaders and managers. "We expect both leadership and management from the same individual" (Manasse, 1986, p. 153). This idea may arise from districts' and schools' structures where superintendents and principals are the primary administrator. Nevertheless, "while we can distinguish management from leadership conceptually, in reality we often find the two roles coexisting in the same positions and the same person" (Manasse, 1986, p. 153). For example, a principal is often responsible for the school's vision as well as the practical steps needed to attain that vision. Teacher leadership also 'coexists' in one person. Traditional teacher leadership roles, such as department heads and textbook adoption committee chairpersons, have been performed by teachers who were responsible for teaching as well as providing leadership (Bellon and Beaudry, 1992; Boles and Troen, 1992; Wasley, 1991).

Another assumption about leaders who change their organisations is that only administrators will be leaders. However this assumption, that change comes only from individuals in top positions, "ignores the invisible leadership of lower-level staff members" (Murphy, 1988, p. 655). While studies of educational leadership have focused on leaders in administrative positions, recent studies are focusing on teachers as leaders (Bellon and Beaudry, 1992; Boles and Troen, 1992; Howey, 1988; Wasley, 1991; Waugh and Punch, 1987). The recent educational reform movements, such as restructuring and site based management, have promoted increased teacher participation and leadership in the decision- making processes of various aspects of school administration. Studies about teachers' roles in these reform efforts are beginning to emerge.

Information about leaders who have guided or provoked their organisations to change is also beginning to emerge. These leaders began with having a vision, developed a shared vision with their co- workers, and valued the organisation's personnel. Leaders who changed their organisations were proactive and took risks. They recognized shifts in the interests or needs of their clientele, anticipated the need to change and challenged the status quo. Educational leaders of change have these characteristics. How these characteristics are manifested by educational leaders is presented in the characteristics section of this paper. Since, limited data exist on educational leaders, the information on the characteristics of these leaders is drawn primarily from the literature on effective schools.

The effective schools movement investigated schools whose students from disadvantaged situations (minority status, low socio-economic levels) were performing at average or above average levels in basic skills on standardized achievement tests (Brookover and Lezotte, 1979; Edmonds, 1979; Sizemore, Brossard, and Harrigan, 1983; Venezky and Winfield, 1979). In the late 1970s, based on contrastive studies of high and low performing schools, researchers began to identify common factors or characteristics of these effective schools. One of the major findings of the effective schools research was the identification of instructional leadership as a significant aspect of effective schools.

Described as a "multidimensional construct" (Heck, Larsen, and Marcoulides, 1990, p. 122), instructional leadership includes characteristics such as high expectations of students and teachers, an emphasis on instruction, provision of professional development, and use of data to evaluate students' progress among others. Instructional leadership has also been found to be a significant factor in facilitating, improving, and promoting the academic progress of students. Although there is a rich description of instructional leaders' behaviors paralleling the findings from the literature on effective leaders, there is limited data about which leadership characteristics facilitate and promote change in educational settings. Instructional leadership characteristics parallel the two dimensions of leadership discussed previously. "A large body of research on schools has consistently demonstrated that the most effective leader behaviour is strong in both initiating structure and consideration" (Hoy and Brown, 1988, p. 27). Effective school leaders are task- and people-oriented. Kohan's (1989) analysis of data concerning superintendents' leadership style supports the findings of effective leaders being high performances in the effective leadership dimensions of initiating structures and consideration. Hoy and Brown (1988) found that teachers responded more favorably to principals with "a leadership style that combines both structure and consideration" (p. 36).

Teacher leadership has been seen in traditional roles such as department heads, textbook adoption committee chairpersons, and union representatives (Bellon and Beaudry, 1992; Wasley, 1991). In addition to being restricted to these three areas, "traditional leadership opportunities for teachers are extremely limited and generally serve an efficiency function rather than a leadership function" (Wasley, 1991, p. 4). However current educational reforms prompt a reconsideration of teacher leadership. Reforms such as site based management and restructuring efforts include broader roles for teacher participation and leadership. Current teacher leadership roles are involving teachers as mentors, team leaders, curriculum developers, and staff development providers and intend to "improve the quality of public education while allowing teachers greater leadership in the development of those improvements" (Wasley, 1991, p 6). These roles involve teachers in decision-making processes and facilitate teachers becoming leaders of change. Nickse (1977) studied teachers as change agents and advocated teachers in leadership roles in change efforts for four reasons:

> Teachers have a vested interest, "they care about what they do and how they do it and feel a sense of responsibility for their efforts";
> Teachers have a sense of history, they are "aware of the norms of their colleagues";
> Teachers know the community, "have information concerning the values and attitudes of the community" and
> Teachers can implement change, they "are where the action is...in the position to initiate planned change on the basis of need" (p. 5).

Yet despite these reasons and attempts to promote teachers as leaders of change and to extend teacher leadership roles, teachers do not view themselves as leaders (Bellon and Beaudry, 1992; Wasley, 1991).

Nevertheless, the data on leaders of educational change and the emerging information on teacher leadership indicate that the characteristics of these individuals mirror those of leaders who have changed other organisations. Leaders of educational change have vision, foster a shared vision, and value human resources. They are proactive and take risks. In addition, they strongly believe that the purpose of schools is to meet the academic needs of students and are effective communicators and listeners. Leaders of educational change have vision, foster a shared vision, and value human resources. They are proactive and take risks.

VISION

Leadership requires vision. It is a force that provides meaning and purpose to the work of an organisation. Leaders of change are visionary leaders, and vision is the basis of their work. "To actively change an organisation, leaders must make decisions about the nature of the desired state" (Manasse, 1986, p. 151). They begin with a personal vision to forge a shared vision with their coworkers. Their communication of the vision is such that it empowers people to act. According to Westley and Mintzberg (1989) visionary leadership is dynamic and involves a three stage process:

> an image of the desired future for the organisation (vision) is
> communicated (shared) which serves to
> "empower those followers so that they can enact the vision" (p. 18).

The important role of vision is also evident in the literature concerning instructional leadership (Blumberg and Greenfield, 1980; Leithwood and Montgomery, 1984; Manasse, 1986; Mazzarella and Grundy, 1989; Pejza, 1985). For educational leaders who implement change in their school or district, vision is "a hunger to see improvement" (Pejza, 1985, p. 10) as well as "the force which molds meaning" (Manasse, 1986, p. 150). Leaders of educational change have a clear picture of what they want to accomplish; they have the "ability to visualize one's goals" (Mazzarella and Grundy, 1989, p. 21). Their vision of their school or district provides purpose, meaning, and significance to the work of the school and enables them to motivate and empower the staff to contribute to the realization of the vision. The American Association of School Administrators' (1986) description of leadership includes the leader's ability to translate a vision into reality as well as the ability to articulate the vision to others. Furthermore, leaders of educational change can transmit that vision to others so that they become motivated to work towards the realization of the vision.

According to Manasse (1986), vision includes the "development, transmission, and implementation of an image of a desirable future" (p. 150). She further states that the sharing of a leader's vision "may differentiate true leaders from mere managers" (p. 151). School leaders have not only a vision but also the skills to communicate that vision to others, to develop a shared vision, a "shared covenant" (Sergiovanni, 1990, p. 216). The "development, transmission, and implementation" of a vision is the focus of leaders of educational change. Leaders invite and encourage others to participate in determining and developing a shared vision. The process of developing a shared vision promotes collegial and collaborative relationships. How educational leaders develop collegial relationships to form a shared vision is discussed in Hord's (1992) companion synthesis to this paper. Sergiovanni (1990) has described this aspect of leadership as "bonding"; leader and followers have a shared set of values and commitment "that bond them together in a common cause" (p. 23) in order to meet a common goal. In Chrispeels's (1990) report of effective schools, she states that "if a school staff has a shared vision, there is a commitment to change" (p. 39). The shared vision becomes a "shared covenant that bonds together leader and follower in a moral commitment" (Sergiovanni, 1990, p. 24).

Vision, a critical leadership characteristic, is also a trait of successful executive educators (Crowson and Morris, 1990; Harrington-Lueker, 1991; Mahoney, 1990; Papalewis,1988). Outstanding superintendents studied by Mahoney (1990) were described as individuals who "knew where their school system ought to be headed and why" (p. 27); he stated that "top school leaders create a vision for their school systems and develop a plan for the future" (p. 27). According to Crowson and Morris's (1990) study of superintendents, vision included "deciding what's the correct thing to do" (p. 54). Vision guides the work of superintendents and influences the work of others. "School leaders are creative visionaries willing to take risks in pursuit of cherished values and able to cling to a vision with a tenacity that is contagious to nearly everyone" (Papalewis, 1988, p. 159).

The importance of principals having a vision also appears in the literature concerning instructional leadership (Blumberg and Greenfield, 1980; Lightfoot, 1983; Méndez-Morse, 1991; Niece, 1989; Pejza, 1985). Principals have a vision — a picture of what they want their schools to be and their students to achieve. Pejza (1985) stated that "leadership requires a vision. Without a vision to challenge followers with, there's no possibility of a principal being a leader" (p. 10). The vision provides guidance and direction for the school staff, students, and administration. Niece (1989) reported that several authorities included "providing vision and direction for the school" (p. 5) as a component of instructional leadership. Principals keep their "vision in the forefront" (Méndez-Morse, 1991, p. 2). "Associated with a vision has to be a plan, a way of reaching the goal" (Pejza, 1985, p. 10).

The terms "mission" and "goal-oriented" are often used in literature to describe this characteristic of principals (Blumberg and Greenfield, 1986; Hallinger, Bickman, and Davis, 1990; Leithwood and Montgomery, 1984). Blumberg and Greenfield (1986) found that effective principals seem to be "highly goal oriented and to have a keen sense of goal clarity" (in Mazzarella and Grundy, 1989, p. 20). Hallinger, Bickman, and Davis (1990) stated that "principals influence student learning by developing a school mission that provides an instructional focus for teachers throughout the school" (p. 28). Leithwood and Montgomery (1984) concluded that "goals are the long term aspirations held by principals for work in their schools. No other dimension of principal behaviour is more consistently linked to school improvement by current empirical research than Goals" (p. 23). The school administrators' values and beliefs shape her or his vision. Vision influences the school climate which includes teachers' instructional behaviors as well as student outcomes.

While administrators' visions tend to focus on district- or school- wide instructional issues, teachers' visions tend to address teacher roles and student outcomes (Bellon and Beaudry, 1992; Boles and Troen, 1992; Murphy, Everston, and Radnofsky, 1991; Wasley, 1991). Murphy, Everston, and Radnofsky (1991) discussed teachers' opinions on restructuring and found that while teachers agreed with the literature concerning restructuring, they emphasized the student and instructional issues. These teachers' visions included changes in the classroom, such as interdisciplinary curricula, varied student grouping patterns, and instruction that included basic literacy as well as "critical thinking, creativity, inquisitiveness, and independence of thought" (Murphy, Everston, and Radnofsky, 1991, p. 144). Teachers' vision also included school changes that would result in more participatory and decision- making roles for teachers. Increased teacher leadership has been reported by Bellon and Beaudry, 1992; Boles and Troen, 1992; and Wasley, 1991. Boles and Troen (1992) found from their personal experience with restructuring that their vision for improved student achievement included changes in instructional approaches and teacher leadership roles. Similarly, other researchers found that teachers included the need to change the school's structures and instructional methods in order to address students' needs (Bellon and Beaudry, 1992; Murphy, Everston, and Radnofsky, 1991; Wasley, 1991). School administrators that have developed a shared vision with their faculty have also created common ground that serves to facilitate or compel action to the realization of this common vision.

The relationship between the teachers' and administrators' vision is important. Administrators' vision tends to encompass the whole system or as described by Manasse (1986) their vision is an organisational vision. Teachers' vision appear to focus primarily on the individual or personal actions for school change. However, closer examination of the two — teachers' and administrators' visions — may reveal that both groups of educators are looking at the same vision but attending to different aspects. School administrators that have developed a shared vision with their faculty have also created common ground that serves to facilitate or compel action to the realization of this common vision. Frequently underlying a shared vision are teachers' and administrators' shared values and beliefs, specifically believing that schools are for students' learning. The next section describes this unifying belief that facilitates school change.

BELIEVING THAT SCHOOLS ARE FOR STUDENTS' LEARNING

The values and beliefs of individuals affect their behaviour and in leaders they influence the vision leaders hold of their school or district. Values are principles an individual considers to be important or desirable, for example honest communication; beliefs are ideas considered to be true and on which people are willing to act, for example, believing that all children can learn. Manasse (1986) stated that vision is "based on personal or personalized professional values" (p. 152). He also states that "visionary leadership demands a clear sense of personal and organisational values" (p. 151). Seeley's (1992) paper on visionary leadership includes discussion of the need to be aware of leaders' values because "there is no way for leaders to avoid moral responsibility"

(p. 24). He states that visions are "normative statements" (p. 24) and consequently "whoever would embrace them or urge others to embrace them are responsible for their moral content" (p. 25). The connection between leaders' values or beliefs and their vision for their organisations is important. Unfortunately, there is minimal information concerning the impact of values and beliefs on the leadership abilities of effective leaders or instructional leaders.

The limited studies of the values and beliefs of effective educators indicate slight differences among superintendents, principals, and teachers. All three groups place high value on students' learning. In addition to believing that schools are for students' learning, effective superintendents are loyal to their community. Effective school principals strongly believe in meeting the instructional needs of all their students. Reports concerning teachers' sense of efficacy indicate that they value students' learning and that students' success is rewarding and motivating to teachers.

The values and beliefs of superintendents influence their vision as well as their actions. Aplin (1984) stated that "clarity of professional values is related to role effectiveness" (p. 3). In her study, she identified five values that guided a superintendent's work. The first value Aplin identified was that the instructional programmes were "the highest priority of the system and decisions were assessed as to whether they enhanced or threatened it" (p. 10). The second value this superintendent had was "equity in person relationships and instructional decisions" (p. 10). "Practices of delegation, teaming, flexibility of process and incremental planning with extensive communication" (p. 11) was the third value listed by Aplin. "The fourth value held was the need to retain a high level of local control....The fifth value disclosed was his belief that the quality of decision is improved if there has been free and honest disclosure among interested parties" (p. 11). Aside from Aplin's in- depth study of one superintendent's values, limited information exists on this aspect of district administrators. However, the studies that do exist provide information on superintendents' values; two common values and beliefs held by these administrators emerge.

The first was a belief that the purpose of their school system is to meet the instructional needs of students (Aplin, 1984; Harrington-Lueker, 1991; Pajack and Glickman, 1989; Papalewis, 1988; Schmuck and Schmuck, 1989). Papalewis (1988) reported that along with remarks about how the superintendent's vision contributed to the district's success, district personnel commented that this administrator "never compromised his goals or philosophy that we are here because of and for the students" (p. 161). Pajack and Glickman (1989) stated that "the specific value that each superintendent seemed to exemplify was simply 'the children come first'" (p. 62). This belief, students' educational needs as the school system's priority, was consistently identified in superintendents that facilitated school improvement (Harrington-Lueker,

1991; Pajack and Glickman, 1989; Papalewis, 1988; Schmuck and Schmuck, 1989). In addition to valuing students as the top priority, superintendents believe that their office can serve to promote this value. According to Pitner and Ogawa (1989), "a major occupational attraction of the superintendency was the expectation that they would be able to wield the influence of their office to improve education" (p. 58).

The second value commonly held by superintendents was loyalty to the community their school district served (Crowson and Morris, 1990; Pitner and Ogawa, 1989; Wilson, 1980). This loyalty includes a keen understanding of the community's values as well as consistent participation in community activities. The latter is supported by Wilson's (1980) observation that outstanding Ohio superintendents were active participants in their communities by being involved in civic and social organisations.

Few studies have revealed a direct link between the superintendents' and communities' values; none discussed the impact of the connection of superintendents' and communities' values to district improvement. The match between a community's values and those of the superintendent appeared in two studies (Crowson and Morris, 1990; Pitner and Ogawa, 1989). Pitner and Ogawa found a commonly held belief of superintendents that they "must see to it that their schools' programmes and methods of operation were consistent with their communities' values" (p. 50). However, it has not been established that a correlation between superintendent and community values promotes school improvement.

Furthermore, additional studies present contradictory data that fuel the need to investigate the impact, if any, of common superintendent and community values. Tyack and Hansot (1982) suggest that superintendents' value orientations have remained constant, representing "old-time" (p. 170) qualities such as hard work, morality, order, and respectability. However, according to the National Center of Education Information's Profiles of School Administrators in the U.S., the views of the general public differed from those of school administrators. Most superintendents and principals gave public schools higher marks and were at odds with the general public and parents of school age children on the issues of busing and sex education. Opinions of school administrators and the general public about the quality of public schools, school improvement, and school performance differ greatly (Feistritzer, 1988). How these major differences between superintendents and the general public regarding public educational systems have an impact on the leadership abilities of executive educators needs to be explored. Beliefs about students' ability to learn and teachers' ability to teach affect a principal's leadership behaviors.

Principals' values and beliefs influence their vision of the school as well as their behaviors (Glasman, 1984; Greenfield, 1991; Hallinger, Bickman, and Davis, 1990; Krug, Scott, and Ahadi, 1990). In an in-depth study of an elementary principal, Greenfield (1991) stated that the "principal's moral orientation is important to understand because it colors practically everything this principal does on a daily basis" (p. 6). Beliefs about students' ability to learn and teachers' ability to teach affect a principal's leadership behaviors. Krug, Scott, and Ahadi's (1990) study "designed to identify and understand the personal beliefs and goals shared by effective school leaders" (p. 2) found that while there was little difference between the activities of effective and ineffective principals, the meanings they attributed to their activities were significantly different. They concluded that "the way a principal interprets a particular activity (beliefs) — [is] of primary importance in explaining differences between effective and less effective principals" (p. 2). Contrasting this finding is Avi-Itzhak's and Ben-Peretz's (1987) study that attempted to determine how values, personal background, and organisational factors influenced principals' change facilitator style. They found that personal background factors, such as type of education, and organisational factors, such as school size, were more important than values.

While effective principals tend to believe that the purpose of the school is to meet the instructional needs of all students, Hallinger and Murphy (1986) have reported that there are differences in the beliefs and the expectations of principals of low and high socio-economic students. "Principals in the high-SES effective schools expected an academic emphasis and task orientations in classrooms but encouraged teachers to implement a broad curriculum. Their counterparts in the low-SES effective schools implemented a more narrowly defined curriculum and allocated more time for basic skill instruction" (Hallinger and Murphy 1986 p. 339).

Teachers value working with students. Compared with the general adult population who identify "a good salary" and "job security" (Feistritzer, 1986, p. iii) as the most satisfying aspects of a job, teachers identify as the three most satisfying aspects of teaching:

"a chance to use your mind and abilities",
"a chance to work with young people — see young people develop", and
"appreciation for a job well done" (Feistritzer, 1986, p. iii).

Greenfield (1991) commented that teachers' work was not "motivated by bureaucratic mandate or directives from superiors, but by a moral commitment to children rooted in their awareness of the needs of these children and their belief about the significance of their roles as teachers, in these children's lives" (p. 8). Murphy, Everston, and Radnofsky's (1991) report on teachers' opinions on general restructuring issues found that teachers' ideas were more student focused, emphasized a school environment where teachers get to know students on a more personal basis and promoted the concept that teachers and students were "colearners" (p. 142). In addition, these teachers emphasized their role in addressing students' social and academic needs such as the need to improve students' self-esteem, to increase student responsibility, and to teach lifelong learning, "encourage students to challenge themselves...develop a sense of excitement about their education" (p. 144).

Teachers believe that they have an impact on student achievement (Rosenholtz, 1987; Sarason, 1982). "The primary rewards for most teachers come from students' academic accomplishments — from feeling certain about their own capacity to affect student development" (Rosenholtz, 1987 p. 188). Sarason (1982) stated that project implementation was influenced by the "belief that the teacher can help even the most difficult or unmotivated students" (p. 77). Teacher participation in pilot site-based decision-making schools was motivated by teachers' believing that the programme would help students (Bellon and Beaudry, 1992). Boles and Troen (1992) reported that their restructuring of teacher roles was prompted by the need to meet the needs of students, especially those participating in pull-out programmes.

Despite teachers' general valuing of working with students and believing that they have an impact on students' learning, there are differences in teachers' beliefs and expectations for high and low socio- economic students. Hallinger and Murphy (1986) reported that even when the low wealth schools were achieving, teachers' expectations were lower than those for students at wealthier schools; they believed they had minimal parental support and therefore assigned less homework and stressed the basic curriculum. "Differences in curricular and instructional practices suggest that the manner in which staff implement curriculum and instruction is filtered through their perceptions, beliefs and expectations concerning student ability and community background" (Hallinger and Murphy, 1986b, p. 154).

How teachers' values and beliefs impact their leadership skills needs to be studied. Teachers valuing working with students and believing they have influence on students' achievement may prove to be significant as teachers assume more leadership roles especially as recent restructuring efforts and site based management are implemented and studied. The limited information on teacher leaders and on correlations between values and leadership abilities of superintendents, principals, and teachers demonstrates the need to investigate this aspect of leadership.

The relationship between educators' values and beliefs and their impact on school improvement needs to be explored. Despite the limited information that does exist, believing that schools are for students' learning frequently surfaced as a common characteristic of leaders that promote school change. Effective superintendents believe that students come first; effective principals believe in meeting the instructional needs of the students. Teachers value working with students and believe that they have an impact on their achievement. They have the shared belief that students' learning is of primary importance. The literature revealed that these individuals' also shared a common value. They valued the human resources — the contributions, talents, and efforts — of others in their organisation. A description of this characteristic follows.

VALUING HUMAN RESOURCES

Leaders for change recognize that the people in the organisation are its greatest resource. "To lead change the leader must believe without question that people are the most important asset of an organisation" (Joiner, 1987 p. 2). This characteristic has three dimensions. The first is the leaders' valuing the professional contributions of the staff, while the second is the leaders' ability to relate to people. The third dimension is fostering collaborative relationship. Valuing people's contributions to an organisation differs from relating to people and building collaboration. The first acknowledges individuals' skills and expertise, while the latter two involve interpersonal skills. Leaders of change not only include the contributions of employees in determining and realizing the vision but also have the interpersonal skills that help them relate with others and develop collaborative relationships, foster environments and work processes to facilitate the organisations' collective efforts, and address the needs of individuals as well as groups (Joiner, 1987; Barnes and Kriger, 1986). Leaders of change trust the strength of others and value their efforts and contributions in the realization of the organisation's vision.

The importance of valuing the personnel of a school or district is also evident in the literature concerning instructional leadership. "One finding to emerge repeatedly in studies of leaders, including studies of educational leaders, is that leaders are people oriented" (Mazzarella and Grundy, 1989, p. 16). The American Association of School Administrators (1986) described this aspect of leadership as renewal: leaders' ability to help the organisation renew itself and keep the organisation dynamic by finding ways to use employees' abilities. Gorton and McIntyre (1978) found that effective principals had as their strongest asset "an ability to work with different kinds of people having various needs, interests, and expectations." (Mazzarella and Grundy, 1989, p. 16). Niece (1989) found in his study of principals that "effective instructional leaders are people oriented and interactional" (p. 5). In addition, he reported that the principals themselves had identified eight additional dimensions of instructional leadership not listed by the experts, six of which targeted people or interpersonal abilities (Niece, 1989).

Effective school administrators have been described frequently as valuing their co-workers' efforts and contributions (Becker, et al. 1971; Bossert, et al. 1982; Crowson, 1989; Gorton and McIntyre, 1978; Hoy and Brown, 1988; Niece, 1989; Sarason, 1982). Mahoney (1990) reported that these superintendents allowed their staff to "do the things they do best with their expertise" (p. 26). Furthermore, he stated that these administrators recommended "creating the conditions under which your subordinates can be successful" (p. 26).

Valuing the faculty's contributions and endeavors was often manifested in the principals' support of teachers' instructional efforts. Support of teachers' efforts was demonstrated in four areas: supporting teachers' instructional methods, their modifications of instructional approaches and materials; providing human and material resources for instruction; providing non-evaluative comments on instructional practices, and protecting teachers' time and efforts from non- instructional tasks (Bossert et al., 1982; Méndez-Morse, 1991). Sarason (1982) stated that principals' contributions to the implementation of a new project rested not in direct, programmatic advice, "but in giving moral support to the staff" (p. 77).

Ability to relate to others is the second dimension of valuing the human resources of a school system and a common characteristic of effective administrators (Aplin, 1984; Crowson and Morris, 1990; Kohan, 1989; Mahoney, 1990; Schmuck and Schmuck, 1989; Wilson, 1980). Crowson and Morris (1990) stated that superintendents frequently commented on the need to have "an ability to relate to people" (p. 54) as an important aspect of their position. One superintendent commented that "in dealing with change, you have to have a capacity to relate well to all types of people" (Crowson and Morris, 1990, p. 52). Schmuck and Schmuck (1989) reported that the people-oriented superintendents they studied had the interpersonal skills that enabled them to "develop a strengthened management team, improve attitudes of students towards school, renew trust between the board and teachers, [and] enhance staff involvement" (p. 4). Wilson (1980) found that the successful superintendent "is a very personable and friendly individual who believes in the importance of human relations skills and demonstrates them daily" (p. 20). Becker, et al. stated that effective principals "had an ability to work effectively with people" (p. 3). Mahoney (1990) investigated the characteristics of outstanding superintendents and included in his list "being able to work effectively with people" (p. 27). School administrators provide an environment that encourages and promotes collaborative relationships.

The ability to relate to others has an impact on the third dimension, fostering collaborative relationships within school systems. School administrators provide an environment that encourages and promotes collaborative relationships. They form teams, support team efforts, develop the skills that groups and individuals need, and provide the necessary human and material resources to realize the school or district vision.

While effective school administrators value and encourage staff efforts and contributions to school improvement, teachers tend to be the recipients of and not the initiators of such support and consequently some teacher leaders report different experiences. Wasley (1991) reported that although the teacher leaders she studied personally benefited from collaborative relationships with fellow teachers, they also experienced additional isolation than that generally experienced by teachers. These teacher leaders were isolated because, according to Wasley's report, in each case the faculty lacked a clear understanding of the role of a teacher leader, and the faculty had not participated in the selection of the teacher leader. This lack of clear understanding and faculty participation undermined these teacher leaders' efforts. Wasley categorized the collaborative relationships into three types: mentoring, division of labour, and partnering, and stated that "each form of collaboration required different kinds of interactions between teachers and suggested various assumptions about the nature of teaching, leading, and learning" (Wasley, 1991, p. 145). While teacher leaders valued the human resources of their peers, their role appeared to hinder their ability to work cooperatively with their fellow teachers. However, Boles and Troen (1992) reported that their team approach to instruction and the three teacher roles of their staff development programme — teacher/researcher, teacher/trainer, and teacher/curriculum writer — enhanced teacher collaboration. These teacher leaders listed opportunities to speak with other teachers about "how student teaching should be structured" (p. 56) and the use of a teacher-developed integrated curriculum that "measurably improved" (p. 56) student work as examples of some of the benefits.

The characteristic of valuing human resources manifests in three dimensions: valuing the contributions and efforts of co-workers, relating effectively with others, and fostering collaboration. Teachers and teacher leaders tend to be the recipients of these three dimensions and not the initiators. However, one example of teachers as the originators of actions that demonstrated this characteristic was found in the report of Boles and Troen (1992). Valuing the human resources of an organisation is a characteristic of effective leaders of school change that is connected to the next descriptor of these leaders: their ability to communicate and listen.

LEADERS OF CHANGE ARE COMMUNICATORS AND LISTENERS.

Foster's (1985) discussion of leadership stresses the importance of communication; he states that "leadership is conditioned on language" (in Mazzarella and Grundy, 1989, p. 18). Mazzarella and Grundy (1989) noted that "effective school leaders in particular, are good at communicating" and have the aptitude and skills "they need to interact well with others; they know how to communicate" (p. 18).

The ability to communicate and listen is a characteristic commonly used to describe effective superintendents (Aplin, 1984; Crowson and Morris, 1990; Mahoney, 1990; Pitner and Ogawa, 1989). According to Pitner and Ogawa (1989), "superintending is communicating" (p. 49). They found that the superintendents they studied considered the "ability to communicate with people as a requisite skill of their job" (p. 51). In addition to being able to communicate, superintendents are good listeners. Mahoney (1990) reported that the superintendents he studied recommended: "Be a good listener....[O]ften, people aren't looking for instant comments or solutions; all they want is for someone to hear them out" (p. 28). Crowson and Morris (1990) included similar advice from superintendents in their study.

Researchers also describe the ability to communicate as a characteristic of effective principals (Blumberg and Greenfield, 1986; Becker et al., 1971; Gorton and McIntyre, 1978; Niece, 1989). Blumberg and Greenfield (1986) found in their in-depth study of eight outstanding principals that, among the five characteristics they held in common, one was "extremely well-developed expressive abilities" (in Mazzarella and Grundy, 1989, p. 18). Principals' communication characteristic includes their listening skills (Becker et al., 1971; Blumberg and Greenfield, 1986; Gorton and McIntyre, 1978). Becker et al. (1971) found that principals of outstanding schools "listened well to parents, teachers, and pupils" (p. 3). Teacher change agents studied by Nickse (1977) reported that strategies such as "developing one-to-one communication with teachers in the lounge" (p. 15) and listening to others, were facilitative in implementing change at these teachers' schools.

The communicating and listening skills of superintendents, principals, and teachers are an important characteristic of leaders who facilitate school change. It is the basis for their ability to articulate a vision, develop a shared vision, express their belief that schools are for the students' learning, and demonstrate that they value the human resources of their peers and subordinates. Being an effective communicator and listener is also a key ingredient of the following characteristics, being proactive and taking risks, of leaders of school change.

LEADERS OF CHANGE ARE PROACTIVE.

They take the initiative, anticipate and recognize changes in their organisational environment, and begin to explore possible courses of action to respond to those changes. Pejza (1985) stated that a "leader continuously scans the environment noticing where change is needed" (p. 10). Leaders of educational change are proactive in their efforts to change and improve their schools and districts. They are "always testing the limits in an effort to change things that no one else believes can be changed" (Mazzarella and Grundy, 1989, p. 23). They are proactive because they challenge the status quo of their organisation to respond to changes that affect the organisation's business. Often these proactive school leaders are described as individuals who do not accept the rules, regulations, or traditions of their schools and districts to limit their change efforts (Blumberg and Greenfield, 1980; Crowson, 1989; Mazzarella and Grundy, 1989; Pezja, 1985; Schmuck and Schmuck, 1989).

Leaders of change recognize shifts in the environment and guide their organisation to be responsive to those changes. They are aware of the realities of their environment and thus guide the organisation to rethink the vision

(Joiner, 1987; Barnes and Kriger, 1986). DeGues (1988) described this ability as organisational learning: "understanding the changes occurring in the external environment and then adapting beliefs and behaviour to be compatible with those changes" (in Stata, 1989, p. 67). Leaders of educational change recognize paradigm shifts in areas such as curriculum issues, student needs, and state level policies (Pezja, 1985; Schmuck and Schmuck, 1989). They also constantly scan their school or district community noticing where change is needed. They anticipate the changing needs of their students and take the initiative to identify the appropriate course of action.

Leaders of change focus the organisation away from maintaining the status quo to exploring various options of the organisation's vision. Joiner's (1987) discussion of these leaders of change included the skill to "access the reality of the present and determine the gaps that exist" (p. 3- 4). They guide the discussion of how continuing the organisation's current way of operating will shortchange the organisation and thus become advocates for a different vision. Educational leaders of change challenge the status quo of their school systems by questioning established procedures when they do not serve the needs of the students or their staff (Becker et al., 1971; Blumberg and Greenfield, 1980; Crowson, 1989; Wynne and McPherson, 1983). Crowson's (1989) study of the ethical aspects of school administrators' decision-making includes the finding that they would use the organisation's structures and procedures against itself "so that the ultimate client, the student, is best served" (p. 413). He found that when decisions contradicted the district's norms, the primary beneficiaries of such decisions were the students and their parents and that the school staff form the secondary group of beneficiaries.

Effective superintendents are proactive and confront rather than avoid, anticipate instead of react to situations and circumstances (Crowson and Morris, 1990; Mahoney, 1990; Pitner and Ogawa, 1989; Schmuck and Schmuck, 1989). Mahoney (1990) reported that "successful superintendents prefer to deal with [problems] head-on — to act on the situation rather than try to avoid it" (p.26). Schmuck and Schmuck (1989) described the proactive activities of two superintendents they studied. One had regularly scheduled meetings to discuss district problems; another superintendent met with African-American and Anglo-American administrators to plan meetings for students, parents and community members to prepare for an impending desegregation ruling in their district. Pitner and Ogawa (1989) reported that superintendents included methods for identifying emerging concerns and attitudes; they communicated with different constituencies to "map out the terrain of opinions and preferences" (p. 50). The strategy included knowing the correct time when an idea would be likely to gain acceptance.

Effective principals also are proactive (Becker et al., 1971; Blumberg and Greenfield, 1986; Crowson, 1989; Hoy and Brown, 1988; Pejza, 1985). Pejza

(1985) stated that "a successful leader is one who aims at something no else can see and hits it" (p. 10). Blumberg and Greenfield (1986) found that the school principals in their research "were continually alert for opportunities to make things happen and if the opportunity didn't present themselves, they created them" (in Mazzarella and Grundy, 1989, p. 20-21). They noted that effective principals did not merely accept all the rules and customs of their schools or districts; they always tested "the limits in an effort to change things that no one else believes can be changed" (in Mazzarella and Grundy, 1989, p. 23). Hoy and Brown (1988) reported that teachers prefer principals to be proactive and warned that "principals who fear to take a stand, who hesitate to initiate structure lest they be accused of being authoritarian, are disadvantaged in leading their teachers; they are likely to lose respect" (p. 36).

Proactive teacher leaders have been discussed in several studies (Bellon and Beaudry, 1992; Boles and Troen, 1992; Nickse, 1977, Wasley, 1991). Wasley (1991) described how the teacher leaders she studied were proactive. Each of these teacher leaders were in positions created to provide assistance in instructional methods intended to improve teachers' effectiveness. One teacher leader proactively conceptualized and organized the position of teacher leader in the district; another tailored the role to better match her knowledge and skills to perform the functions of the teacher leader position. The pilot site-based decision- making programme studied by Bellon and Beaudry (1992) included descriptions of teachers taking the initiative to be part of this programme. Boles and Troen (1992) reported their personal experiences as teachers in the efforts to restructure their school. Some of the proactive strategies they used were: write articles, present ideas at conferences, allocate money, and establish a collaborative relationship with a nearby college. Similar proactive activities were reported by Nickse (1977) in his study of teacher change agents. Teacher leaders' proactive activities are beginning to appear in the literature and more can be anticipated as teachers assume a more participatory role in site based management and restructuring efforts.

Superintendents, principals and teachers that are effective leaders of school change are proactive. They initiate action, anticipate and recognize changes in their environment that will affect their schools and districts, and challenge the status quo, the established ways of operating, that interfere with realization of their organisations' vision. This characteristic of being proactive merges with the following descriptor of leaders of school change — being a risk taker.

LEADERS OF EDUCATIONAL CHANGE ARE RISK TAKERS.

"Change must be initiated by leaders who are willing to risk their reputations for the future benefit of their companies" (Joiner, 1987 p. 4). Risks are not taken haphazardly but tend to be considered as opportunities that will improve the organisation. Crowson (1989) describes the risks principals took when they disobeyed or bent the rules when making ethically laden decisions as "creative insubordination" (p. 412). His study reveals that when certain decisions would not serve the needs of their students, staff or the school, these principals chose to disobey or at least bend the district's rules. He reports that principals risked "be[ing] 'insubordinate' in the face of organisational/professional norms or rules" (p. 429) in to serve student, staff and school needs. The ethical choices principals had to make were such that the "principals feel they owe it to their children and to their school to be insubordinate if necessary in the children's interest" (p. 430).

Leaders of change provide the needed stimulus for change. Calling attention to the possibilities, they take risks and encourage others to initiate change. School leaders encourage their staff to experiment with various instructional methods to meet the academic needs of the students. They guide and provoke the staff to explore options that more adequately address the needs of their students and provide the environment that makes risk-taking safer. They provide their staff with opportunities to consider and implement curriculum changes as well as encourage experimentation with different arrangements of organisational structures, such as schedules and class size. However, as Mazzarella and Grundy (1989) noted "even though effective leaders stretch the rules, they are not rebels; they do play the game" (p. 2). Crowson and Morris (1990) reported similar findings in their study of successful superintendents and stated that absent from their career histories "was an avoidance of risk" (p. 40). Becker, et al. (1971) found that successful principals "found it difficult to live within the constraints of the bureaucracy; they frequently violated the chain of command, seeking relief for their problems from whatever sources that were potentially useful" (p. 3) and yet these principals "expressed concern for the identification of the most appropriate procedure through which change could be secured" (p. 3). School leaders encourage their staff to experiment with various instructional methods to meet the academic needs of the students.

Few examples of teachers as risk takers are found in the literature. Waugh and Punch (1987) found that teachers' participation in the implementation of a change depended on variables including "the extent that fears and uncertainties associated with the change are alleviated" (p. 243). Nickse (1977) stated that one reason for limited teacher leadership in change, which involves risk taking, was "their fear of reprisal, not only from administrators but also from some of their colleagues" (p. 6). He described some of the experiences of the teacher change agents he studied as, "bureaucratic frustrations, fear of retaliation" (p. 14-15) and found that despite these reactions, the teachers learned that "you must believe totally in your goal, have all the data, stick to your topic, study each aspect without flinching and then charge ahead" (p. 17). Boles and Troen (1992) described themselves as "two tenured teachers, with no power, beholden to no one, and with nothing to lose" (p. 53) as they began their restructuring efforts. Even as these two teacher leaders experienced various setbacks and rejections during their initial restructuring efforts, they continued. Their programme gained support and eventually expanded to other schools. Reports concerning the limitations on risk taking by teachers and teacher leaders are emerging and more can be anticipated as teachers become more involved in leadership roles in site based management and restructuring efforts.

Principals and superintendents that lead and guide others in school change take risks but not carelessly or without forethought. Furthermore they encourage others to be innovative by providing an environment that makes this safer. Teachers appear to be reluctant risk takers for a variety of reason although Boles and Troen (1992) provided an example of their risk taking during their restructuring efforts. Current educational reform efforts may change this hesitance in teachers.

THE CHANGE PROCESS AS "UNFREEZING, CHANGING AND REFREEZING"

The process of change has been characterized as having three basic stages: unfreezing, changing, and re-freezing. This view draws heavily on Kurt Lewin's adoption of the systems concept of homeostasis or dynamic stability. What is useful about this framework is that it gives rise to thinking about a staged approach to changing things.

Looking before you leap is usually sound practice. What is not useful about this framework is that it does not allow for change efforts that begin with the organisation in extremis nor does it allow for organisations faced with the prospect of having to ¯hang loose for extended periods of time. In other words, the beginning and ending point of the unfreeze-change-refreeze model is stability — which, for some people and some organisations, is a luxury. For others, internal stability spells disaster. A tortoise on the move can overtake even the fastest hare if that hare stands still.

THE CHANGE PROCESS AS PROBLEM SOLVING AND PROBLEM FINDING

A very useful framework for thinking about the change process is problem solving. Managing change is seen as a matter of moving from one state to another, specifically, from the problem state to the solved state. Diagnosis or problem analysis is generally acknowledged as essential. Goals are set and achieved at various levels and in various areas or functions. Ends and means are discussed and related to one another. Careful planning is accompanied by efforts to obtain buy-in, support and commitment. The net effect is a transition from one state to another in a planned, orderly fashion. This is the planned change model.

The word—problem carries with it connotations that some people prefer to avoid. They choose instead to use the word—opportunity. For such people, a problem is seen as a bad situation, one that shouldn't have been allowed to happen in the first place, and for which someone is likely to be punished—if the guilty party can be identified. We will set aside any cultural or personal preferences regarding the use of —problem or—opportunity. From a rational, analytical perspective, a problem is nothing more than a situation requiring action but in which the required action is not known. Hence, there is a requirement to search for a solution, a course of action that will lead to the solved state. This search activity is known as—problem solving. From the preceding discussion, it follows that—problem finding is the search for situations requiring action. Whether we choose to call these situations—problems or whether we choose to call them—opportunities is immaterial. In both cases, the practical matter is one of identifying and settling on a course of action that will bring about some desired and predetermined change in the situation.

THE CHANGE PROBLEM

At the heart of change management lies the change problem, that is, some future state to be realized, some current state to be left behind, and some structured, organized process for getting from the one to the other. The change problem might be large or small in scope and scale, and it might focus on individuals or groups, on one or more divisions or departments, the entire organisation, or one or on more aspects of the organisation's environment. At a conceptual level, the change problem is a matter of moving from one state to another state. Moving from A to A' is typically accomplished as a result of setting up and achieving three types of goals: *transform*, *reduce*, and *apply*. Transform goals are concerned with identifying differences between the two states. Reduce goals are concerned with determining ways of eliminating these differences.

Apply goals are concerned with putting into play operators that actually effect the elimination of these differences. As the preceding goal types suggest, the analysis of a change problem will at various times focus on defining the outcomes of the change effort, on identifying the changes necessary to produce these outcomes, and on finding and implementing ways and means of making the required changes. In simpler terms, the change problem can be treated as smaller problems having to do with the how, what, and why of change.

CHANGE AS A "HOW" PROBLEM

The change problem is often expressed, at least initially, in the form of a ˉhow question. How do we get people to be more open, to assume more responsibility, to be more creative? How do we introduce self-managed teams in Department W? How do we change over from System X to System Y in Division Z? How do we move from a mainframe-centered computing environment to one that accommodates and integrates PCs? How do we get this organisation to be more innovative, competitive, or productive? How do we raise more effective barriers to market entry by our competitors? How might we more tightly bind our suppliers to us?

How do we reduce cycle times? In short, the initial formulation of a change problem is means-centered, with the goal state more or less implied. There is a reason why the initial statement of a problem is so often means-centered and we will touch on it later. For now, let g”s examine the other two ways in which the problem might be formulated □g” as ¯what or as ¯why questions.

CHANGE AS A “WHAT” PROBLEM

To frame the change effort in the form of ¯how questions is to focus the effort on means. Diagnosis is assumed or not performed at all. Consequently, the ends sought are not discussed. This might or might not be problematic. To focus on ends requires the posing of ¯what questions. What are we trying to accomplish? What changes are necessary? What indicators will signal success? What standards apply? What measures of performance are we trying to affect?

CHANGE AS A “WHY” PROBLEM

Ends and means are relative notions, not absolutes; that is, something is an end or a means only in relation to something else. Thus, chains and networks of ends-means relationships often have to be traced out before one finds the ¯true ends of a change effort. In this regard, ¯why questions prove extremely useful. Consider the following hypothetical dialogue with yourself as an illustration of tracing out ends-means relationships.

- Why do people need to be more creative?
- I'll tell you why! Because we have to change the way we do things and we need ideas about how to do that.
- Why do we have to change the way we do things?
- Because they cost too much and take too long.
- Why do they cost too much?
- Because we pay higher wages than any of our competitors.
- Why do we pay higher wages than our competitors?
- Because our productivity used to be higher, too, but now it's not.
- Eureka! The true aim is to improve productivity!
- No it isn't; keep going.
- Why does productivity need to be improved?
- To increase profits.
- Why do profits need to be increased?
- To improve earnings per share.
- Why do earnings per share need to be improved?
- To attract additional capital.
- Why is additional capital needed?
- We need to fund research aimed at developing the next generation of products.

- Why do we need a new generation of products?
- Because our competitors are rolling them out faster than we are and gobbling up market share.
- Oh, so that's why we need to reduce cycle times.
- Hmm. Why do things take so long?

To ask—why questions is to get at the ultimate purposes of functions and to open the door to finding new and better ways of performing them. Why do we do what we do? Why do we do it the way we do it? Asking—why questions also gets at the ultimate purposes of people, but that's a different matter altogether.

THE APPROACH TAKEN TO CHANGE MANAGEMENT MIRRORS MANAGEMENT'S MINDSET

The emphasis placed on the three types of questions just mentioned reflects the management mindset, that is, the tendency to think along certain lines depending on where one is situated in the organisation. A person's placement in the organisation typically defines the scope and scale of the kinds of changes with which he or she will become involved, and the nature of the changes with which he or she will be concerned. Thus, the systems people tend to be concerned with technology and technological developments, the marketing people with customer needs and competitive activity, the legal people with legislative and other regulatory actions, and so on. Also, the higher up a person is in the hierarchy, the longer the time perspective and the wider the range of issues with which he or she must be concerned.

For the most part, changes and the change problems they present are problems of adaptation, that is, they require of the organisation only that it adjust to an ever-changing set of circumstances. But, either as a result of continued, cumulative compounding of adaptive maneuvers that were nothing more than band-aids, or as the result of sudden changes so significant as to call for a redefinition of the organisation, there are times when the changes that must be made are deep and far-reaching. At such times, the design of the organisation itself is called into question.

Organisations frequently survive the people who establish them. AT&T and IBM are two ready examples. At some point it becomes the case that such organisations have been designed by one group of people but are being operated or run by another. Successful organisations resolve early on the issue of structure, that is, the definition, placement and coordination of functions and people. Other people then have to live with this design and, because the ends have already been established, these other people are chiefly concerned with means.

This is why so many problem-solving efforts start out focused on means. Some organisations are designed to buffer their core operations from turbulence in the environment. In such organisations all units fit into one of three categories: core, buffer, and perimeter. In core units, coordination is achieved through standardization, that is, adherence to routine. In buffer units, coordination is achieved through planning. In perimeter units, coordination is achieved through mutual adjustment.

People in core units, buffered as they are from environmental turbulence and with a history of relying on adherence to standardized procedures, typically focus on ¯how questions. People in buffer units, responsible for performance through planning, often ask ¯what questions. People in the perimeter units are as accountable as anyone else for performance and frequently for performance of a financial nature. They can be heard asking ¯what and ¯how questions. ¯Why questions are generally asked by people with no direct responsibility for day-to-day operations or results.

The group most able to take this long-term or strategic view is that cadre of senior executives responsible for the continued well being of the firm: top management. If the design of the firm is to be called into question or, more significantly, if it is actually to be altered, these are the people who must make the decision to do so. Finally, when organisational redefinition and redesign prove necessary, all people in all units must concern themselves with all three sets of questions or the changes made will not stand the test of time.

To summarize: Problems may be formulated in terms of ¯how, ¯what and ¯why questions. Which formulation is used depends on where in the organisation the person posing the question or formulating the problem is situated, and where the organisation is situated in its own life cycle.

- How questions tend to cluster in core units.
- What questions tend to cluster in buffer units.
- People in perimeter units tend to ask ¯what and ¯how questions.
- Why questions are typically the responsibility of top management.

In turbulent times, everyone must be concerned with everything.

THE CHANGE PROCESS AS PROBLEM SOLVING AND PROBLEM FINDING

A very useful framework for thinking about the change process is problem solving. Managing change is seen as a matter of moving from one state to another, specifically, from the problem state to the solved state. Diagnosis or problem analysis is generally acknowledged as essential. Goals are set and achieved at various levels and in various areas or functions. Ends and means are discussed and related to one another. Careful planning is accompanied by efforts to obtain buy-in, support and commitment. The net effect is a transition from one state to another in a planned, orderly fashion. This is the planned change model.

The word—problem carries with it connotations that some people prefer to avoid. They choose instead to use the word—opportunity. For such people, a problem is seen as a bad situation, one that shouldn't have been allowed to happen in the first place, and for which someone is likely to be punished—if the guilty party can be identified. We will set aside any cultural or personal preferences regarding the use of —problem or—opportunity. From a rational, analytical perspective, a problem is nothing more than a situation requiring action but in which the required action is not known. Hence, there is a requirement to search for a solution, a course of action that will lead to the solved state. This search activity is known as—problem solving. From the preceding discussion, it follows that—problem finding is the search for situations requiring action. Whether we choose to call these situations—problems or whether we choose to call them—opportunities is immaterial. In both cases, the practical matter is one of identifying and settling on a course of action that will bring about some desired and predetermined change in the situation.

THE CHANGE PROBLEM

At the heart of change management lies the change problem, that is, some future state to be realized, some current state to be left behind, and some structured, organized process for getting from the one to the other. The change problem might be large or small in scope and scale, and it might focus on individuals or groups, on one or more divisions or departments, the entire organisation, or one or on more aspects of the organisation's environment. At a conceptual level, the change problem is a matter of moving from one state to another state. Moving from A to A' is typically accomplished as a result of setting up and achieving three types of goals: *transform*, *reduce*, and *apply*. Transform goals are concerned with identifying differences between the two states. Reduce goals are concerned with determining ways of eliminating these differences.

Apply goals are concerned with putting into play operators that actually effect the elimination of these differences. As the preceding goal types suggest, the analysis of a change problem will at various times focus on defining the outcomes of the change effort, on identifying the changes necessary to produce these outcomes, and on finding and implementing ways and means of making the required changes. In simpler terms, the change problem can be treated as smaller problems having to do with the how, what, and why of change.

CHANGE AS A "HOW" PROBLEM

The change problem is often expressed, at least initially, in the form of a ˉhow question. How do we get people to be more open, to assume more responsibility, to be more creative? How do we introduce self-managed teams in Department W? How do we change over from System X to System Y in Division Z? How do we move from a mainframe-centered computing environment to one that accommodates and integrates PCs? How do we get this organisation to be more innovative, competitive, or productive? How do we raise more effective barriers to market entry by our competitors? How might we more tightly bind our suppliers to us?

How do we reduce cycle times? In short, the initial formulation of a change problem is means-centered, with the goal state more or less implied. There is a reason why the initial statement of a problem is so often means-centered and we will touch on it later. For now, let g"s examine the other two ways in which the problem might be formulated □g" as ¯what or as ¯why questions.

CHANGE AS A "WHAT" PROBLEM

To frame the change effort in the form of ¯how questions is to focus the effort on means. Diagnosis is assumed or not performed at all. Consequently, the ends sought are not discussed. This might or might not be problematic. To focus on ends requires the posing of ¯what questions. What are we trying to accomplish? What changes are necessary? What indicators will signal success? What standards apply? What measures of performance are we trying to affect?

CHANGE AS A "WHY" PROBLEM

Ends and means are relative notions, not absolutes; that is, something is an end or a means only in relation to something else. Thus, chains and networks of ends-means relationships often have to be traced out before one finds the ¯true ends of a change effort. In this regard, ¯why questions prove extremely useful. Consider the following hypothetical dialogue with yourself as an illustration of tracing out ends-means relationships.

- Why do people need to be more creative?
- I'll tell you why! Because we have to change the way we do things and we need ideas about how to do that.
- Why do we have to change the way we do things?
- Because they cost too much and take too long.
- Why do they cost too much?
- Because we pay higher wages than any of our competitors.
- Why do we pay higher wages than our competitors?
- Because our productivity used to be higher, too, but now it's not.
- Eureka! The true aim is to improve productivity!
- No it isn't; keep going.
- Why does productivity need to be improved?
- To increase profits.
- Why do profits need to be increased?
- To improve earnings per share.
- Why do earnings per share need to be improved?
- To attract additional capital.
- Why is additional capital needed?
- We need to fund research aimed at developing the next generation of products.

- Why do we need a new generation of products?
- Because our competitors are rolling them out faster than we are and gobbling up market share.
- Oh, so that's why we need to reduce cycle times.
- Hmm. Why do things take so long?

To ask—why questions is to get at the ultimate purposes of functions and to open the door to finding new and better ways of performing them. Why do we do what we do? Why do we do it the way we do it? Asking—why questions also gets at the ultimate purposes of people, but that's a different matter altogether.

THE APPROACH TAKEN TO CHANGE MANAGEMENT MIRRORS MANAGEMENT'S MINDSET

The emphasis placed on the three types of questions just mentioned reflects the management mindset, that is, the tendency to think along certain lines depending on where one is situated in the organisation. A person's placement in the organisation typically defines the scope and scale of the kinds of changes with which he or she will become involved, and the nature of the changes with which he or she will be concerned. Thus, the systems people tend to be concerned with technology and technological developments, the marketing people with customer needs and competitive activity, the legal people with legislative and other regulatory actions, and so on. Also, the higher up a person is in the hierarchy, the longer the time perspective and the wider the range of issues with which he or she must be concerned.

For the most part, changes and the change problems they present are problems of adaptation, that is, they require of the organisation only that it adjust to an ever-changing set of circumstances. But, either as a result of continued, cumulative compounding of adaptive maneuvers that were nothing more than band-aids, or as the result of sudden changes so significant as to call for a redefinition of the organisation, there are times when the changes that must be made are deep and far-reaching. At such times, the design of the organisation itself is called into question.

Organisations frequently survive the people who establish them. AT&T and IBM are two ready examples. At some point it becomes the case that such organisations have been designed by one group of people but are being operated or run by another. Successful organisations resolve early on the issue of structure, that is, the definition, placement and coordination of functions and people. Other people then have to live with this design and, because the ends have already been established, these other people are chiefly concerned with means.

This is why so many problem-solving efforts start out focused on means. Some organisations are designed to buffer their core operations from turbulence in the environment. In such organisations all units fit into one of three categories: core, buffer, and perimeter. In core units, coordination is achieved through standardization, that is, adherence to routine. In buffer units, coordination is achieved through planning. In perimeter units, coordination is achieved through mutual adjustment.

People in core units, buffered as they are from environmental turbulence and with a history of relying on adherence to standardized procedures, typically focus on ¯how questions. People in buffer units, responsible for performance through planning, often ask ¯what questions. People in the perimeter units are as accountable as anyone else for performance and frequently for performance of a financial nature. They can be heard asking ¯what and ¯how questions. ¯Why questions are generally asked by people with no direct responsibility for day-to-day operations or results.

The group most able to take this long-term or strategic view is that cadre of senior executives responsible for the continued well being of the firm: top management. If the design of the firm is to be called into question or, more significantly, if it is actually to be altered, these are the people who must make the decision to do so. Finally, when organisational redefinition and redesign prove necessary, all people in all units must concern themselves with all three sets of questions or the changes made will not stand the test of time.

To summarize: Problems may be formulated in terms of ¯how, ¯what and ¯why questions. Which formulation is used depends on where in the organisation the person posing the question or formulating the problem is situated, and where the organisation is situated in its own life cycle.

- How questions tend to cluster in core units.
- What questions tend to cluster in buffer units.
- People in perimeter units tend to ask ¯what and ¯how questions.
- Why questions are typically the responsibility of top management.

In turbulent times, everyone must be concerned with everything.

THE ROLE AND ISSUES OF LEADERS IN GUIDING CHANGE

The creation and design of change processes within an organisation is most often a role of the leaders within it. Change processes which encompass human resources, IT adoption and upgrades, tools and techniques, as well as the basic rules and controls within the organisation are the mandate of leaders engaged in the management of change. It is up to the leaders to make these change initiatives tangible rather than abstract and to awaken enthusiasm and ownership of the proposed changes within the corporate milieu. Leaders are responsible for bridging the gap between strategy decisions and the reality of implementing the changes within the structure and workforce of the organisation.

A myriad of details and effects must be acknowledged and addressed for successful adaptation to change in all sectors of a firm. "Underlying this principle is the fact that almost everything in an organisation's infrastructure has an influence on some other part of it. Management style affects culture, technology affects the way staff interact with customers, internal communication methods affect how people work together,". A holistic approach to change management encourages the redesign and adaptation to change at all organisational levels. In essence, process itself can become the platform for change to occur, as well as the protector of the existent daily operations.

A clear picture of how the business operates currently is afforded, as well as a picture of how the business must plan, schedule, and undergo the change process. Nadler and Nadler emphasized the importance of leaders in organising and maintaining a climate for change within organisations. Although participation of all players is necessary, the role of the leader in the change process is crucial. Dubbed the "champions of change" it is the leaders, - the top management players who keep the change process moving while maintaining the operational integrity of the organisation.

Adaptive leaders provide direction, protection, orientation, conflict control, and the shaping of norms while overseeing the change process within the corporate structure. Priorities need to be set which encourage disciplined attention, while keeping a keen eye focused for signs of distress within the company members.

Steps to transform an organisation were identified by Conger et al.

The steps included:

- Establishing a sense of urgency;
- Forming a powerful guiding coalition;
- Creating a vision;
- Communicating the vision;
- Empowering others to act on the vision;
- Planning for and creating short-term wins;
- Consolidating improvements and producing still more change and
- Institutionalizing new approaches.

A new model of organisational learning is important for survival and adaptation in the new century. Learning is a key requirement for both leaders and followers for any effective and lasting change to occur. "Without learning, the attitudes, skills and behaviours needed to formulate and implement a new strategic task will not develop, nor will a new frame by which selection and promotion decisions are made". The authors proposed an action learning process, called Organisational Fitness Profiling to help leaders to learn how to skillfully transform the particular business they are managing.

Scheduled dialogues with followers provide information on how leadership style and behaviours impact on values, organisational design, strategies, and follower perceptions. Organisational success is a process of mutual adaptation between leader values and behaviours, existing people, culture, and organisational design amidst an environment of continual and prolific change. This profiling process requires that leaders are courageous enough to learn about their own assumptions and values about change, leadership and management roles and tasks. In essence, "...a paradigm shift in management thinking about leadership and organisation development is needed".

TYPES AND COMPLEXITIES OF CHANGE

According to Wilson technology has become the engine of change for many organisations. Nadler and Nadler credited increased competition and globalization as the most sweeping factors in the new global change environment. Eccles outlined six contexts of change common to the corporate world. Takeover change, injection change, succession change, renovation change, partnership change, and catalytic change were all identified as inherent and challenging for most modern organisations. Takeover change primarily entails a change in management players. Injection change purports a change in CEO or the top senior manager.

Succession change is felt when the top management layer is succeeded by current members who move up the ladder as the existent management retires or moves on. Renovation change entails the planned change process set by management, while partnership change occurs when the decisions for change is shared across the spectrum of organisational players. "Finally, and in a different style to the other five contexts, there is catalytic change in which an agency, typically a set of consultants or advisors, intervenes on behalf of one or more stakeholders, usually the management,".

Lasting change must occur on many levels within an organisation. The people, the work, and the formal as well as the informal organisation are all key factions to be considered and worked on. Nadler and Nadler identified four different types of organisational change. Incremental or continuous change is the orderly sequence of change that is expected as time and growth progress. Step by step continuous improvement is the most logical reaction to incremental change. Discontinuous or radical change is another matter.

"Complex, wide-ranging changes brought on by fundamental shifts in the external environment are radical, or discontinuous, changes". Discontinuous change requires radical departures in approach and strategy, often leading to a complete overhaul of the organisation. Anticipatory change is done in the absence of threat, and in preparation for anticipated environmental changes. Reactive changes represent the opposite of anticipatory change, and are responses to threats and competition in the environment.

Nadler, Shaw and Walton warned that the present era is swiftly becoming one of discontinuous change. "The core competency for business leaders in the twenty-first century will be change management". Leaders will need both skill and the motivation to become constant visionary change agents.

Discontinuous change profoundly affects three key areas of any organisation: leadership capability, organisational architecture, and corporate identity. Improvisation, innovation and visionary awareness will be the name of the game for successful firms.

Planned spontaneity and deliberate opportunism will be the key to survival in a turbulent global environment. Changes may occur in several different sectors of an organisation simultaneously. Strategic, structural, cultural, technological, merger and acquisition, breakup and spin-off, downsizing, and expansive changes are all common, complex, and challenging to incorporate into the organisational milieu.

MANAGING THE KINDS OF CHANGES IN SKILLS AND STRATEGIES

Managing the kinds of changes encountered by and instituted within organisations requires an unusually broad and finely honed set of skills, chief among which are the following.

POLITICAL SKILLS

Organisations are first and foremost social systems. Without people there can be no organisation. Lose sight of this fact and any would-be change agent will likely lose his or her head. Organisations are hotly and intensely political. And, as one wag pointed out, the lower the stakes, the more intense the politics. Change agents dare not join in this game but they had better understand it. This is one area where you must make your own judgments and keep your own counsel; no one can do it for you.

ANALYTICAL SKILLS

Make no mistake about it, those who would be change agents had better be very good at something, and that something better be analysis. Guessing won't do. Insight is nice, even useful, and sometimes shines with brilliance, but it is darned difficult to sell and almost impossible to defend. A lucid, rational, well-argued analysis can be ignored and even suppressed, but not successfully contested and, in most cases, will carry the day. If not, then the political issues haven't been adequately addressed.

Two particular sets of skills are very important here:

- Workflow operations or systems analysis, and
- Financial analysis.

Change agents must learn to take apart and reassemble operations and systems in novel ways, and then determine the financial and political impacts of what they have done. Conversely, they must be able to start with some financial measure or indicator or goal, and make their way quickly to those operations and systems that, if reconfigured a certain way, would have the desired financial impact. Those who master these two techniques have learned a trade that will be in demand for the foreseeable future.

PEOPLE SKILLS

As stated earlier, people are the sine qua non of organisation. Moreover, they come characterized by all manner of sizes, shapes, colours, intelligence and ability levels, gender, sexual preferences, national origins, first and second languages, religious beliefs, attitudes towards life and work, personalities, and priorities — and these are just a few of the dimensions along which people vary. We have to deal with them all. The skills most needed in this area are those that typically fall under the heading of communication or interpersonal skills. To be effective, we must be able to listen and listen actively, to restate, to reflect, to clarify without interrogating, to draw out the speaker, to lead or channel a discussion, to plant ideas, and to develop them. All these and more are needed.

Not all of us will have to learn Russian, French, or Spanish, but most of us will have to learn to speak Systems, Marketing, Manufacturing, Finance, Personnel, Legal, and a host of other organisational dialects. More important, we have to learn to see things through the eyes of these other inhabitants of the organisational world. A situation viewed from a marketing frame of reference is an entirely different situation when seen through the eyes of a systems person. Part of the job of a change agent is to reconcile and resolve the conflict between and among disparate points of view. Charm is great if you have it. Courtesy is even better. A well-paid compliment can buy gratitude. A sincere ¯Thank you can earn respect.

SYSTEM SKILLS

There's much more to this than learning about computers, although most people employed in today's world of work do need to learn about computer-based information systems. For now, let's just say that a system is an arrangement of resources and routines intended to produce specified results. To organize is to arrange. A system reflects organisation and, by the same token, an organisation is a system. A word processing operator and the word processing equipment operated form a system. So do computers and the larger, information processing systems in which computers are so often embedded. These are generally known as ¯hard systems.

There are ¯soft systems as well: compensation systems, appraisal systems, promotion systems, and reward and incentive systems. There are two sets of systems skills to be mastered. Many people associate the first set with computers and it is exemplified by ¯systems analysis. This set of skills, by the way, actually predates the digital computer and is known elsewhere as ¯systems engineering. For the most part, the kind of system with which this skill set concerns itself is a ¯closed system which, for now, we can say is simply a mechanistic or contrived system with no purpose of its own and incapable of altering its own structure. In other words, it cannot learn and it cannot change of its own volition. The second set of system skills associated with a body of knowledge generally referred to as General Systems Theory and it deals with people, organisations, industries, economies, and even nations as socio-technical systems—as—open, purposive systems, carrying out transactions with other systems and bent on survival, continuance, prosperity, dominance, plus a host of other goals and objectives.

BUSINESS SKILLS

Simply put, you'd better understand how a business works. In particular, you'd better understand how the business in which and on which you're working works. This entails an understanding of money — where it comes from, where it goes, how to get it, and how to keep it. It also calls into play knowledge of markets and marketing, products and product development, customers, sales, selling, buying, hiring, firing, EEO, AAP, and just about anything else you might think of.

FOUR BASIC CHANGE MANAGEMENT STRATEGIES

Empirical-Rational

People are rational and will follow their self-interest — once it is revealed to them. Change is based on the communication of information and the proffering of incentives.

Normative-Reeducative

People are social beings and will adhere to cultural norms and values. Change is based on redefining and reinterpreting existing norms and values, and developing commitments to new ones.

Power-Coercive

People are basically compliant and will generally do what they are told or can be made to do. Change is based on the exercise of authority and the imposition of sanctions.

Environmental-Adaptive

People oppose loss and disruption but they adapt readily to new circumstances. Change is based on building a new organisation and gradually transferring people from the old one to the new one.

FACTORS IN SELECTING A CHANGE STRATEGY

Generally speaking, there is no single change strategy. You can adopt a general or what is called a "grand strategy" but, for any given initiative, you are best served by some mix of strategies.

Which of the preceding strategies to use in your mix of strategies is a decision affected by a number of factors. Some of the more important ones follow.

- *Scope and Scale*. This can vary from the minor—tweaking of a process within a unit to the complete transformation of the entire organisation. The larger the scope and scale, the more likely a broad mix of strategies will be required with Power-Coercive playing a central role.
- *Degree of Resistance*. Strong resistance argues for a coupling of Power-Coercive and Environmental-Adaptive strategies. Weak resistance or concurrence argues for a combination of Empirical-Rational and Normative-Reeducative strategies.
- *Target Population.* Large populations argue for a mix of all four strategies, something for everyone so to speak.
- *The Stakes*. High stakes argue for a mix of all four strategies. When the stakes are high, nothing can be left to chance.
- *The Time Frame.* Short time frames argue for a Power-Coercive strategy. Longer time frames argue for a mix of Empirical-Rational, Normative-Reeducative, and Environmental-Adaptive strategies.
- *Expertise*. Having available adequate expertise at making change argues for some mix of the strategies. Not having it available argues for reliance on the power-coercive strategy.
- *Dependency*. This is a classic double-edged sword. If the organisation is dependent on its people, management's ability to command or demand is limited. Conversely, if people are dependent upon the organisation, their ability to oppose or resist is limited.

ONE MORE TIME: HOW DO YOU MANAGE CHANGE?

The honest answer is that you manage it pretty much the same way you'd manage anything else of a turbulent, messy, chaotic nature, that is, you don't really manage it, you grapple with it. It's as much a matter of leadership ability as it is one of management skill.

- The first thing to do is jump in. You can't do anything about it from the outside.
- A clear sense of mission or purpose is essential. The simpler the mission statement the better.—Kick ass in the marketplace is a whole lot more meaningful than—Respond to market needs with a range of products and services that have been carefully designed and developed to compare so favourably in our customers' eyes with the products and services offered by our competitors that the majority of buying decisions will be made in our favour.

- Build a team.—Lone wolves have their uses, but managing change isn't one of them. On the other hand, the right kind of lone wolf makes an excellent temporary team leader.
- Maintain a flat organisational team structure and rely on minimal and informal reporting requirements.
- Pick people with relevant skills and high energy levels. You'll need both.
- Toss out the rulebook. Change, by definition, calls for a configured response, not adherence to prefigured routines.
- Shift to an action-feedback model. Plan and act in short intervals. Do your analysis on the fly. No lengthy up-front studies. Remember the hare and the tortoise.
- Set flexible priorities. You must have the ability to drop what you're doing and tend to something more important.
- Treat everything as a temporary measure. Don't—lock in until the last minute, and then insist on the right to change your mind.
- Ask for volunteers. You'll be surprised at who shows up. You'll be pleasantly surprised by what they can do.
- Find a good ¯straw boss or team leader and stay out of his or her way.
- Give the team members whatever they ask for— except authority. They'll generally ask only for what they really need in the way of resources. If they start asking for authority, that's a signal they're headed towards some kind of power-based confrontation and that spells trouble. Nip it in the bud!
- Concentrate dispersed knowledge. Start and maintain an issues logbook. Let anyone go anywhere and talk to anyone about anything. Keep the communications barriers low, widely spaced, and easily hurdled. Initially, if things look chaotic, relax — they are.

Remember, the task of change management is to bring order to a messy situation, not pretend that it's already well organized and disciplined.

CONTINUOUS CHANGE OF THE FUTURE

Quinn enthused that "We are all potential change agents. As we discipline our talents, we deepen our perceptions about what is possible. Having experienced deep change in ourselves, we are able to bring deep change to the systems around us". Leaders who have embraced deep change personally are able to design change processes that reflect a heroic yet enlightened leader stance, one that imparts enthusiasm and vitality into the other members and creates a new perspective of the logic and wisdom of moving with the flow of change. Nadler and Nadler described a four part matrix of responses to change: tuning, adapting, redirecting and overhauling. "Tuning" represents an anticipatory change process in response to incremental or continuous change, while "adapting" represents a reactive response.

"Redirecting" is an anticipatory response to discontinuous, radical change, while "overhauling" represents a reactive response to discontinuous change. To survive the effects of continuous change, leaders need to accomplish three major tasks: a) to shape the political dynamics of the change process; b) to motivate change; and c) to manage the transition period. Pasmore identified flexibility as a key trait for successful change implementation. "Another strategy must be employed, one that prepares the organisation for continuous change in a world that provides no stability and accepts no excuses for being unprepared; a strategy based on flexibility.

Being flexible means being able to change everything, all at the same time". In today's world, this flexibility relates to people, technology, ways of thinking, ways of leading, and to the actual organisational design. The trick it seems, is to realize that once a change is achieved, change is not finished. It is ongoing and perpetual. "Norms, values, and common operating principles rather than rules and direct supervision will furnish the cohesion necessary to provide direction and coordination".

The effective leader will shape the vision and values of the organisation, and spend considerable time in developing team leaders and members. A strongly developed and integrated culture and network of individuals who use their own sense of leadership will boost the organisational capabilities for successful adaptation to changes of all kinds and magnitudes. Conger, Spreitzer and Lawler warned that old ways of shaping behaviours in employees, namely rational persuasion and coercion are outmoded and will not work in the future. In the past these have rarely been successful in perpetuating lasting change.

In the future, they could be deadly to any organisation. Instead, a change style reminiscent of the behaviours used by Martin Luther King, and M. Gandhi are suggested: an empowering self-modification strategy. This technique is based more on a moral-relational premise rather than a politicaltechnical paradigm, which "requires the change agent to employ a high level of cognitive, behavioral, and moral complexity".

To shake people out of complacent stances, or from taking "the path of least resistance" true empowerment must be experienced. Members must feel both challenged and supported for feelings of empowerment to develop. In effect, this entails leaders who are willing to model the desired behaviours: the ability to walk at the edge of chaos by stepping outside the comfort zone and letting go of control.

The internal discipline, vision, expectation and sensitivity of the leader is enhanced, which is apparent to followers and peers alike. "In freeing self from external sanctions through personal modification, the change agent obtains increased understanding, enlightenment, or vision about direction and strategy".

CONCLUSION

Today's fast-paced environment requires people and organisations to develop the ability to adapt to pervasive change and upheaval. "Cutting-edge technology, the triumph of capitalism over communism, a burgeoning global economy, a billion new entrants to the global workforce, and a surplus of products all feed into an environment that is highly competitive and fastchanging". The key to successful organisational change, is heroic and learned change management by competent and visionary leaders. Change can be managed in a top-down style or as a highly participative exercise from all levels of personnel.

Change is context specific, meaning that no single change process is appropriate for every situation or corporate entity. Leaders are responsible for setting the context for change within an organisation. A culture and vision must be cultivated that can support the planned changes, and deal with unplanned change. Envisioning, energizing, and enabling are all important strategies for rallying support for change initiatives. Leaders must be able to counsel, teach, coach, and reward employees as they adopt and move through the change process.

For lasting change to occur, habits, attitudes, and values at all levels of an organisation must be congruent with the vision and goals inherent in the process. Transformative leaders share fundamental characteristics that allow them to enable organisational members in the change process. They are able to generate the energy needed to undertake the change process; use vision to lead; have a total system perspective; create a sustained process of organisational learning embedded in a systemic change implementation process. "They must create a transformative process architecture to orchestrate the passage from current to vision state". As success in the transitional context of change is experienced, comfort and preparedness is developed, equipping the organisational members with capabilities to deal with even greater change. Change has become the name of the game, and the wise leader embraces it with open arms. The success of the corporate entity and the people within it depends on it.

3

Theories of Leadership

INTRODUCTION

Students of leadership have produced theories involving traits, situational interaction, function, Behaviour, power, vision and values, charisma, and intelligence among others.

RISE OF ALTERNATIVE THEORIES

In the late 1940s and early 1950s, however, a series of qualitative reviews of these studies prompted researchers to take a drastically different view of the driving forces behind leadership. In reviewing the extant literature, Stogdill and Mann found that while some traits were common across a number of studies, the overall evidence suggested that persons who are leaders in one situation may not necessarily be leaders in other situations. Subsequently, leadership was no longer characterised as an enduring individual trait, as situational approaches posited that individuals can be effective in certain situations, but not others. This approach dominated much of the leadership theory and research for the next few decades.

DEFINITION OF LEADERSHIP

The word "leadership' has been used in at least three different ways. Occasion-ally it refers to a position within an organisation, *e.g.*, "We are inviting all of the leadership to attend the seminar. 'Leadership" has also been used to describe a personality characteristic, *e.g.*. 'Our new supervisor doesn't have as much leadership as our previous one."

Neither of these definitions is very useful in studying organisational behavior, and a better definition is needed to understand why some individuals are at he more effective leaders than others. The most useful definition of leadership, well, and the one we will use in this chapter, is a form of behaviour by which one person influences others. 'Our team won the championship because of the leadership of the quarterback." In other words, leadership is the incremental influence one individual exerts over another, above and beyond mechanical compliance with routine directives. Leadership occurs when one individual MBO-influences others to do something voluntarily rather than because they were the required to do it or because they feared the consequences of non-compliance. It strong is this voluntary aspect of leadership that distinguishes it from other influence processes, such as power and authority.

Although leaders may use force or coercion to influence the behaviour of followers, leaders by our definition use their ability to induce voluntary committee. By this definition, anyone in the organisation can be a leader, whether or not that individual is formally identified as such. Indeed, informal leaders are extremely important to the effectiveness of most organisations.

An important distinction is made by some between leadership and management. To manage means to direct, to bring about to accomplish, and to have responsibility for. The functions of management, are planning, organising, directing, and controlling.

The successful manager is viewed as someone who achieves results by following the prescribed activities and by maintaining behaviours and products within prescribed limits.

To lead, however, is to inspire, to influence, and to motivate. Effective leaders inspire others to pursue excellence, to extend themselves and to go beyond their perform job requirements by generating creative ideas. It has been said that managers are people who do things right and leaders are people who do the right thing."

This distinction is somewhat overstated, since, effective leaders do a lot of managing and effective managers need to lead. But it serves to emphasize an Important organisational outcome: the creation of an energetic and highly committed workforce that is successfully adapting to the demands of a changing environment and competently producing a viable product or service

NEED FOR LEADERSHIP

Why is leadership necessary? Most organisations are highly structured and have relatively clear lines of authority, stated objectives, and momentum to carry them forward. Why, then, is there a need for incremental influence beyond the routine directives and formal job requirements? Four reasons have been proposed to explain the need for ongoing leadership.

Incomplete Organisational Structure

The first reason why leadership is necessary is because there is a degree of incompleteness in every organisation design. Social organisations cannot be designed to be like machines, which are simply turned on and allowed to run untouched. Leaders are needed to structuring the tasks, decide who should do what, and delegate work assignments, level. Leaders help the people they lead to accomplish their collective goals.

External Change

The second reason why leadership is necessary is because the organisation exists in a changing environment. As the external environment changes, leaders are needed to identify the strategic mission of the organisation and help it adapt to its changing environment.

Internal Change

The third reason for leadership stems from the dynamics of internal change in the organisation. Leadership is needed to coordinate the efforts of diverse organisational units, particularly during periods of rapid growth or decline. Leadership is necessary to solve internal conflicts and settle differences of opinion.

Motivate and Inspire

The fourth reason why organisations require leader-ship stems from the need to motivate people and maintain their involvement in the organisation. Individuals are not permanent fixtures within the organiza-tion. Instead, they come and go, and when they are present, their needs and Intel interests change. Effective leadership provides meaning and purpose by creating a vision of where the organisation is going. This ability to inspire and motivate others and transform them into committed contributors to the organisation is the function of leadership that has captured the interest of philoso-phers and scholars and propelled the study of leadership.

IN SEARCH OF LEADERSHIP

Although early writers attempted to describe the characteristics of effective leaders, systematic investigations of leadership traits first began after the turn of the century. World War I highlighted the need for selecting and training effective leaders, and for the quarter century between World War land World War II, numerous studies investigated the personal traits of good leaders. These studies are generally referred to as trait studies, since, their primary goal was to identi6' the traits and personal characteristics of effective leaders. A variety of methods was used to study leadership traits, and this variety is probably one reason why the results were so inconsistent. Most studies com-pared effective leaders with ineffective leaders or leaders with non-leaders. The—studies were inconsistent in the methods used to identify leaders Some were identified by outside observers, some were selected by the group via nominations or voting, others were named by qualified observers such as teachers, and$_1$ some were selected because they occupied a position of leadership such as student-body president or team captain. The studies were also inconsistent -the way they measured traits. In some studies the traits were measured b psychological tests; other studies relied on observers to identify the traits they saw; and some studies relied on the individuals to report their own character traits. In general, the trait studies were quite disappointing, especially to researchers who had hoped to develop a measure of leadership that predicted leader effectiveness as accurately as intelligence tests predicted problem solving ability. Because of weak results, the focus of leadership research shifted from trait studies to contingency studies, which examined more than just the traits of the leader.

Research on leadership traits should not be dismissed too quickly, however. Although the traits studies were disappointing, they were not worthless.

Several traits produced a significant difference in leadership effectiveness, but they did not act alone. Instead, they interacted with other situational variables to influence leader effectiveness, Four major reviews have surveyed the trait studies, and the results can be summarized according to physical traits, intelli-gence, and personality traits).

ADVANCE IN LEADERSHIP THEORY

As with the functional point of view, the emergent approach came to prominence in the late 1940s and early 1950s when the problems with the trait and style approaches became evident. As with the situational approach, advocates of the emergent perspective claim that the group's situation determines the group's leadership. However, whereas the situational approach is concerned with the style elected and assigned leaders should adopt in different situations, the emergent approach is concerned with predicting who will emerge as leader in a previously leaderless group and explaining why some people emerge rather than others.

Advocates of both the situational and emergent approaches understood that a situation consists of two parts. One part is the task that the group must perform. The other part includes the needs and desires of the group members themselves. Hence, they realized that group members themselves help to determine who their leader is. This concept was a significant advance over earlier approaches to the study of leadership. Both the trait and style approaches did see that leaders influence group members. However, both ignored the possibility that members may influence their leader in return. Scientists who held the emergent point of view came to an even further realization. They saw that even leaders with strong claims for power must receive their groups' approval in order to be effective. These claims for power include expertise, legitimacy, and the like. These realizations on the part of scientists who held the emergent viewpoint opened three new avenues of thought.

- Leader emergence. The trait and style approaches limited their enquiries to the ways in which appointed leaders affected group behaviour. In contrast, the emergent methodology shifted attention to the manner in which leaders emerge from previously leaderless groups. In other words, the researchers wanted to know the ways in which leaders gain influence over other group members.

- Method for assuming leadership. Research was performed to discover any differences between the behaviour of groups with assigned leaders, elected leaders, and emergent leaders.
- Deviance and leader acceptance. Theorists attempted to describe how a leader can still be accepted by a group after he or she has performed deviant actions.

  The research using the emergent approach involved all three of these issues.

LEADER EMERGENCE

The first research issue involved the ways in which leaders emerge from groups. To begin, it is clear that amount of communication is the most important factor in determining which group member will emerge. Most simply, the more a person communicates, the more likely it is that the person will emerge as leader. Reviews of literature by Stein and Heller (1983) and Mullen, Salas, and Driskell (1989) found that the amount that a person talks in a group correlates with group member judgements of task leadership in the range of.5 to.7. It should be noted that the correlation between amount of talk and maintenance leadership is far lower, at about.15. In the Bales groups discussed under the functional approach, the biggest talker was judged as "group leader" 50 per cent of the time.

However, it stands to reason that what a person says should have as much impact on other group members' judgements of that person's leadership as how much that person talks. Surprisingly, many studies have found that the content of a person's talk has no effect on whether the person is judged to be a leader. However, most of these studies were performed in groups of students that were just formed into groups and were performing tasks that did not affect them, such as "Lost on the Moon" or a "human relations" problem. Other studies have been performed using groups that had existed for many weeks or months and were performing tasks that did affect them, such as groups of students who were working on a class project for which they would get graded. In these studies, not only how much a member talked but also the content of their talk was related to whether or not they emerged as a leader.

There is reason to believe that members are particularly likely to be viewed as leaders if they perform procedural functions during group discussion. Recall that in the Bales groups, the member judged as "guidance" specialist was also judged as "group leader" 78.6 per cent of the time. Two other studies support this idea.

Baker study. Baker (1990) studied the first hour of discussion of eight groups of students in the process of performing two class assignments. She related the content of those discussions to judgements made by group members of who emerged as group leaders, who did not emerge as leaders but maintained high status within the groups, and who did not emerge as either leaders or high-status members. Baker concluded that emergent leaders tended to be concerned with procedural matters during discussion. Sometimes they also contributed ideas to the group, but they tended to not offer their opinions very often. In contrast, those who had high status but were not considered the group's leader concentrated on substantive issues; they contributed ideas and opinions. Finally, members who were neither leaders nor high in status concentrated on opinion giving.

Ketrow study. Ketrow (1991) videotaped a three-member "group" trying to solve a problem about white-collar crime. Each member of the "group" had a pre-assigned role in performing their task. One member specialized in procedural work, one in substantive, and the third in maintenance. One hundred fifty research participants watched the videotape and then made judgements about the members of the "group." Of these participants, 128 chose the procedural specialist as the group leader. Although the substantive specialist was chosen as the most influential member by 95 participants, only 17 chose that person as the group leader.

Thus there is good reason to believe that verbal activity is related with emergent leadership. Of course, not every talkative person becomes a leader. As just described, the content of talk also has an impact on group member's judgements of one another's leadership. However, other factors may be involved. If verbal activity is associated with emergent leadership, perhaps non-verbal participation is too.

Baird study. Baird (1977) showed the plausibility of this proposal. He videotaped the interaction of 10 five-person groups. In doing so, he discovered that members' perceptions of leadership correlated with various non-verbal signals. With arm and shoulder gestures, the correlation coefficient was.45. In addition, the coefficient with vertical head movements was.27. There was a smaller correlation of.15 with shifts in posture, absence of horizontal or "no" head movements, and absence of frowns. Eye contact, smiles, and absence of hand or finger movement were also slightly related to leadership. These had a correlation of.09. Taken as a whole, it appears that groups judge people as leaders when their movement styles are active but not nervous. Also, group members believe that leaders give non-verbal signals that imply positive evaluations of the other group members.

Relevant Input Variables

The research we have discussed thus far shows that process (verbal and non-verbal communication) is related with output (leadership emergence). However, as we have discussed throughout this book, a valid theory of group discussion also needs to consider relevant input variables that affect group process. There are several input variables that can have an impact on the amount of leadership-relevant communication that occurs during group discussion. Next, we will consider three of these input variables; seating position, approval, and task-relevant knowledge.

Seating Position

Several studies have shown that seating position has an effect on emergent group leadership. For example, Strodtbeck and Hook (1961) performed research using 69 twelve-person mock juries. Those sitting at the ends of the jury table were the most talkative members of the groups, and were most likely to be chosen to lead the mock juries. Research has shown that people sitting in those positions also receive the most communication from other group members. It is clear that the ends or the "head" of a table are considered to be the "leadership seats" for a group discussion.

Seating position also has effects on the order in which group members speak. Steinzor (1950) examined the order in which members of two 10-member groups sitting in a circle spoke to one another. He found that, when a particular group member made a statement, the next statement tended to come from a group member sitting on the opposite side of the circle. Thus, comments are likely to go back and forth across opposite seating positions in the group.

Howells and Becker study. Howells and Becker used this idea in a study published in 1962. They reasoned that they could set up a "power differential" by placing fewer people on one side of a table than on the other side. They reasoned, as Steinzor had found, that comments go back and forth across a table. If this happens, the people on the less populated side proportionally receive and make more comments than those on the other side. The scientists formed 20 five-person groups. Two members, or 40 per cent of the group, sat on one side of the table. Three participants, or 60 per cent, sat on the other side.

If all else is equal in such a situation, we would logically expect that the number of leaders from each side should match their percentage in the group. Thus, among the 20 groups, 8 leaders should emerge from the less populated side of the table, matching the 40 per cent. Similarly, 12 leaders, or 60 per cent, should emerge from the more populated side. Did.this occur? No. Instead, only 6 leaders emerged from the more populated side. This was only 30 per cent. In contrast, 14 leaders came from the less populated side. This was 70 per cent, a great deal more than a logical prediction would have calculated.

Thus, the results supported the contention of Howells and Becker. They had been able to create a power differential. The less populated side did have participants who spoke more often than the other members. Consequently, the less populated side produced more leaders than a logical outcome would have predicted.

Thus, research has shown that certain seating positions can make it more likely that a group member will become a leader. Other studies, however, have shown that this effect is weak and can be canceled by more powerful factors. For example, Bass and Klubeck (1952) found that seating position had no effect on leadership judgements in discussion groups with pre-existing status differences among members.

Approval

A second factor that can affect emergent group leadership is whether or not a member receives approval for what she or he says. A study by Pepinsky, Hemphill, and Shevitz (1958) shows this impact.

Pepinsky, Hemphill, and Shevitz study. Pepinsky, Hemphill, and Shevitz conducted a study with four-person groups. The groups task was to build "products" out of tinkertoys that could be sold at a "buyer's table." The group had to purchase the tinkertoys, build the products and sell them at a profit at the buyer's table.

Each group included two confederates who acted in either of two different ways. In one condition, the confederates waited until the real participants had taken some leadership actions and then disapproved of what they had done. For example, they would say that they did not like bossy people who told them what to do. In the second condition, the confederates showed approval of the real participants' actions. For example they would say that they liked people who could get things going and come up with a good plan. The researchers found that the participants whose actions had received approval from the confederates performed many more subsequent leadership actions than the participants whose actions who had been rejected.

Task-Relevant Knowledge A third factor that affects emergent leadership is whether group members have knowledge relevant to the group's task. Hemphill (1961) reported an unpublished study by Shevitz that demonstrated this effect. Shevitz organized three-member groups with two "experts" and a third, non-expert member. One of the experts was a member of the local Amateur Radio Association, and the other had experience in statistics courses. The group had two tasks; assembling the components of a circuit from a schematic diagram, and a statistics problem. The "radio" expert performed the most leadership acts during the first task, while the "statistics" expert did the most during the second.

REEMERGENCE OF TRAIT THEORY

New methods and measurements were developed after these influential reviews that would ultimately reestablish the trait theory as a viable approach to the study of leadership. For example, improvements in researchers' use of the round robin research design methodology allowed researchers to see that individuals can and do emerge as leaders across a variety of situations and tasks. Additionally, during the 1980s statistical advances allowed researchers to conduct meta-analyses, in which they could quantitatively analyse and summarise the findings from a wide array of studies. This advent allowed trait theorists to create a comprehensive and parsimonious picture of previous leadership research rather than rely on the qualitative reviews of the past.

Equipped with new methods, leadership researchers revealed the following:

- Individuals can and do emerge as leaders across a variety of situations and tasks.
- Significant relationships exist between leadership and such individual traits as:
  - Intelligence.
  - Adjustment.
  - Extraversion.
  - Conscientiousness.
  - Openness to experience.
  - General self-efficacy.

While the trait theory of leadership has certainly regained popularity, its reemergence has not been accompanied by a corresponding increase in sophisticated conceptual frameworks. Specifically, scholars noted that trait theories still:

- Focus on a small set of individual attributes such as Big Five personality traits, to the neglect of cognitive abilities, motives, values, social skills, expertise, and problem-solving skills.
- Fail to consider patterns or integrations of multiple attributes.
- Do not distinguish between those leader attributes that are generally not malleable over time and those that are shaped by, and bound to, situational influences.
- Do not consider how stable leader attributes account for the Behavioural diversity necessary for effective leadership.

ATTRIBUTE PATTERN APPROACH

Considering the criticisms of the trait theory, several researchers have begun to adopt a different perspective of leader individual differences - the leader attribute pattern approach. In contrast to the traditional approach, the leader attribute pattern approach is based on theorists' arguments that the influence of individual characteristics on outcomes is best understood by considering the person as an integrated totality rather than a summation of individual variables. In other words, the leader attribute pattern approach argues that integrated constellations or combinations of individual differences may explain substantial variance in both leader emergence and leader effectiveness beyond that explained by single attributes, or by additive combinations of multiple attributes.

BEHAVIOURAL AND STYLE THEORIES

In response to the early criticisms of the trait approach, theorists began to research leadership as a set of Behaviours, evaluating the Behaviour of 'successful' leaders, determining a Behaviour taxonomy and identifying broad leadership styles. David McClelland, for example, Leadership takes a strong personality with a well developed positive ego. Not so much as a pattern of motives, but a set of traits is crucial. To lead; self-confidence and a high self-esteem is useful, perhaps even essential. Kurt Lewin, Ronald Lipitt, and Ralph White developed in 1939 the seminal work on the influence of leadership styles and performance. The researchers evaluated the performance of groups of eleven-year-old boys under different types of work climate.

In each, the leader exercised his influence regarding the type of group decision making, praise and criticism and the management of the group tasks according to three styles:

- Authoritarian,
- Democratic and
- Laissez-faire.

Authoritarian climates were characterised by leaders who make decisions alone, demand strict compliance to his orders, and dictate each step taken; future steps were uncertain to a large degree. The leader is not necessarily hostile but is aloof from participation in work and commonly offers personal praise and criticism for the work done. Democratic climates were characterised by collective decision processes, assisted by the leader. Before accomplishing tasks, perspectives are gained from group discussion and technical advice from a leader.

Members are given choices and collectively decide the division of Labour. Praise and criticism in such an environment are objective, fact minded and given by a group member without necessarily having participated extensively in the actual work. *Laissez faire* climates gave freedom to the group for policy determination without any participation from the leader. The leader remains uninvolved in work decisions unless asked, does not participate in the division of Labour, and very infrequently gives praise.

The results seemed to confirm that the democratic climate was preferred. The managerial grid model is also based on a Behavioural theory. The model was developed by Robert Blake and Jane Mouton in 1964 and suggests five different leadership styles, based on the leaders' concern for people and their concern for goal achievement. B.F. Skinner is the father of Behaviour Modification and developed the concept of positive reinforcement. Positive reinforcement occurs when a positive stimulus is presented in response to a Behaviour, increasing the likelihood of that Behaviour in the future. The following is an example of how positive reinforcement can be used in a business setting. Assume praise is a positive reinforcer for a particular employee. This employee does not show up to work on time every day.

The manager of this employee decides to praise the employee for showing up on time every day the employee actually shows up to work on time. As a result, the employee comes to work on time more often because the employee likes to be praised. In this example, praise is a positive reinforcer for this employee because the employee arrives to work on time more frequently after being praised for showing up to work on time. The use of positive reinforcement is a successful and growing technique used by leaders to motivate and attain desired Behaviours from subordinates. Organisations such as Frito-Lay, 3M, Goodrich, Michigan Bell, and Emery Air Freight have all used reinforcement to increase productivity. Empirical research covering the last 20 years suggests that reinforcement theory has a 17 per cent increase in performance. Additionally, many reinforcement techniques such as the use of praise are inexpensive, providing higher performance for lower costs.

SITUATIONAL AND CONTINGENCY THEORIES

Situational theory also appeared as a reaction to the trait theory of leadership. Social scientists argued that history was more than the result of intervention of great men as Carlyle suggested. Herbert Spencer said that the times produce the person and not the other way around. This theory assumes that different situations call for different characteristics; according to this group of theories, no single optimal psychographic profile of a leader exists. The theory, "what an individual actually does when acting as a leader is in large part dependent upon characteristics of the situation in which he functions." Some theorists started to synthesise the trait and situational approaches.

Building upon the research of scholars academics began to normatise the descriptive models of leadership climates, defining three leadership styles and identifying which situations each style works better in. The authoritarian leadership style, for example, is approved in periods of crisis but fails to win the "hearts and minds" of their followers in the day-to-day management; the democratic leadership style is more adequate in situations that require consensus building; finally, the laissez faire leadership style is appreciated by the degree of freedom it provides, but as the leader does not "take charge", he can be perceived as a failure in protracted or thorny organisational problems. Thus, theorists defined the style of leadership as contingent to the situation, which is sometimes classified as contingency theory.

Four contingency leadership theories appear more prominently in the recent years: Fiedler contingency model, Vroom-Yetton decision model, the path-goal theory, and the Hersey-Blanchard situational theory. The Fiedler contingency model bases the leader's effectiveness on what Fred Fiedler called situational contingency.

This results from the interaction of leadership style and situational favourableness. The theory defined two types of leader: those who tend to accomplish the task by developing good-relationships with the group and those who have as their prime concern carrying out the task itself. There is no ideal leader. Both task-oriented and relationship-oriented leaders can be effective if their leadership orientation fits the situation. When there is a good leader-member relation, a highly structured task, and high leader position power, the situation is considered a "favourable situation". Fiedler found that task-oriented leaders are more effective in extremely favourable or unfavourable situations, whereas relationship-oriented leaders perform best in situations with intermediate favourability. Victor Vroom, in collaboration with Phillip Yetton and later with Arthur Jago, developed a taxonomy for describing leadership situations, taxonomy that was used in a normative decision model where leadership styles were connected to situational variables, defining which approach was more suitable to which situation.

This approach was novel because it supported the idea that the same manager could rely on different group decision making approaches depending on the attributes of each situation. This model was later referred as situational contingency theory. The path-goal theory of leadership was developed by Robert House and was based on the expectancy theory of Victor Vroom. The essence of the theory is "the meta proposition that leaders, to be effective, engage in Behaviours that complement subordinates' environments and abilities in a manner that compensates for deficiencies and is instrumental to subordinate satisfaction and individual and work unit performance.

The theory identifies four leader Behaviours, achievement-oriented, directive, participative, and supportive, that are contingent to the environment factors and follower characteristics. In contrast to the Fiedler contingency model, the path-goal model states that the four leadership Behaviours are fluid, and that leaders can adopt any of the four depending on what the situation demands. The path-goal model can be classified both as a contingency theory, as it depends on the circumstances, but also as a transactional leadership theory, as the theory emphasises the reciprocity Behaviour between the leader and the followers. The situational leadership model proposed by Hersey and Blanchard suggests four leadership-styles and four levels of follower-development. For effectiveness, the model posits that the leadership-style must match the appropriate level of followership-development. In this model, leadership behaviour becomes a function not only of the characteristics of the leader, but of the characteristics of followers as well.

FUNCTIONAL THEORY

Functional leadership theory is a particularly useful theory for addressing specific leader behaviours expected to contribute to organisational or unit effectiveness. This theory argues that the leader's main job is to see that whatever is necessary to group needs is taken care of; thus, a leader can be said to have done their job well when they have contributed to group effectiveness and cohesion. While functional leadership theory has most often been applied to team leadership, it has also been effectively applied to broader organisational leadership as well.

In summarising literature on functional leadership These functions include:

- Environmental monitoring,
- Organising subordinate activities,
- Teaching and coaching subordinates,
- Motivating others, and
- Intervening actively in the group's work.

A variety of leadership behaviours are expected to facilitate these functions. In initial work identifying leader behaviour, Fleishman observed that subordinates perceived their supervisors' behaviour in terms of two broad categories referred to as consideration and initiating structure. Consideration includes behaviour involved in fostering effective relationships. Examples of such behaviour would include showing concern for a subordinate or acting in a supportive manner towards others. Initiating structure involves the actions of the leader focused specifically on task accomplishment. This could include role clarification, setting performance standards, and holding subordinates accountable to those standards.

TRANSACTIONAL AND TRANSFORMATIONAL THEORIES

Eric Berne first analysed the relations between a group and its leadership in terms of Transactional Analysis. The transactional leader is given power to perform certain tasks and reward or punish for the team's performance. It gives the opportunity to the manager to lead the group and the group agrees to follow his lead to accomplish a predetermined goal in exchange for something else. Power is given to the leader to evaluate, correct and train subordinates when productivity is not up to the desired level and reward effectiveness when expected outcome is reached. The transformational leader motivates its team to be effective and efficient. Communication is the base for goal achievement focusing the group on the final desired outcome or goal attainment. This leader is highly visible and uses chain of command to get the job done. Transformational leaders focus on the big picture, needing to be surrounded by people who take care of the details. The leader is always looking for ideas that move the organisation to reach the company's vision.

EMOTIONS

Leadership can be perceived as a particularly emotion-laden process, with emotions entwined with the social influence process. In an organisation, the leader's mood has some effects on his/her group.

These effects can be described in 3 levels:

- The mood of individual group members. Group members with leaders in a positive mood experience more positive mood than do group members with leaders in a negative mood. The leaders transmit their moods to other group members through the mechanism of emotional contagion. Mood contagion may be one of the psychological mechanisms by which charismatic leaders influence followers.

- The affective tone of the group. Group affective tone represents the consistent or homogeneous affective reactions within a group. Group affective tone is an aggregate of the moods of the individual members of the group and refers to mood at the group level of analysis. Groups with leaders in a positive mood have a more positive affective tone than do groups with leaders in a negative mood.
- Group processes like coordination, effort expenditure, and task strategy. Public expressions of mood impact how group members think and act. When people experience and express mood, they send signals to others. Leaders signal their goals, intentions, and attitudes through their expressions of moods. For example, expressions of positive moods by leaders signal that leaders deem progress Towards goals to be good.The group members respond to those signals cognitively and Behaviourally in ways that are reflected in the group processes.

In research about client service, it was found that expressions of positive mood by the leader improve the performance of the group, although in other sectors there were other findings. Beyond the leader's mood, her/his behaviour is a source for employee positive and negative emotions at work. The leader creates situations and events that lead to emotional response. Certain leader behaviours displayed during interactions with their employees are the sources of these affective events. Leaders shape workplace affective events. Examples – feedback giving, allocating tasks, resource distribution. Since, employee Behaviour and productivity are directly affected by their emotional states, it is imperative to consider employee emotional responses to organisational leaders. Emotional intelligence, the ability to understand and manage moods and emotions in the self and others, contributes to effective leadership in organisations. Leadership is about being responsible.

NEO-EMERGENT THEORY

The Neo-emergent leadership theory espouses that leadership is created through the emergence of information by the leader or other stakeholders, not through the true actions of the leader himself. In other words, the reproduction of information or stories form the basis of the perception of leadership by the majority. It is well known that the great naval hero Lord Nelson often wrote his own versions of battles he was involved in, so that when he arrived home in England he would receive a true hero's welcome. In modern society, the press, blogs and other sources report their own views of a leader, which may be based on reality, but may also be based on a political command, a payment, or an inherent interest of the author, media or leader. Therefore, it can be contended that the perception of all leaders is created and in fact does not reflect their true leadership qualities at all.

ENVIRONMENTAL LEADERSHIP THEORY

The environmental leadership model describes leadership from a group dynamics perspective incorporating group psychology and self awareness to nurture "Environments" that promote self-sustaining group leadership based on personal emotional gratification from the activities of the group. The Environmental Leader creates the psychological structure by which employees can find and attain this gratification through work or activity.

It stems from the idea that each individual has various environments that bring out different facets from their own Identity, and each facet is driven by emotionally charged perceptions within each environment... The Environmental Leader creates a platform through education and awareness where individuals fill each others emotional needs and become more conscious of when, and how they affect personal and team emotional gratifications. This is accomplished by knowing why people "react" to their environment instead of act intelligently. "Environmental Leadership is not about changing the mindset of the group or individual, but in the cultivation of an environment that brings out the best and inspires the individuals in that group.

It is not the ability to influence others to do something they are not committed to, but rather to nurture a culture that motivates and even excites individuals to do what is required for the benefit of all.

It is not carrying others to the end result, but setting the surrounding for developing qualities in them to so they may carry each other. The role of an Environmental Leader is to instill passion and direction to a group and the dynamics of that group. This leader implements a psychological support system within a group that fills the emotional and developmental needs of the group.

INTRINSIC MOTIVATION THEORIES

INTRINSIC MOTIVATION

Some theorists (*e.g.*, Combs, 1982; Purkey and Schmidt, 1987; Purkey and Stanley, 1991) maintain that there is only a single kind of intrinsic motivation, which can be described as a motivation to engage in activities that enhance or maintain a person's self-concept. Most theorists define the term more broadly.

Note that even though the following pages will describe intrinsic motivation ashighly desirable, most of the activities in which teachers, students, and other human beings engage are most directly influenced by extrinsic rather than intrinsic motivation. For example, most people use a knife and a fork in a certain way or follow conventions in a restaurant not because they find knife and fork use to be intrinsically motivating, but because the correct use of these utensils leads to such intrinsic benefits as a good meal or the respect of people we care about. This is not a serious problem, unless the person feels coerced or in some other way alienated by having to use the utensils.

However, extrinsic motivators may lead to merely short-range activity while actually reducing long-range interest in a topic. If this does not happen, the result is likely to be areduction in the very behaviour we want to promote.

One of the most frequent failures in education is that students rarely say that they find studying to be intrinsically rewarding. This is a critical problem. One of the most straightforward conclusions of research from the past two decades is that extrinsic motivation alone is likely to have precisely the opposite impact that we want it to have on student achievement.

FUNDAMENTAL DISTINCTION IN THE MOTIVATION

There is a fundamental distinction in the motivation literature between intrinsic motivation and extrinsic motivation. When individuals are intrinsically motivated they do activities for their own sake and out of interest in the activity. When extrinsically motivated, individuals do activities for instrumental or other reasons, such as receiving a reward. There is continuing debate about the pros and cons of intrinsic and extrinsic motivation, and a growing consensus that these two constructs should not be treated as polar opposites. Rather, they often both operate, and may even form a continuum.

Much of the work on intrinsic motivation stemmed from White's (1959) seminal article on effectance motivation, in which he argued persuasively that both people and at least some animals are motivated by curiosity and interest in developing their competence, rather than just by rewards or the satisfaction of basic bodily needs. This influential article had a strong influence on the views of Edward Deci and Richard Ryan, whose self-determination theory of intrinsic motivation is the main focus in this section.

Self-determination theory. Deci, Ryan, and their colleagues' self-determination theory (SDT) is an organismic theory of development that has a particular focus on the role of motivation in development and learning (*e.g.*, Deci and Ryan, 1985; 2002a; Deci, Vallerand, Pelletier, and Ryan, 1991; Ryan and Deci, 2000a). Broadly, self-determined behaviour is behaviour that originates from the self and, results from the individual utilising his or her volition. Deci, Ryan, and their colleagues suggest that when individuals' behaviour is self-determined they are psychologically healthier, and tend to be intrinsically motivated. Indeed, they make a specific link between intrinsic motivation and self-determination, arguing that intrinsic motivation is only possible when individuals freely choose their own actions; that is, they are self-determined.

A fundamental aspect of this theory is that Deci, Ryan, and their colleagues propose that there are three basic or fundamental human psychological needs:

the need for competence, the need for autonomy, and the need for relatedness. In order for healthy development to occur these needs must be met. Further, these needs are a basis for motivation. For instance, the need for competence is the major reason why people seek out optimal stimulation and challenging activities. The need for autonomy refers most directly to volition and self-determination; Deci and Ryan argue that this sense of volition is necessary for optimum motivation. Ryan (1992) discussed the importance of distinguishing between competence and autonomy. He argued that models that focus primarily on competence, like self-efficacy theory, do not make this distinction clearly enough. Individuals can act competently and demonstrate their competence but still be doing so under the control of others. Ryan compared such actions to those of a robot, rather than a self-determined individual, and argued that intrinsic motivation only occurs when individuals are both autonomous and competent. As we will see, the proposal that autonomy is a basic human need has led to much interesting research on topics such as choice and how providing children and adults with choice influences their intrinsic motivation. Relatedness refers to the need to be connected with others. This need was added to the theory after the other two, and reflects Deci and Ryan's beliefs that individuals must have strong connections to others for optimum development to occur. In their view autonomy does not imply total independence; connections with others are key to optimum development.

Deci, Ryan, and colleagues go beyond the extrinsic - intrinsic motivation dichotomy in their discussion of internalization, the process of transferring the regulation of behaviour from outside to inside the individual. They developed a taxonomy to describe different types of motivation involved in the process of going from external to more internalized regulation of motivation. This taxonomy forms a continuum. At one extreme is amotivation, which as the name implies means an absence of motivation to act. Next are several types of extrinsic motivation that range from least to most autonomous. In order these are external, or regulation coming from outside the individual; introjected, or internal regulation based on feelings that he or she should or has to do the behaviour; identified, or internal regulation of behaviour that is based on the utility of that behaviour (*e.g.*, studying hard to get grades to get into college), and finally, integrated, or regulation based on what the individual thinks is valuable and important to the self. Each of these levels also is associated with different kinds of motivation. For instance, extrinsic rewards are most salient for external regulation, and at each subsequent level motivation become more internalized.

Deci, Ryan, and their colleagues have developed scales to measure these different levels of regulation They have tested their continuum idea by looking at how related the different kinds of motivation are. For instance, Ryan and Connell (1989) assessed children's external, introjected, identified, and intrinsic reasons for doing schoolwork, and found that these correlations formed a simplex pattern. That is, the levels of regulation closer to one another in the continuum were more highly related than those further apart, which they took as evidence for their placement on the continuum. Further, they found that the more extrinsically motivated the students were the less invested they were in their schoolwork.

One major focus of Deci, Ryan, and their colleagues' research and theorizing has been how extrinsic rewards can undermine intrinsically motivated behaviour. They call this portion of their theory Cognitive Evaluation Theory. They and others described different conditions under which rewards can be undermining; the most notable is when rewards are controlling, which reduces the individual's perceptions of autonomy over their own learning. When rewards provide individuals with information about how they are doing rather than focus on controlling them, the undermining effects do not occur. In 1994 Cameron and Pierce published a meta-analysis of this research in which they questioned the strength of these undermining effects, arguing that they occurred only in very limited circumstances if at all. This article led to a series of commentaries and reactions and further meta analyses of the findings regarding the undermining effects of rewards on intrinsically motivated behaviour, with many claims and counter-claims about the adequacy of the meta-analytic techniques used and ways of parsing the findings. We believe that Deci, Ryan, and their colleagues have replied effectively to Cameron and Pierce's various arguments against the undermining effects of extrinsic motivation. Yet this debate was useful because it served to clarify the conditions under which extrinsic motivators do undermine intrinsically motivated behaviours, and so moved the field ahead in important ways.

SDT has been a dominant theoretical model and one that has generated a great deal of research. It is a broad model that encompasses a variety of constructs, and integrates many important issues with respect to the development of motivation. The theory, however, has been the subject of some criticism.

A number of questions have been raised about Deci and Ryan's contention that there are three basic psychological needs. Other questions have been raised about the universality of these needs and whether they operate similarly in different cultures. For instance, in cultures defined as less individualistic and more collectivist does the need for autonomy take on the same importance? This question currently is the focus of a great deal of research. There also has been debate within SDT on the role of choice in helping children fulfill their need for autonomy. Finally, although the continuum from extrinsic to intrinsic motivation is intriguing, there is some concern that intrinsic motivation as defined in this way only describes a very limited set of activities that people do in the normal course of their daily lives. This perhaps constrains intrinsic motivation too much.

Flow theory. Csikszentmihalyi (1988) discusses intrinsically motivated behaviour in terms of the immediate subjective experience that occurs when people are engaged in the activity. Interviews with climbers, dancers, chess players, basketball players, and composers revealed that these activities yield a specific form of experience - labelled flow - characterized by: (1) holistic feelings of being immersed in, and of being carried by, an activity, (2) merging of action and awareness, (3) focus of attention on a limited stimulus field, (4) lack of self-consciousness, and (5) feeling in control of one's actions and the environment. Flow is only possible when people feel that the opportunities for action in a given situation match their ability to master the challenges. The challenge of an activity may be something concrete or physical like the peak of a mountain to be scaled, or it can be something abstract and symbolic, like a set of musical notes to be performed, a story to be written, or a puzzle to be solved. Further research has shown that both the challenges and skills must be relatively high before a flow experience becomes possible.

At first sight, the theories of Deci and Ryan and Csikszentmihalyi seem to be very different. Deci and Ryan (1985, 2002a) explain intrinsic motivation by assuming innate, basic needs, whereas Csikszentmihalyi stresses subjective experience. We suggest, however, that this difference reflects two sides of the same coin. As Schneider (1996) has argued, one has to distinguish between immediate reasons (*e.g.*, enjoyment) and ultimate reasons of behaviour (*e.g.*, survival). Intrinsically motivated behaviour can be conducive to ultimate goals even though the actor is only motivated by immediate incentives. A typical case is exploratory or play behaviour. Both types of behaviour help to increase an individual's competence but they are usually performed because they are exciting, pleasurable, or enjoyable. This distinction between immediate and ultimate causes of behaviour makes it possible to reconcile the positions of Deci and Ryan and Csikszentmihalyi. Deci and Ryan (1985) focus on ultimate reasons of behaviour, whereas Csikszentmihalyi (1988) focuses mainly on immediate reasons. Csikszentmihalyi and Massimini (1985) have suggested that the experience of flow is a reward that ensures that individuals will seek to increase their competence. According to Csikszentmihalyi, the repeated experience of flow is only possible when individuals seek out increasingly challenging tasks and expand their competencies to meet these challenges. Thus, the experience of flow should reinforce behaviours underlying development.

Individual difference theories of intrinsic motivation. Until recently intrinsic motivation researchers like Deci and Ryan and Csikszentmihalyi have dealt with conditions, components, and consequences of intrinsic motivation without making a distinction between intrinsic motivation as a state versus intrinsic motivation as a trait-like characteristic. However, interest in trait-like individual differences in intrinsic motivation has increased recently, particularly among educational psychologists. These researchers define this enduring intrinsic motivational orientations in terms of three components: (1) preference for hard or challenging tasks, (2) learning that is driven by curiosity or interest, and (3) striving for competence and mastery. The second component is most central to the idea of intrinsic motivation. Both preference for hard tasks and striving for competence can be linked to either extrinsic or more general need achievement motivation. non-etheless, empirical findings suggest that the three components are highly correlated. In addition, evidence suggests that high levels of trait-like intrinsic motivation facilitate positive emotional experience and well-being, self-esteem, high academic achievement (Cordova and Lepper, 1996; Schiefele and Schreyer, 1994), creativity, self-regulation and persistence (Cordova and Lepper, 1996; Pelletier, Fortier, Vallerand, and Brière, 2001; Pintrich and Schrauben, 1992; Schiefele and Schreyer, 1994). As a consequence, many have suggested that the development of an intrinsic motivational orientation should be fostered in the home and the classroom (*e.g.*, Brophy, 1999; Dewey, 1913; Lepper and Chabay, 1985).

INTEREST THEORIES

Closely related to the notion of intrinsic motivation is work on the concept of "interest". Hidi and Harackiewicz (2001) propose that interest is more specific than intrinsic motivation, which is a broader motivational characteristic. Researchers studying interest differentiate between individual and situational interest. Individual interest is a relatively stable evaluative orientation towards certain domains; situational interest is an emotional state aroused by specific features of an activity or a task. Two aspects or components of individual interest are distinguishable: feeling-related and value-related valences. Feeling-related valences refer to the feelings that are associated with an object or an activity itself - feelings like involvement, stimulation, or flow. Value-related valences refer to the attribution of personal significance or importance to an object.

In addition, both feeling-related and value-related valences are directly related to the object rather than to the relation of this object to other objects or events. For example, if students associate mathematics with high personal significance because mathematics can help them get prestigious jobs, then we would not speak of interest. Although feeling-related and value-related valences are highly correlated, it is useful to differentiate between them because some individual interests are likely based primarily on feelings, while others' interests are more likely to be based on personal significance. Further research is necessary to validate this assumption.

Much of the research on individual interest has focused on its relation to the quality of learning. In general, there are significant but moderate relations between interest and text learning. More importantly, interest is more strongly related to indicators of deep-level learning (*e.g.*, recall of main ideas, coherence of recall, responding to deeper comprehension questions, representation of meaning) than to surface-level learning. Findings by Ainley, Hidi, and Berndorff (2002) and Hidi (2001) suggest that attentional processes, affect, and persistence mediate the effects of interest on text learning.

There is also ample evidence that subject matter interest is positively related to school achievement. Recent studies suggest that interest particularly predicts achievement when there is a context that allows for choice. Specifically, Köller, Baumert, and Schnabel (2001) found that interest in mathematics predicts achievement only at higher grade levels when students have a choice between more or less advanced courses. The "effect" of interest on achievement was partly mediated by choice of course level. However, there was also a direct path from interest to achievement even when controlling for prior achievement.

Most of the research on situational interest has focused on the characteristics of academic tasks that create interest. Among others, the following text features were found to arouse situational interest: personal relevance, novelty, vividness, and comprehensibility. Empirical evidence has provided strong support for the relation between situational interest and text comprehension and recall.

Goal Theories

Work on achievement goals and goal orientations has flourished since, the publication of our previous chapter. This work can be organized into three relatively distinct areas. One group of researchers has focused on the properties of goals for specific learning activities. These researchers focus on goals' proximity, specificity, and level of challenge and have shown that specific, proximal, and somewhat challenging goals promote both self-efficacy and improved performance. A second group of researchers defined and investigated broader goal orientations students have to their learning, focusing primarily on three broad orientations: a mastery or learning orientation, an ego or performance orientation, and a work avoidant orientation. These orientations refer to broader approaches children take to their learning, rather than goals for specific activities, although of course goal orientations can also influence the approach one takes to a specific task. A third group focuses on the content of children's goals, proposing that there are many different kinds of goals individuals can have in achievement settings, including both academic and social goals. We focus in this section on the work of the latter two groups.

Goal orientation theory. Researchers initially distinguished two broad goal orientations that students can have towards their learning. One orientation, called a learning, task involved, or mastery goal orientation, means that the child is focused on improving their skills, mastering material, and learning new things. Questions such as "How can I do this task?" and "What will I learn?" reflect task-involved goals. A second goal orientation, called performance or ego orientation, means that the child focuses on maximizing favourable evaluations of their competence and minimizing negative evaluations of competence. Nicholls and his colleagues and Meece (1991, 1994) also have described a work avoidant goal orientation, which means that the child does not wish to engage in academic activities.

The different terms used to label these goal orientations occurred because different researchers were working on them simultaneously, with each having a somewhat distinctive view of each orientation. For instance, Dweck and Leggett (1988) proposed that children's goal orientations stem from their theories of intelligence that were described earlier. Children believing intelligence is malleable tend to hold a learning (mastery) goal orientation, and children adopting the entity view take on performance goals. By contrast, Ames (1992) focused primarily on classroom antecedents of these goal orientations, rather than characteristics of children, which implies that goal orientations are more a product of context rather than the person, and so may vary more widely across different achievement situations. We acknowledge that the different terminology used by these theorists reflects some important distinctions in the conceptualization of these" goal orientations, but also believe that the similarities are stronger than the distinctions between them. We will use the terms mastery and performance goal orientations in this chapter.

One of the newer directions in goal orientation theory is further differentiation of these two broad goal orientations into approach and avoidance components. This occurred first for the performance goal orientation, beginning with work by Elliot and Harackiewicz (1996) and Skaalvik (1997), among others. These further distinctions emerged for two main reasons. Empirically, findings concerning the outcomes of having a performance goal orientation were somewhat contradictory, leading researchers to wonder why this occurred. Theoretically, Elliot and Harackiewicz noted that traditional achievement motivation theories, such as Atkinson's (1957) expectancy-value model, included both approach and avoidance motives. By contrast, most modern theories focus primarily on the approach aspect, thus overlooking the importance of avoidance motivation.

Therefore, Elliot and Harackiewicz (1996) proposed approach and avoidance aspects of performance goals, as did Skaalvik (1997). Performance-approach goals refer to the students' desire to demonstrate competence and outperform others. Performance-avoidance goals involve the desire to avoid looking incompetent. Researchers began to disentangle the effects of these two kinds of performance orientations. As we will see later, there is evidence that performance-approach goals can have a positive impact on different outcomes such as grades, whereas the impact of performance-avoidance goals is nearly always negative. Elliot and Pintrich (2000c) proposed that the mastery goal orientation also may be divided into approach and avoid components. Elliot and

McGregor stated that the assumption likely was made that mastery goals always referred to approach situations, rather than avoidance situations, which they believe does not provide a full characterization of situations to which mastery goals apply. They argued that mastery-avoidance goals include such things as working to avoid misunderstanding, or the use of standards to not be wrong when doing an achievement activity. As Elliot and McGregor and Pintrich both note, perfectionists may be characterized as holding mastery avoidance goals. Elliot and McGregor (2001) developed items to assess mastery avoidant goals, and found (in a study of college students) that these items factored separately from items measuring the other three kinds of goal orientations. The antecedents (as perceived by the participants) of mastery-avoidance goals were not as positive as antecedents of mastery-approach goals. These results are intriguing, but much more work is needed to establish the meaningfulness of this new category.

There is a growing body of research documenting the consequences of adopting one or the other of these goal orientations. Researchers have used a variety of methodologies in this work, including classroom observations, interviews, and questionnaire-based studies, often using Midgley and her colleagues' Patterns of Adaptive Learning Scale (PALS). Experimental manipulations of students' goal orientations also have been done, by introducing achievement tasks in a way that fosters either mastery or performance goals. The results concerning mastery orientation are quite consistent and positive. When children are mastery oriented they are more highly engaged in learning, use deeper cognitive strategies, and are intrinsically motivated to learn. Elliot and McGregor (2001) found that mastery-avoidance goals are associated with a mixture of outcomes, including subsequent test anxiety, mastery-approach goals, and performance-approach goals. Based on this and other work researchers have proposed that schools should work to foster mastery goal orientations rather than performance goal orientations, and school reform efforts to do just that have been undertaken.

As noted above the research on performance goals is somewhat less consistent, in part because of the methodological confounding of performance avoidance and approach goals. When these two aspects of performance goals are unconfounded, researchers find that performance avoid goals have negative consequences for students motivation and learning. Performance approach goals relate positively to academic self-concept, task value, and performance (at least in college students), but not to intrinsic motivation to learn.

The distinction between performance approach and avoid goals, and evidence showing that performance-approach goals relate to positive motivational and achievement outcomes, led Harckiewicz, Barron, and Elliot (1998) and Pintrich (2000a,c) to call for a revision of goal theory that acknowledges the positive effects of performance-approach goals, and also the need to look at how different goals relate to different outcomes. Traditional (or normative, to use the term adopted by Harackiewicz et al) goal theory argues for the benefits of mastery goals and the costs of performance goals. Pintrich (2000b) studied 8th grade students' goal orientations, and identified four groups of children crossing high and low mastery and performance goal orientations. He found that students with a combination of high mastery and high performance-approach goal orientations were similar with respect to a variety of motivational outcomes to a group of students who were high in mastery but low in performance goal orientations. This finding does not support the normative theory view that only mastery goal orientations lead to positive developmental outcomes, and was one impetus for the call for a revised goal orientation theory.

Midgley *et al.* (2001) disputed these claims, arguing that the costs of performance avoidance goals are clearly documented and that the benefits of performance approach goals are not as clearly established in the literature. They also noted that performance approach goals may benefit some students (boys, older students) rather than others (girls, younger students), and that we do not yet have enough information about how performance-approach goals operate in other groups of children. They also pointed out that benefits of performance goals identified by researchers may be in part due to the focus of our educational system on standards, assessments, and performance rather than effort and improvement, which they argue is a better approach to schooling.

In response, Harackiewicz *et al.* (2002) argued that the evidence for the positive effects of performance-approach goals is clearer than Midgley *et al.* stated that it was, and continued to propose the multiple goal perspective (that both mastery and performance goals can benefit different educational outcomes) is the more viable approach to goal orientation theory. They noted a number of areas of research that now are needed to assess each of these perspectives.

In a final response Kaplan and Middleton (2002) took a broader perspective and focused on what the purposes of schooling should be. In their view the purposes of schooling should be knowledge growth and the fostering of a love of learning, rather than performance *per se*, and thus for them a mastery orientation continues to be more desirable, even if performance-approach goals relate to some positive educational outcomes in our current educational system. So this debate appears to be at different levels. At one level is the concern for how the specific goal orientations relate to different kinds of outcomes within our current educational system.

The second level concerns what that system should focus on, rather than an acceptance of the current system and its strong performance emphasis. This healthy debate among goal orientation theorists should move the field ahead, as more research is done to look at the benefits and costs of different kinds of goal orientations, and as we consider further the nature and purposes of schooling and their influence on the development of students' motivation. We believe the move beyond the perhaps too simplistic two-goal orientation theory is welcome, but acknowledge that more work is needed both on performance approach and (especially) mastery-avoidance goals to evaluate their effects, and in the case of mastery-avoid goals, document their existence. Work on achievement goal orientations also needs to look more carefully at how different achievement domains (math, science, English) might impact achievement goal orientations and their effects.

The goal content approach: Academic and social goals. Building on Ford's (1992) work defining a taxonomy of human goals, Wentzel has examined the multiple goals of children in achievement settings. Her view on goals differs from the goal orientation theorists in that she focuses on the content of children's goals to guide and direct behaviour, rather than the criteria a person uses to define success or failure (*i.e.*, mastery versus performance). In this sense, these goals are like the goals and self-schema that relate to attainment value hierarchies in the Eccles *et al.* expectancy value. However, she does view these goals as contributing to children's competence in particular situations. Wentzel primarily has focused on academic and social goals and their relations to a variety of outcomes.

Wentzel has demonstrated that both social and academic goals relate to adolescents' school performance and behaviour (Wentzel, 2002b). For instance, she found that the goals related to school achievement include seeing oneself as successful, dependable, wanting to learn new things, and wanting to get things done.

Higher-achieving students have higher levels of both social responsibility and achievement goals than lower achieving students. Similarly, Wentzel (1994) documented the association among middle school children's pro-social goals of helping others, academic pro-social goals like sharing learning with classmates, peer social responsibility goals like following through on promises made to peers, and academic social responsibility goals like doing what the teacher says to do. Pro-social goals (particularly academic pro-social goals) related positively to peer acceptance. She also found positive relations between prosocial goals and children's grades and even IQ scores.

While it appears valuable to have multiple goals, Wentzel (2002b) discussed the difficulty some children may have coordinating these multiple goals. Can students manage a variety of social and academic goals? This question also applies to the multiple goal perspective in goal orientation theory. Having multiple goals may be especially challenging for younger children, whose resources to manage such goals may be limited.

SOCIAL CURRENCIES AND SENIOR LEADERSHIP

One of the innate social exchange algorithms that all people seem to have is the ability to trade favours in order to build social relationships and systems of mutual obligation. In the traditional societies long-studied by anthropologists, this is manifested in gift exchange systems where social obligations are created and repaid through the exchange of gifts. Even without a physical accounting of who owes what to whom, people are very proficient at keeping score, not only in terms of knowing how much is owed, but what is owed—favours, goods, payments, or special privileges.

The exchange of gossip is a very powerful "social glue" and plays a vital role in keeping a group together and informed of the status of its members. Different social groups have different systems of exchange, different kinds of tokens—what we call *social currencies* – for creating affinities, building relationships of mutual advantage, and enabling the valuing and trading of different kinds of skills, privileges, and goods. In other words, people in social and work networks create their own markets around their particular skills and resources and use these transactions to build social cohesion and trust within and across social networks.

Social currencies are typically denominated in the types of skills and resources that define a social network. For example, in some *professional* networks, the prevalent social currencies are knowledge, expertise, and access to important events and people; in other *soical* networks, social status and privilege of membership can be the principle inducement.

In many cases, the social currencies that fuel the many informal networks that make up businesses and formal organisations are often more powerful than other more traditional forms of inducement, such as financial incentives. Indeed, most large organisations are made up of peer networks of constituencies who, by virtue of shared skills and mutual interests, act more on the behalf of their network than for benefit of the overall organisation. Members within these networks realise that their peer relationships have more influence over their future success than the formal organisation or enterprise.

Successful senior leaders, for example, know what the currencies are for such peer networks and they know when and how to cash in their chips to advance their interests and those of their peer networks.

This kind of behaviour is often dismissed as politics, and when undertaken in an opaque, self-serving, and episodic manner, can completely undermine the trust and efficacy of an organisation. Non-etheless, it is through such shrewd negotiations that truly effective and credible senior leaders arise, and it is as natural as breathing for most accomplished senior leaders.

These senior leaders, however, tend to combine for a variety of leadership roles, with particular emphasis on connector leadership skills. They tend not to be visionaries or truth-tellers, who by bent of personality can be so committed to their vision and truth telling that they fail to build the requisite social capital with their peers to advance to more senior levels. Examples in the military are Billy Mitchell, George Patton, and John A. Boyd. The leadership roles that emerge under these circumstances are the connector, fixer, and facilitator.Such leadership roles seem better adapted to reading and responding to complex social signals and building the requisite social capital to assume senior leadership roles. In this camp, one would find Dwight Eisenhower, Omar Bradley, and George Marshall. Only under the rarest of circumstances do you find military leaders who combine visionary roles and skills with those of the connector, exemplar, and fixer: Lord Nelson, the Duke of Wellington, Carl Phillip von Clausewitz, Otto von Bismarck, and George Marshall.

The challenge is not to eradicate such Behaviour, but to harness it by making the coining, exchange, accrual, and cashing in of social currencies wholly transparent and driven by criteria that support the mission and capabilities of the entire organisation. One of the most ubiquitous and natural of social currencies is reputation.

It is not surprising that it is the driving force behind so many different Open Source and peer production networks. Individuals can have multiple reputations and a reputation in one field may not be easily transferable into another, because reputation is highly contextspecific and subject to the conditions of local rules.

Nonetheless, just as trust can be transitive—*e.g.*, I trust whom you trust—especially if it is predicated on strong ties established over long periods of time, so can reputation be transitive even when circumstances may not warrant it. For example, someone who is a great hockey player may not be a great businessperson, but because of the desire of one group to affiliate with another, reputation points or social currencies garnered in one area are often convertible into another.

Careers can often be built by leveraging a highly visible success in one area of endeavor to a succession of successes in other areas of endeavor such as athletics, business, academia, politics, and public service. The challenge is to trade up and to increase the cumulative value of a personal currency.

Great "cross network players" include George Washington, Benjamin Franklin, Henry Kissinger, Ronald Reagan, Arnold Schwarzenegger, and Rupert Murdock. A remarkable fact is the extent to which high reputation ratings are transferable across domains, especially in the case of "world class" ratings where Nobel Laureates, NBA athletes, film stars, and media commentators can form a common peer group, irrespective of glaringly different competencies.

It would seem that extremely high competency creates a peer network of celebrity and achievement. In terms of building robust social networks that offer the right combination of leadership roles to achieve a larger organisational purpose, what might be good for the individual may not be good for the organisation. Visionaries, for instance, may provide needed innovation and achieve significant personal and organisational success through their visions. Yet if such visions are not challenged by truth-teller leaders and held accountable by enforcers, they may result in "false" successes and inappropriate learnings at the cost of the organisation's success.

Visionary leaders, on the other hand, would have moved on to other organisations and social networks based upon their proclaimed "success". Similarly, an excess of truth telling and enforcement leadership can stifle both innovation and risk taking, just as an excess of connector leadership within private firms can result in acquisitions that are neither strategic nor synergistic.

Associate Dean of the Yale School of Management and head of the CEO Institute, companies tend to go through a succession of CEO leadership roles without a coherent understanding of how they relate to either one another or to the interest of the corporation and its shareholders.

CONCLUSION

Leadership is essentially a subject of management research. It is however a theme that is relevant to all human endeavours. Business enterprises and corporations have embraced the application of leadership principles and have found them to be agents of productivity and profitability. The time is therefore ripe for the Library and Information Professionals, particularly in this part of the world, to take a cue from the latter s experiences to enhance professionalism, information service delivery as well as social/educational relevance of practitioners. The leadership qualities of a person create a niche for him and a combination of leadership competencies of managers in the workplace brings corporate success. It is also expedient to add that the phenomenon of the knowledge society has made cross-fertilisation of ideas imperative in the process of knowledge acquisition. This, without mincing words, is the surest way of survival in an extremely competitive world.

4

Styles of Leadership

INTRODUCTION

In the past several decades, management experts have undergone a revolution in how they define leadership and what their attitudes are towards it. They have gone from a very classical autocratic approach to a very creative, participative approach. Somewhere along the line, it was determined that not everything old was bad and not everything new was good. Rather, different styles were needed for different situations and each leader needed to know when to exhibit a particular approach.

LEADERSHIP STYLES

A leadership style is a leader's style of providing direction, implementing plans, and motivating people. There are many different leadership styles that can be exhibited by leaders in the political, business or other fields.

Authoritarian

The authoritarian leadership **style** or autocratic leader keeps strict, close control over followers by keeping close regulation of policy's and procedures given to followers. To keep main emphasis on the distinction of the authoritarian leader and their followers, these types of leaders make sure to only create a distinct professional relationship. Direct supervision is what they believe to be key in maintaining a successful environment and follower ship. In fear of followers being unproductive, authoritarian leaders keep close supervision and feel this is necessary in order for anything to be done.

Examples of authoritarian communicative behaviour: a police officer directing traffic, a teacher ordering a student to do his or her assignment, and a supervisor instructing a subordinate to clean a workstation. All of these positions require a distinct set of characteristics that give the leader the position to get things in order or get a point across. Authoritarian Traits: sets goals individually, engages primarily in one-way and downward communication, controls discussion with followers,and donates interaction.

Paternalistic Leadership

The way a Paternalistic leader works is by acting as a father figure by taking care of their subordinates as a parent would. In this style of leadership the leader supplies complete concern for his followers or workers. In return he receives the complete trust and loyalty of his people. Workers under this style of leader are expected to become totally committed to what the leader believes and will not strive of and work independently. The relationship between these co-workers and leader are extremely solid. The workers are expected to stay with a company for a longer period of time because of the loyalty and trust. Not only do they treat each other like family inside the workforce, but outside too. These workers are able to go to each other with any problems they have regarding something because they believe in what they say is going to truly help them. "

One of the downsides to a paternalistic leader is that the leader could start to play favourites in decisions. This leader would include the workers more apt to follow and start to exclude the ones who were less loyal. In today's market paternalism is more difficult to come by according to Padavic and Earnest who wrote "business dimensional and Organisational Counseling." They believe this because there have become more lay-offs and stronger unionization. This affects paternalistic leaders because the co-workers may not believe that their jobs are 100 per cent ensured. When this happens, workers begin to look for bigger and better job opportunities instead of staying at one company for a longer period of time. Because of this, The leader may be thinking that you could be leaving and not fully believe you when you tell them something about a job opportunity. This could put the workers and leader at risk for a bad situation. "

According to B. M. Bass who wrote Leadership and Performance Beyond Expectations, workers who follow paternalistic leadership also have better organisation skills. The leader encourages organisation because they allow the workers to complete tasks so that they can stay on top of their work. The workers complete tasks this boosts self-confidence and it makes them work harder to reach a goal and exceed the goal to prove to their boss they are working hard. Having this style of leadership can also help implement a reward system. This system will allow their workers to work even better because there is something for them at the end of the tunnel. While doing this they will also be able to accomplish more work in a set time frame.

Democratic

The democratic leadership style consists of the leader sharing the decision-making abilities with group members by promoting the interests of the group members and by practicing social equality.

This style of leadership encompasses discussion, debate and sharing of ideas and encouragement of people to feel good about their involvement. The boundaries of democratic participation tend to be circumscribed by the organisation or the group needs and the instrumental value of people's attributes (skills, attitudes, etc.). The democratic style encompasses the notion that everyone, by virtue of their human status, should play a part in the group's decisions. However, the democratic style of leadership still requires guidance and control by a specific leader. The democratic style demands the leader to make decisions on who should be called upon within the group and who is given the right to participate in, make and vote on decisions. Traits of a Good Leader compiled by the Santa Clara University and the Tom Peters Group:

- Honest — Display sincerity, integrity, and candor in all your actions. Deceptive behaviour will not inspire trust.
- Competent — Base your actions on reason and moral principles. Do not make decisions based on childlike emotional desires or feelings.
- Forward-looking — Set goals and have a vision of the future. The vision must be owned throughout the organisation. Effective leaders envision what they want and how to get it. They habitually pick priorities stemming from their basic values.
- Inspiring — Display confidence in all that you do. By showing endurance in mental, physical, and spiritual stamina, you will inspire others to reach for new heights. Take charge when necessary.
- Intelligent — Read, study, and seek challenging assignments.
- Fair-minded — Show fair treatment to all people. Prejudice is the enemy of justice. Display empathy by being sensitive to the feelings, values, interests, and well-being of others.
- Broad-minded — Seek out diversity.
- Courageous — Have the perseverance to accomplish a goal, regardless of the seemingly insurmountable obstacles. Display a confident calmness when under stress.
- Straightforward — Use sound judgement to make a good decisions at the right time.
- Imaginative — Make timely and appropriate changes in your thinking, plans, and methods. Show creativity by thinking of new and better goals, ideas, and solutions to problems. Be innovative!

Research has found that this leadership style is one of the most effective and creates higher productivity, better contributions from group members and increased group morale. Democratic leadership can lead to better ideas and more creative solutions to problems because group members are encouraged to share their thoughts and ideas. While democratic leadership is one of the most effective leadership styles, it does have some potential downsides. In situations where roles are unclear or time is of the essence, democratic leadership can lead to communication failures and uncompleted projects. Democratic leadership works best in situations where group members are skilled and eager to share their knowledge. It is also important to have plenty of time to allow people to contribute, develop a plan and then vote on the best course of action.

Laissez-Faire

The laissez-faire leadership style was first described by Lewin, Lippitt, and White in 1938, along with the autocratic leadership and the democratic leadership styles. The laissez-faire style is sometimes described as a "hands off" leadership style because the leader delegates the tasks to their followers while providing little or no direction to the followers. If the leader withdraws too much from their followers it can sometimes result in a lack of productivity, cohesiveness, and satisfaction. Laissez-faire leaders allow followers to have complete freedom to make decisions concerning the completion of their work. It allows followers a high degree of autonomy andself-rule, while at the same time offering guidance and support when requested. The laissez-faire leader using guided freedom provides the followers with all materials necessary to accomplish their goals, but does not directly participate in decision making unless the followers request their assistance.

This is an effective style to use when:

- Followers are highly skilled, experienced, and educated.
- Followers have pride in their work and the drive to do it successfully on their own.
- Outside experts, such as staff specialists or consultants are being used.
- Followers are trustworthy and experienced.

LEADERSHIP ORGANISATIONS

Leadership has been closely studied over the years, both as a matter of academic interest and with an eye to making leadership easier and more effective in organisations. There is no formal and agreed definition of leadership (or even of its functions), although there are common features to many of the definitions available.

In 1988, Warren G Bennis completed writing his classic book On Becoming A Leader. This richly praised book details: how people become leaders; how they lead; and how organisations encourage or indeed, stifle leaders. Underlying the 'how's,' he goes onto claim that leaders must understand the context in which they are working in and notes: "The changes in the last generation have been so radical that it seems...not just that the rules have changed (but that) it is a different game".

Indeed, for the RAF, the pace of change in the last 30 years alone has been extraordinary, with simultaneous changes in both international security and domestic society. Therefore, in this dynamic and fast-changing environment, strong leadership is required at every level of the organisation; there is nothing more important to an organisation than the quality of its leadership and indeed, of its leadership philosophy. However, one criticism of today's organisations is that they are over managed and under led: they (organisations) are overly concerned with policies, practices, procedures and rule books and not concerned enough with the important issues like trust, mission and an overarching and compelling vision.

Indeed, Warren Bennis has detailed 4 things that people want from their leaders:

- Purpose, direction and meaning (a strong determination to achieve a goal).
- Trust.
- A sense of we-can-do-it (optimism).
- Results.

Everyone knows that excellent leadership can be felt throughout an organisation; leadership gives pace and energy to the work and empowers the workforce, which is most evident in 4 themes: people feel significant (everyone feels that he or she makes a difference to the success of the organisation); learning and competence matter (leaders value learning and mastery and so do the people who work for leaders); people are part of the community (where there is leadership, there is a team – a family a unit); and work is exciting (where there are leaders, work is stimulating, challenging, fascinating and fun).

Therefore, in simple terms, leaders create vision, trust, meaning, success and healthy environments – if they survive the bureaucracy. A better definition of leadership, therefore, is how to achieve worthwhile goals through other people via a vision. Critically, to survive in the 21st Century, the RAF will require a new generation of leaders – leaders, not managers. This distinction is an important one: leaders conquer the context, the volatile, turbulent, ambiguous surroundings that sometimes seem to conspire against the organisation, whilst managers surrender to the bureaucracy! Effective leadership, therefore, is very important to unlocking the immense talent in any organisation, including the RAF. Moreover, organisational vision can also challenge people to stretch beyond their current capabilities and often beyond their limitations. As Nanus comments: "There is no more powerful engine driving an organisation towards excellence and long range success, than an attractive, worthwhile and achievable vision of the future, that is widely shared".

This vision must be alive in every command level of the RAF and a corporate vision must operate at 3 levels:

- Strategic – The RAF's overriding philosophy.
- Operational – That philosophy in action.
- Tactical – That philosophy manifested in the behaviour of each airman/ woman.

Thus, the leaders responsibilities include disseminating vision to all 3 levels and this vision needs to permeate throughout the organisation.

Finally, leaders must evaluate vision, before the vision fails or is inadequate to handle new challenges. Vision needs constant attention in light of the dynamic environment in which we live and work in and leaders who are not strategists are simply caretakers and gatekeepers. Though they may run efficient and effective organisations (*i.e.* they are managers), they do not really serve the long-term interests of their institutions unless they plan, set goals and provide strategic vision. Leaders who care about their missions and about their people normally want to leave their organisation in better shape and with a clearer strategic direction, than when they took over.

In summary, the difference between a good unit and a bad unit is leadership: sound leadership within a dynamic environment, is at the heart of the RAF's institutional character. It is the most important bond among airmen and is the foundation for successful Air Force achievements in peace and war; of the many skills and abilities used in the profession of arms, none is prized more highly. Enhancing leadership as we transform to meet the challenges of this millennium can strengthen the foundation of mutual trust and respect among ranks and across the organisation as a whole.

AUTOCRATIC LEADERSHIP STYLE

This is often considered the classical approach. It is one in which the manager retains as much power and decision-making authority as possible. The manager does not consult employees, nor are they allowed to give any input. Employees are expected to obey orders without receiving any explanations. The motivation environment is produced by creating a structured set of rewards and punishments. This leadership style has been greatly criticised during the past 30 years. Some studies say that organisations with many autocratic leaders have higher turnover and absenteeism than other organisations. Certainly Gen X employees have proven to be highly resistant to this management style.

These studies say that autocratic leaders:

- Rely on threats and punishment to influence employees.
- Do not trust employees.
- Do not allow for employee input.

Yet, autocratic leadership is not all bad. Sometimes it is the most effective style to use.

These situations can include:

- New, untrained employees who do not know which tasks to perform or which procedures to follow.
- Effective supervision can be provided only through detailed orders and instructions.
- Employees do not respond to any other leadership style.

- There are high-volume production needs on a daily basis.
- There is limited time in which to make a decision.
- A manager's power is challenged by an employee.
- The area was poorly managed.
- Work needs to be coordinated with another department or organisation.

The autocratic leadership style should not be used when:

- Employees become tense, fearful, or resentful.
- Employees expect to have their opinions heard.
- Employees begin depending on their manager to make all their decisions.
- There is low employee morale, high turnover and absenteeism and work stoppage.

BUREAUCRATIC LEADERSHIP STYLE

Bureaucratic leadership is where the manager manages "by the book" Everything must be done according to procedure or policy. This manager is really more of a police officer than a leader. He or she enforces the rules.

This style can be effective when:

- Employees are performing routine tasks over and over.
- Employees need to understand certain standards or procedures.
- Employees are working with dangerous or delicate equipment that requires a definite set of procedures to operate.
- Safety or security training.
- Is being conducted.
- Employees are performing tasks that require handling cash.

This style is ineffective when:

- Work habits form that are hard to break, especially if they are no longer useful.
- Employees lose their interest in their jobs and in their fellow workers.
- Employees do only what is expected of them and no more.

DEMOCRATIC LEADERSHIP STYLE

The democratic leadership style is also called the participative style as it encourages employees to be a part of the decision making. The democratic manager keeps his or her employees informed about everything that affects their work and shares decision making and problem solving responsibilities. This style requires the leader to be a coach who has the final say, but gathers information from staff members before making a decision. Democratic leadership can produce high quality and high quantity work for long periods of time. Many employees like the trust they receive and respond with cooperation, team spirit, and high morale.

Typically the democratic leader:

- Develops plans to help employees evaluate their own performance.
- Allows employees to establish goals.
- Encourages employees to grow on the job and be promoted.
- Recognises and encourages achievement.

Like the other styles, the democratic style is not always appropriate. It is most successful when used with highly skilled or experienced employees or when implementing operational changes or resolving individual or group problems.

The democratic leadership style is most effective when:

- The leader wants to keep employees informed about matters that affect them.
- The leader wants employees to share in decision-making and problem-solving duties.
- The leader wants to provide opportunities for employees to develop a high sense of personal growth and job satisfaction.
- There is a large or complex problem that requires lots of input to solve.
- Changes must be made or problems solved that affect employees or groups of employees.
- You want to encourage team building and participation.

Democratic leadership should not be used when:

- There is not enough time to get everyone's input.
- It's easier and more cost-effective for the manager to make the decision.
- The business can't afford mistakes.
- The manager feels threatened by this type of leadership.
- Employee safety is a critical concern.

Laissez-Faire Leadership Style

The laissez-faire leadership style is also known as the "hands-off" style. It is one in which the manager provides little or no direction and gives employees as much freedom as possible. All authority or power is given to the employees and they must determine goals, make decisions, and resolve problems on their own.

This is an effective style to use when:

- Employees are highly skilled, experienced, and educated.
- Employees have pride in their work and the drive to do it successfully on their own.
- Outside experts, such as staff specialists or consultants are being used and,
- Employees are trustworthy and experienced.

This style should not be used when:

- It makes employees feel insecure at the unavailability of a manager.
- The manager cannot provide regular feedback to let employees know how well they are doing.
- Managers are unable to thank employees for their good work.
- The manager doesn't understand his or her responsibilities and is hoping the employees can cover for him or her.

VARYING LEADERSHIP STYLE

While the proper leadership style depends on the situation, there are three other factors.

That also influence which leadership style to use:

- The manager's personal background. What personality, knowledge, values, ethics, and experiences does the manager have. What does he or she think will work?
- The employees being supervised. Employees are individuals with different personalities and backgrounds. The leadership style managers use will vary depending upon the individual employee and what he or she will respond best to.
- The company. The traditions, values, philosophy, and concerns of the company will influence how a manager acts.

A NETWORK DEFINITION OF LEADERSHIP

One of the great unknowns in the business and organisational development literature is what accounts for great leadership. It is one of the softest areas of the social sciences, having defied rigorous analysis for decades. Yet, leadership is considered one of the key ingredients for the success of any organisation. The position taken here is that leadership is both born and nurtured. The evidence for the biological and evolutionary basis underlying the personality associated with leadership is compelling and growing. Individuals have innately different leadership capacities in the same way that they have different mental and physical capacities.

These personality traits are some of the genetic variables that evolution periodically and randomly shuffles. But what makes a personality trait—such as the ability to interpret emotional cues, to connect with other people, to detect cheaters, to gossip and trade favours—a property of the social network are the rules that govern how individual members interact and cooperate.

In this sense, leadership is a network effect that can result in highly responsive and effective leaders, or contrarily, degradation into kleptocracy or demagoguery.

On the other hand, if networked organisations can be designed that select for certain leadership roles and competencies that can be measured, evaluated, and improved upon, then leadership ceases to be an ineffable quality, but becomes a tangible asset that can be learned, improved upon, and replicated.

Table, summarises some of the potential metrics of network leadership that are associated with the eight different leadership roles. These lists are not meant to be definitive, but rather illustrative of how explicit network metrics might be related to both the definition network roles and the self-management of those rules through the appropriate metrics and feedback.

Table. Network Properties of Leadership.

Network Roles	Signature Pattern	Types of Links	Performance Metrics	Social Currencies
Exemplar	star, asymmetric	inform, challenge, assert	independence, trust, reach, completion rate, reputation	expertise, reputation trust, access
Gatekeeper	asymmetric, gateway, hub, weak links, power law	invite, offer, uninvite	transparency independence, completion, reputation	access, information, reputation
Visionary	star, sparse asymmetric, strong ties, weak links	inform, question, challenge, assert	social capital , reputation, initiation, reach, trust	expertise, information, reputation
Truth-Teller	dense, sub-networks, strong ties,	question, request, inform, assess, challenge	independence, reputation, transparency, trust	reputation, trust
Fixer	strong ties, weak links, hub, power law	request, offer, question, assess, directive	completion rate reputation, reach	access, goods, services, income, reputation
Connector	symmetric, gateway, weak links, small world	inform, access, invite, offer, request	density, diversity, redundancy, reach, trust	access, favours, reputation
Enforcer	strong ties, subnetwork, power law	directives, compliance, request, question	completion rate reputation, transparency, trust	access, favours, reputation
Facilitator	gateway, sparse, GFN	invite, request, offer	completion rate diversity, initiation,	reputation, access, favours reputation

SIGNATURE PATTERN

Much of the research on social networks stresses the fact that an individual's role in a social network is dependent upon their structural position in the network. Individuals who act as go-betweens or connectors are typically seen as having a network signature measured in terms of how many other members are linked to them and the directionality of these links. The field of social network analysis is still in its early phases of development, and there are many different types of network measures: density, power laws, hub-and-spoke, small world effects, reach, strong ties, weak ties, stars, subnetworks, clusters, clumpiness, constraints, redundancy, effective sise, etc., These measures for the most part ignore the type of links and try to derive a description of a network principally from its topology. As Barabasi observed in noting the limitations of his own analysis of scale-free networks and as Watts noted in his critique of small world effects, the types of links are very important, as are the rules governing the addition and removal of links. Hence, a description in terms of structure alone is insufficient.

TYPES OF LINKS: TAGGED

The fact that two parties are only removed by three to six links is no guarantee that one party can access another. It all depends upon the nature of the links. Not everyone can or ever will have access to one another. There are social, cultural, and economic rules that preclude certain forms of interaction. More importantly, for the purposes for understanding network leadership roles, the tagging of the links is associated with the nature of the leadership role. Visionaries' characteristically originate informational links, and, unlike fixers, are not in the business of asking people to commit to completing tasks, whereas gatekeepers are periodically inviting and uninviting people to join a group. The notion of tagged links as discussed here is very similar to Searle's notion of "speech acts," forms of dialogue that people use to get other people to do things. This is a fertile and highly developed field of linguistics—discourse analysis and pragmatics—that offers significant promise for identifying the grammars of interactions among members of a social network. There are rules or social protocols for the addition and removal of combinations of such links, thereby making most complex social networks not scalefree.

PERFORMANCE METRICS

Given the visibility that being a member of a network provides and the opportunity to track and measure interactions, it then becomes possible to provide relatively simple, straightforward, empirically based measures related to the quality of leadership. For example, a leader should not lose track of people, resources, or projects, but have a high completion rate for the number of commitments or "loops" that he has initiated. Measures can tell how many loops remain open, how fast they are being closed, and who is the bottleneck. In a world of such visibility, there can be real accountability. Perhaps the initial metrics are not correct and do not reflect true performance. They then could be modified over time through feedback, and adjusted to drive the desired Behaviours.

As was noted in the earlier analysis of peer-to-peer networks, reputation is a widely shared performance metric and a profound driver of Behaviour. There are more sophisticated measures such as reciprocity and social capital measures, but every performance measure would have to be adjusted for the particular needs and circumstances of the networked organisation. This can be an important measure because each network and leadership role evolves its own social currency, and these currencies are relational measures indicating the status of an individual's relationships with others in the network. The ability to amass significant amounts of social currencies can translate into effective leadership. The ability to convert from one social currency account into another can greatly facilitate a leadership role, such as a connector or a fixer. This is an important dimension of network interactions and needs to be understood in order to direct overall network Behaviours.

DEVELOPING NETWORK LEADERS

VISIBILITY AND DIGITISATION

As more and more interactions become digitised and observable, opportunities abound for using the naturally occurring data about the volume and the nature of the interactions among members of network organisations. Collaborative technologies, as simple and ubiquitous as e-mail, make it possible to make visible the millions of social interactions among the participants in networked organisations and thereby gain insight and eventual control over how members manage their work relationships. Not only is it possible to capture data about who is interacting with whom, but it is also possible through analytics to identify some of the emergent network leadership roles. Simple modifications to existing collaborative platforms make it possible to identify the network signatures of different types of leadership roles.

By making different members' Behaviours visible to one another, and by developing metrics for rating leadership performance, many of the techniques that are used in peer production systems—Open Source, eBay, and even MMORPGs—can be applied to the self-synchronised management of networked organisation. For example when setting up multifunctional or cross-organisational teams through e-mail, it was possible for all the members to see who communicated with whom about what topics and how frequently. A new kind of self-enforcing accountability could be introduced.

Furthermore, by providing metrics of responsiveness, connectedness, loop closing, and peer ratings, not only would shared awareness be increased but new forms of self-synchronisation would emerge. As more data on the interactions of social networks becomes available, it should not be too long before network leadership roles are identified in much the same way that different roles are identified in online games and peer production systems. It is just a matter of time before network leadership roles become digital, and by virtue of their becoming digital become measurable, teachable, and systematically deployed to maximise network performance.

IDENTIFY PERFORMANCE METRICS FOR NETWORK LEADERS

Social network analysis has identified some of the preliminary network structures associated with different kinds of leadership roles, such as the importance of connectors and hubs in network organisations, or how small world effects can be achieved. With the advent of social software to manage social interactions, form *ad hoc* groups, close decision loops, and enable self-synchronisation Behaviours, leadership qualities that had been unmanageable intangibles for so long can be measured, improved, and taught in a way that was never before possible. With the wide-scale adoption of RFID and mote technologies for tracking physical assets in real time, and the enormous strides in information sharing, improved awareness, collaboration, and self-synchronisation demonstrated by the war in Iraq, the time is not so distant when leadership roles will be measured and tracked digitally and become an integral part in how networked organisations are managed. These cumulative innovations will significantly reduce agency costs and improve the flexibility and productivity of large-scale organisations by orders of magnitude. New metrics will make it possible to measure the degree of trust, reciprocity, successes, failures, social capital, diversity, network value, etc., within an edge organisation. By making all assets—physical, human, content, and interactions— observable and providing for the selective disclosure of information and the dynamic allocation and revocation of security access, it will be possible to have much more secure and robust networked organisations.

CAREER PATHS

In order for new models of network leadership to be adopted and become an integral part of networked organisations, there have to be clear career paths that reward the skills of network leadership as a recognised part of career development. In military organisations where the alpha leadership role is still wedded to certain traditional combat roles, identifying new alpha roles that exemplify important and valued competencies outside those of the traditional military culture could prove challenging. In forms of warfare that are increasingly informational, analytic, sensemaking, and collaborative, communication and interaction skills are becoming increasing important.

New kinds of competencies will be selected and need to be rapidly incorporated into the training of all recruits. By having explicit, real-time measures not only of important leadership traits but also the demand for different types of leadership roles, human resource departments will have an easier time not only in developing credible and practical work performance criteria, but also in anticipating the demand for current and new types of leaders and skills. As suggested earlier, through the real-time content analysis and tagging of messages, primarily e-mail and instant messaging, it would be possible to differentiate visionary leadership roles from truth-tellers. The analysis might reveal a dearth of truth telling interactions and that visionary-type communications dominate the interactions within the social network, leading to bad decisions and failed missions.

Individuals could be evaluated in terms of how well they are able to fulfil different network leadership roles and recommended for the roles that they are best suited for. There are specific metrics associated with different types of leadership roles and these measures could derived from naturally occurring metadata that are the byproduct of e-mail interactions. Given these capabilities in the future, not only could there be a "real-time inventory and stocking system" for leadership skills and roles, but real-time systems for evaluating the performance of human assets and knowing when to replace or upgrade them. Such metrics will also be used to conduct forensic analyses of different missions where there have been leadership successes, failures, or the need for new kinds of leadership roles or combinations of roles. Given the explicitness of the leadership models, lessons learned from one networked organisation can be rapidly applied to another, thereby accelerating organisational learning and innovation adoption.

ANTECEDENTS

The subject of leadership has been described as a very imperative one that can never be over-flogged in management research. More imperative is the relevance of the theme in library and information management profession. While literature abound on the topic in management research, books on the subject as it relates to the library and information services are still terse. Western researchers even affirmed this and noted that not until the recent times that we have journal articles and short communications on the subject in LIS literature. General observation revealed that formal leadership training, if not totally absent in our library and information establishments, is very scarce.

EXIGENCIES

There is concern within the library profession that we are short of leaders. Why is this such a common lament. Those of us who are responsible for recruitment in our organisations often get together to scratch our heads and complain about the apparent lack of colleagues within the profession who will take up leadership roles. Why is this? The quote simply leads us to the first statement of exigency that:

- There is a dearth of library and information profession leaders.

Of course, leadership is also hard work – managing, persuading, motivating, inspiring others is not easy, although it can definitely be rewarding. I suspect many people are scared off by what is required....

The second statement of exigency is that:

- Leadership qualities, skills, and competencies are hard to come by.

One theory is that the typical value set of those who work in libraries are not compatible with managing people or managing physical resources such as budgets, or operating confidently in a political and business environment.

Some blame the library qualification providers for not attracting the right people.

The third statement of exigency is that:

- Even if people are not born leaders, the library and information schools should do better in teaching leadership skills to prospective library and information practitioners.

Librarianship as a profession has entered an area where its workforce is ageing and its leadership is becoming more "graying".

Fifty eight percent of librarians in the U.S. are projected to reach the retirement age of 65 between 2005 and 2019 and forty percent of library directors plan to retire in less than nine years. There is also an international trend of graying.

In Australia, over 52 per cent of librarians are currently more than 45 years old. If they retire, at the age of 60, then about half of the population of Australian librarians are expected to retire within the next 10 to 15 years.

The fourth statement of exigency as derived from the above is that:

- The library and information system need succession planning – Hence, the need for leaders.

To meet the demands of today's fast-paced and competitive business environment, people at all levels are being asked to step up and assume leadership behaviours... companies are investing millions of dollars annually in leadership development training to meet this challenge.

The fifth statement of exigency is that:

- The library and information system profession should take a cue from the business and corporate world by having leadership development agenda.

ISSUES IN LEADERSHIP IN THE LIBRARY AND INFORMATION ENVIRONMENT: FOCUS ON LIBRARY DIRECTORS

Despite all the theoretical bases for leadership, the leadership role of a leader cannot be divulged from his basic functions in a specific situation. Therefore, for practicability, this portion of this presentation will hang essentially on the propositions of Versosa as depicting the functional/leadership roles of the library leadership.

The highlights as submitted in her presentation are given as thus:

- Leadership is just one dimension of the managers work.
- It involves "the exercise of social influence by infusing the parent organisation with purpose and direction in order to achieve its goals.
- Leadership requires that the library director should influence members of the parent institutions to provide resources in order to:

- Support expansion plans.
- Accept the goals of the library as valid and deserving support.

- The 3 dimensions used to measure library leadership are:
  i. Leader activities.
  ii. Management of organisational change and
  iii. Reputational Effectiveness.

Leader Activities:

- Managerial role activities.
- Professional activities and involvement.
- Membership on community committees.
- Strategies for influencing the environment.

The managerial role/activities are further broken into six:

- Which involves directing the work of subordinates; integrating subordinates goals with the librarys goals and objectives; allocating human resources to tasks; evaluating subordinates job performance; resolving conflicts between subordinates and providing new staff with training.
- Involves attending social functions for contacts; attendance at conferences/meetings; maintaining informal communication networks; and relating with people outside.
- Includes initiating new ideas for services and operations; keeping up with professional trends/changes; keeping abreast of technological developments; scanning the environment for new opportunities to improve services/operations; collecting information about users touring facilities to observe and reading reports of other units.
- Involves planning and implementing changes in the library, initiating change in the library and solving problems by instituting changes in the library.
- Includes serving as an expert or advising people outside the library; keeping others abreast of developments in the library, attending to correspondences, and serving on committees, and representing the library.
- Changes in organisational domain *vis-a-vis* other community/cognate entities; Internal changes

REPUTATIONAL EFFECTIVENESS

Includes considerations of:

- Years in managerial positions.
- Libraries worked in.
- Continuing education.
- Professional journals scanned/read.
- No. of publications.
- Membership of Association, and
- Services to University/Parent Establishment.

THE LIBRARY/INFORMATION PROFESSIONALS LEADERSHIP AGENDA/STRATEGY

The following initiatives are desirable and could be found rewarding:

- Creation of awareness for need of leadership development skills among professionals.
- Self-development in leadership skills by Librarians and Information Professionals.
- Integration of leadership development into the library/information centre strategic planning.
- Leadership Development Programme to run through the ladder
- Library and Information Schools to integrate Leadership Skills development into their curricula.
- Need for librarians and information professionals to maintain strong network within and without their organisation to enhance development of skills and knowledge.

NETWORK STRUCTURES AND LEADERSHIP ROLES

Social networks self-organise to acquire and allocate resources such as information, goods, favours, access, privileges, and protection. As discussed earlier, the specialisation of roles in social networks has been demonstrated to have strong long-term survival value, and therefore has been biologically encoded through evolutionary forces as innate psychological or personality traits.

These traits are reflected in how people read social cues, detect cheaters, create and share ideas, and form affinities with strangers. In addition to having innate social exchange competencies, some alpha or exemplar individuals are especially proficient at a skill or exhibit a prised trait that warrants widespread emulation and imitation. Typically, alpha individuals have a special physical prowess, physical attraction, intelligence, social proficiency, or some combination of these traits. When one considers Cosmides and Tooby's findings on innate social exchange algorithms and Damasio's analysis of the neuro-physiology of social emotions combined with Dunbar's studies on the role of grooming and language in social groups, a compelling argument can be made that these different roles are an evolutionary stable strategy that makes possible the efficient functioning of any self-organising social network.

Few of these network roles have any intrinsic individual value. However, when combined with other roles, they enable the organisation and functioning of complex networks of exchange relationships. Leadership in this context can be regarded as a proficiency in any one or combination of these network roles.

In this sense, some individuals may have greater innate talents than others, but the effectiveness of these gifts is dependent upon the overall qualities of the network and the roles of other members of the network. Network leadership roles assume different levels of importance depending upon the phase of evolution of a networked organisation. This fact is often not fully appreciated in the business leadership literature where visionary leaders are periodically revered and reviled depending upon the ebb and flow of their company's earnings. The value of such leadership roles might be more fruitfully understood by attempting to determine the conditions under which a visionary role is adaptive and when it is not, thereby recognising that it is one of many combinations of leadership roles that is required. Likewise, the absence of certain critical leadership roles, such as truth telling, can contribute to the failure of corporate governance or the excesses of overly zealous visionaries.

A further example of the importance of different kinds of network leadership roles can be found in the failure of large organisations to manage relationships across functional and organisational boundaries. Here the high "agency costs" of coordinating across organisational or functional boundaries is largely due to the absence of leaders who are connectors and who know how to interact and affiliate with third parties to build trust. These are what Burton identifies as the *tertiaries*, the brokers between organisational networks. In each of these examples, there are leadership roles whose value and appropriateness depend upon the state of the network.

The effective governance of a networked organisation should therefore involve knowing the status of the organisational network, being able to assess the strengths and weaknesses of different roles, and then allocating the appropriate leadership assets to improve the overall performance of the network. This is something that Louis Gerstner understood when he first took the job of CEO at IBM. Initially, he was criticised for being insufficiently visionary, to which he responded that the company had become too enamored of its own vision and detached from reality. What was needed, he contended, was a good dose of truth telling, an operational overhaul, and then a new vision. These were different leadership roles that he seemed to switch in and out of comfortably and effectively.

JOINT LEADERSHIP AND META-LEADERSHIP

Just as there are different leadership roles *within* social networks, there are also metaleadership roles that cut *across* networked organisations. When it comes to leading across different organisations, such as coalition partners, partnerships, alliances, joint command, or multi-agency missions, a new set of meta-leadership roles comes into play. These roles are different from those in a hierarchical organisation where subordinates are required to execute orders or follow management directives and are held accountable for doing so.

In joint command efforts, on the other hand, collaboration is peer-based, consensual, and mutual. There are no prior histories for building reciprocity, trust, or transparency. Therefore these have to be created anew over time.

Moreover, as the leadership role is more one of governance than of command, the issue becomes how to cooperatively develop metrics and protocols that respect the integrity of each of the respective organisations. That being said, creating new meta-networks is much the same as creating any peer networked organisation, except that the units are significantly larger and each has its own distinctive culture.

Certain leadership roles have to be established for all participants—specifically, what Behaviours or traits best exemplify the qualities and standard being sought of the meta-network. Since, leadership in joint efforts typically rotates over time, exemplar leadership roles should be filled by those who have qualities that are not closely identified with any one particular organisation or Service. Rather, an effort should be made to give this networked organisation its own independent identity.

An early visionary can act as the exemplar member and personify the desired qualities, thereby setting a precedent for others to follow. However, there should be an effort to identify other network leadership roles and the associated metrics and protocols that the different representatives of the joint organisations would undertake.

This networked approach to joint leadership differs significantly from the traditional, hierarchical Napoleonic staff codes wherein a small number of fixed staff personnel with limited specialisation perform most of the joint leadership support functions. The networked approach more closely resembles former Marine General Anthony Zinni's proposal for a Modular Commander Center, which stresses specialisation and flexibility. As a former CENTCOM commander, General Zinni recognised that commanders had variable missions requiring combinations of different functions, resources, and partners.

In effect, the command structure had to be agile enough to adapt to the different circumstances of the mission from unilateral humanitarian missions to coalition-based major combat. The combinations of skills for each differed significantly and therefore would entail specialised social network protocols and combinations of different network leadership roles and skills. Under such conditions where it is difficult for one coalition partner to exert authority over another, as many of the organisations are sovereign and independent, the only form of effective control is the selective exclusion of partners or the minimisation of their role.

The qualities of the connector and the facilitator network leadership roles are especially important at this senior level and have their own specialised "social protocols" and skills for setting and coordinating joint missions.

LEADERSHIP AND SCOPE OF CONTROL

In hierarchical and bureaucratic organisations, leadership is often confused with scope of control and authority—power. In such organisations, leaders are given the latitude, even the expectation, to exercise significant control at all levels of the organisation. This is often expressed in budgetary terms: the willingness and the ability to control, cut, or redirect a subordinate's budget.

The power of a superior is virtually absolute in such organisations as they have the authority to project control all the way down the organisation. There are no autonomous layers, and in this sense, decision rights are not protected but revocable and alienable. Usurping local control and autonomy through topdown budgetary restrictions can undermine the efficacy and self-organising capabilities of an organisation and thereby prevent it from effectively learning and adapting.

The integrity of local rules and allocation protocols have to be maintained, and while there can be a decrement in the gross resources available to a subordinate or sub-network, these resources should not be explicitly earmarked or constrained, as such interventions will prevent the network from being self-organising. This is the same type of issue as the requirement for tactical autonomy in a command system, where the supra-ordinate strategic layer determines the objectives and the assets to be allocated, but the subordinate commander has the authority and the responsibility to make the tactical decisions. In a networked organisational model where there are also independent layers of selforganisation and different types of protocols for interaction, the transecting of layers by a supra-ordinate to a subordinate, in effect, micromanaging and second-guessing, is dangerous for the well-being of the network.

It transforms a collective, networked asset into an episodic individualised asset, thereby undermining trust and accountability. This may happen out of frustration by a senior manager wanting to get things done and going outside official channels.

However, in every case it undermines the collective capability of a networked organisation to self-organise. For this reason, it is very important to move away from the individualised model of leadership and authority and to develop governance mechanisms that build up the overall ongoing assets of the networked organisation. Network leadership roles that are held accountable to the interests of the whole will yield far more efficient, effective, and accountable organisational structures than those that are governed through sporadic and episodic interventions that undermine local authority.

THE STYLE APPROACH TO LEADERSHIP

The basic premise of the style approach to leadership is that a leader's "style" determines his or her success. A style is the method of leading that a person uses. Kurt Lewin was the theorist most responsible for this approach. We have discussed Lewin's theoretical contributions to small-group research throughout this book. It is now time to discuss the man himself. His life affected how he viewed leadership. Lewin was a German Jew who gained an international reputation for his research on perception during the 1920s. During the 1930s, Lewin was able to escape the fate that the Nazis planned for the Jewish citizenry of Germany by immigrating to the United States. As a new American, Lewin was enamored with our democratic traditions and decided to research leadership. He wished to show that democratic leadership is better than the authoritarianism that Hitler was using in Germany at the time.

As we explained, he conceived of a life-space for every person and group. There are regions within this life-space. Forces attract people to or repel them from the various regions. As we have described, we can represent the group itself as an entity that moves around its own life-space.

Lewin believed that a leader has the ability to manipulate the group's life-space and direct its movement towards various goals. Thus, the leader has power over the group. Lewin decided that there are three styles of leadership. The styles are based on the relationship that the leader has with his or her group. A leader has a "democratic" style if he or she manipulates the life-space to help the group reach its own goals. A leader with an "authoritarian" style manipulates the group's life-space to force the group to reach the leader's goals. A leader with a "laissez faire" style does not manipulate the group's life-space at all.

Findings

Lewin *et al.* performed a detailed analysis of the behaviour of the boys during their meetings. They also interviewed the boys concerning their feelings about the sessions. This work resulted in a mass of information from the study.

Maintenance output. First, the researchers found that the democratic leadership style led to greater satisfaction with the group experience than either the authoritarian or the laissez faire styles. The experimenters asked the 20 boys if they preferred the democratic or the authoritarian leaders. Nineteen of them said that they favoured the democratic leaders. The scientists then asked 10 of the boys to compare the democratic and the laissez faire-style leaders. Out of these 10, 7 said that they preferred the democratic leadership method.

Second, the groups that had the democratic-style leaders appeared to be the most cohesive. During the study, one of the methods that scientists used to measure levels of cohesiveness was to determine the ratio between how often the members used group-oriented pronouns, such as "we" and "us," and how often they used individual-oriented pronouns, such as "I" and "me." In addition, the researchers looked at other indicators of cohesiveness, including the levels of friendly statements, mutual praise, sharing of work materials, and playfulness. The democratic groups had the highest levels of these factors. The laissez faire groups were also fairly cohesive, perhaps in response to their "nonleading" leaders.

In contrast, the groups with leaders who used an authoritarian style were far less cohesive than the other groups. Observers compared the behaviour of the boys in the authoritarian-led groups with the behaviour of those in the democratic-led groups. They noted 30 times as many acts of hostility and 8 times as many acts of aggression in the authoritarian groups. In addition, authoritarian-led sessions had the highest levels of statements of discontent and the largest levels of absenteeism.

Task output. As for their work output, both the authoritarian and the democratic groups outpaced the laissez faire groups. The boys in the authoritarian groups worked 74 per cent of the time when their leaders were present. This compared with a work level of 50 per cent for boys in democratic groups and 33 per cent in the laissez faire groups. However, when the leaders left the room, these percentages changed. Groups following a democratic leader continued to work at a 46 per cent level. In contrast, the work time for authoritarian groups fell drastically to only 29 per cent, implying that the members of the authoritarian groups had little desire to work. On the other hand, groups with leaders using a laissez faire style actually worked more when their leaders left the room. Their work time increased to 52 per cent. This result implies that these members remained motivated.

Finally, the researchers judged the work of democratic groups highly. They considered this work to be of higher quality and originality than the performance of authoritarian and laissez faire groups.

CONTINGENCY THEORY OF LEADERSHIP

The most popular and extensively researched situational theory of leadership was first proposed by Fred Piedler during the 1960s. Fiedler's model claims that group performance depends on the interaction of the leader style and the favourableness of the situation. Fiedlers major contributions consist of(1) iden-tifying the leadership orientation of the leader and developing a way to measure it, and (2) identifying three situational factors influencing leadership and developing a method of measuring them

Leader orientation. Fiedler's definition of the leader's orientation emerged largely from earlier studies in which leaders were classified as either relationship-oriented or task-oriented. Relationship-oriented leaders look at others as coworkers and see close interpersonal relations as a requirement for accomplishing the task. Task-oriented leaders show a strong emotional reaction against people with whom they have difficulty working. If they are forced to make a choice between getting the job done or worrying about interpersonal relations, they choose the task first and worry about interpersonal relations later. Following earlier research, Fiedler suggested that individuals could be placed along one continuum characterized by two basic leader orientations: relationship-oriented versus task-oriented.

LPC scale. Leadership orientation is measured by the least preferred coworker (LPC) scale, as illustrated in Exhibit 16.5. Individuals are asked to think of a person with whom they have worked who they least preferred as a coworker, and describe this person using sixteen scales. When the responses arc summed, an individual with a favourable description of the least preferred coworker would have a high LPC score, suggesting a relationship-oriented leader. An unfavourable description of the least preferred coworker would result in a low score, suggesting a task-oriented leader.

Difficulty in interpreting the LPC scores has been a problem for Fiedler's contingency theory. The LPC scale is not related to any of the well-known personality measures. In spite of uncertainty about what exactly it measures, however, the evidence indicates that it is a reliable measure of something, and Fiedler concludes that "there can be little doubt that we are dealing with a very important aspect of personality." A review of 25 years of research using th~3 LPC scale concluded that high LPC leaders are primarily relationship-oriented while low LPC leaders are primarily task-oriented consistent with Fiedler's claims.' In general, a low LPC leader is more directive, more structuring, more goal-oriented, and more concerned with efficiency. A high LPC leader is more considerate, more human relations oriented, more participative, and more sensitive to the feelings of others.

Situational favourableness. Fiedler's model claims that whether a high LPC leader or low LPC leader will be more effective depends upon the favourableness of the situation. In some situations, a high LPC leader is most effective, while a unenthusiastic low LPC leader is more effective in other situations. Fiedler claimed that the favourableness of the situation is determined by three variables: (1) whether the relationships between the leader and the members are good or poor. (2) whether the task is relatively structured or unstructured, and (3) whether the power position of the leader is relatively strong or weak.

In studies testing the model, Fiedler and his colleagues developed instruments to measure each of these three situational variables." Of the three situational variables, the leader-member relations variable was considered to be the most important for determining the favourableness of the situation. Leader-member relations were measured using a simple questionnaire with ten scales on which the leader was asked to describe the group. This instrument was called a "group atmosphere scale" and two sample items are shown here.

The second most important situational variable was the task structure which was evaluated by judges who examined four aspects of the task structure.

- *Coal clarity:* the degree to which the requirements of the job are clearly stated and known by the people performing then,
- *Coal-path multiplicity:* the degree to which the problems encounter in the job can be solved by a variety of procedures.
- *Decision verifiability:* the degree to which the correctness of the solutions or decisions can be demonstrated and ascertained.

- *Decision specificity:* the degree to which there is generally more than one correct solution involved in performing the task.

In a highly structured task, goals are very clear, there is on! y one correct procedure for performing the task, the correctness of the decisions can be immediately verified, and there is only one correct solution. Obviously, a highly structured task does not require leaders to provide additional structure.

The third situational variable was the power position of the leader. This factor was measured by a series of questions asking whether the leaders could recommend rewards or promotions, whether they could assign tasks and evaluate performance, and whether they had been given official titles by the organisation to differentiate them from subordinates.

By determining whether a group is high or low on each of the three situational factors, Fiedler classified each group into one of eight categories, which ranged along a scale from extremely favourable situations to extremely unfavourable situations for the leader. A highly favourable situation consisted of good leader-member relations, a highly structured task, and a strong power position, as illustrated in Exhibit 16.6. On the other hand, an extremely unfavourable situation existed when the leader-member relations were poor, the task was unstructured, and the leader possessed a weak power position.

Group effectiveness. Fiedler examined the relationship between the leaders' LPC score and the effectiveness of the group in a variety of situations. The results indicated that a high LPC leader was most effective when the situation was moderately favourable. If the situation was extremely favourable or unfavourable, however, the low LPC leaders tended to have the most effective groups. These relationships are illustrated in Exhibit 16.7.

Although these results may look rather complex and difficult to understand, they seem plausible after a brief consideration. Relationship-oriented leaders (high LPC) tend to excel in situations of intermediate favourableness where concern for the group members is apparently a necessary prerequisite for motivating them to perform well. In these situations, people want to have leaders who care about them. Task-oriented leaders (low LPC), however, are more effective when the situation is either very favourable or very unfavourable. In a highly favourable situation, the personal needs of members are apparently already satisfied and what is needed is a task-oriented leader to get the job done. In an extremely unfavourable situation, however, satisfying individual needs is probably impossible. A task-oriented leader who simply focuses on getting the work done is more effective than a relationship-oriented leader who spends time fruitlessly trying to build good relationships in an impossible situation.

Fiedler's theory has some interesting implications for the selection and training of leaders in organisations. Candidates for leadership positions should be evaluated to assess their basic orientations, and they should be placed in jobs consistent with their leadership orientation. The favourableness of a situation should be assessed before assigning a leader to that position. Leaders who are struggling may need to be placed in a different situation, or their current situation may need to be changed.

When leaders are not successful, it is tempting to suggest that they need to change their leadership orientation. Fiedler does not recommend this approach, however, and argues that the basic leadership orientation of an individual is a relatively stable personality characteristic that cannot be easily changed. Rather than changing the leader to fit the situation, Fiedler recommends changing the situation to fit the leader through what he calls job engineering. Job engineering consists of changing one of the situational factors to increase or decrease the favourability of the situation. For example, the task structure and power position can be effectively changed through job redesign programmes or changes in personnel policies.

The validity of Fiedler's contingency theory has been examined in numerous studies. Although most of the studies have been supportive, there have been enough contradictory findings for the model to remain somewhat controversial among leadership scholars. The most serious controversy about Fiedler's model concerns the LPC scale. Although the theory seems to predict leader effectiveness, the ambiguity over what the LPC score is actually measuring is disturbing.

Path-Goal Model

Another situational leadership theory is the path-goal model developed primarily by Robert House. This model is fairly well known because it is based upon a popular theory of motivation — expectancy theory. The path-goal model ex-plains how leaders can facilitate task performance by showing subordinates how their performance can be instrumental in achieving desired rewards. Expectancy theory explains how an individual's attitudes and behaviour are influenced by the relationships between effort and performance (goal paths) and the valence of the rewards (goal attractiveness). Therefore, individuals are satisfied and productive when they see a strong relationship between their effort and performance and when their performance results in highly valued rewards. The path-goal model claims that the most effective leaders are those who help subordinates folio's the path to receiving valued rewards.

Essentially, the model explains what leaders should do to influence the perceptions of subordinates about their work, the personal goals of subordinates, and the various paths to goal attainment. The model claims that leader behaviour is motivating and satisfying to the extent that it clarifies the paths to the goals and increases goal attainment,**Leader behaviours.** The path-goal model suggests that leadership consists of two basic functions. The first function is path clarification: the leader helps subordinates understand which behaviours are necessary to accomplish the tasks. The second function is to increase the number of rewards available to subordinates by being supportive and paying attention to their personal needs. To perform these functions, leaders may adopt a variety of leadership styles.

Four distinct leadership styles are explained in the model:

1. *Directive leadership:* tells subordinates what is expected of them and provides specific guidance, standards, and schedules of work.
2. *Supportive leadership:* treats subordinates as equals and shows concern for their well-being, status, and personal needs; attempts to develop pleasant interpersonal relationships among group members.
3. *Achievement-oriented leadership:* sets challenging goals expects subordinates to perform at their highest level, and continually seeks improvement in performance.
4. *Participative leadership:* consults with subordinates and uses their suggestions and ideas in decision making. Unlike Fiedler's model, which suggested that leadership style was resistant to change, the path-goal model suggests that these four styles can be performed by the same manager at different times and in different situations. In other words, the path-goal theory suggests that if a directive leader discovers the situation has changed and now requires a participative leader, it is possible. For the leader to change. The appropriate leadership style depends on the situation. Although the path-goal model does not explain how to identify the appropriate leadership leader style, the model does present a list of situational factors that need to be consid-ered.

Situational factors. Two types of situational factors are proposed—the characteristics of the follower and environmental factors. Three characteristics of the followers have been identified as significant variables determining the appropriate leadership style:

- *Locus of control:* Locus of control refers to the individual's belief concerning the determinants of reward. Individuals with an internal locus of control believe their rewards are based on their own efforts, while those with an external locus of control believe their rewards are controlled by external forces. Internals prefer a participative leadership style while externals are generally more satisfied oh are with a directive leadership style.
- *Authoritarianism:* Authoritarianism refers to an individual's willing to accept the influence of others. High authoritarian followers tend to be less receptive to a participative leadership style and more responsive to directive leadership.
- *Abilities:* The ability and experience of the followers will influence leader whether they are able to work more successfully with an

achievement oriented leader who sets challenging goals and expects high perform-ance, or a supportive leader who is willing to patiently encourage and instruct them. The path-goal model identifies three environmental factors moderating the effects of leadership styles: (1) the nature of the task, (2) the formal authority system within the organisation, and (3) the group norms and dynamics. These environmental factors can influence the effectiveness of different leadership styles in a variety of ways. A highly structured task, for example, may reduce the need for a directive leader and even make a directive leader's attempt to pro-vide additional structure seem unwarranted and unwanted. However, a direc-tive leader would be more likely to succeed than a participative leader if the organisation had a highly formal authority structure that followed a strict chain of command. Likewise, a concern for the personal needs of subordinates by a supportive leader may seem superficial and unnecessary in a highly cohesive work group. The basic elements of the path-goal model of leadership axe illustrated in Exhibit 16J. This model shows how leadership styles interact with follower-characteristics and environmental factors to influence the personal percep-tions and motivation of the followers. The perceptions of the followers concerning the situation and the followers' level of motivation determine their job satisfaction, performance, and acceptance of the leader.

Some simplified applications of the path-goat model are shown in Exhibit 16.9. In the first two situations, subordinates have an ambiguous job or they feel insufficiently rewarded. Both situations call for a directive leader who explains the job and helps subordinates know how to get rewarded for performing it. The next two situations, boring work and a lack of self-confidence call for a support- leader. Repetitive jobs are not as boring if a supportive leader helps subordi-nates see that their work is meaningful and significant. Likewise, a supportive leader can help subordinates feel greater self-confidence by coaching them and praising their accomplishments. In situation 5, subordinates are not challenged by the task. An achievement-oriented leader will set high goals and emphasize the intrinsic and extrinsic rewards from more effort. Finally, situation 6 in-volves a task that is unstructured and poorly defined, calling for participative leadership. By participating in the decision making, subordinates help to create an effective solution to the problem and, as a result of their involvement, feel committed to making it work.

Research on the path-goal model. The relationships specified by the path-goal model have been examined in a modest number of empirical studies. This research has tested the theory's predictions concerning the moderators of lead-ership effectiveness to determine whether the situational variables interacted with the leadership styles in the predicted manner. The evidence seems to indicate that the model does quite well in predicting how the situational variables and leader styles combine to influence individual satisfaction and group morale? However, the model has not been-shown to be a good predictor of individual or group performance. Perhaps the greatest disadvantage in trying to' validate the model empirically is that it contains too many variables and tries to explain too much. An experiment testing the full pat-goal model is difficult because too many variables have not been clearly identified and instruments -have not been developed to measure them. Nevertheless, the available studies tend to support the model, although they suggest that it understates the com-plexity of the situation. Furthermore, the research suggests that other variables, such as conflict and structure, also need to be incorporated into it.

Perhaps the major contribution of the path-goal model is that it provides a method for viewing leadership in terms of the rewards and punishments administered by the leader. The path-goal model explains why a particular style works best because of the reward contingencies determined by the environment and the leader's capacity to administer rewards and punishments. As more research accumulates, this type of explanation will have practical applications for those interested in the leadership process.

ANTI-SOCIAL AND PROSOCIAL LEADERSHIP STYLE

Running along side explorations of personality have been many efforts to distinguish leadership styles using different constructs. For example, Maslow distinguished democratic from authoritarian leaders; McClelland distinguishes the affiliative from the power orientated; Eisler distinguishes dominator (masculine) from partnership (feminine) styles; Kalma *et al.*, distinguish between sociable and aggressive leaders. And elsewhere I have distinguished the prosocial from the anti-social leader.

So there is no single system of understanding and all have their insights and limitations. Much may depend on where you look of course, *i.e.*, whether you focus on the tasks, results or on interpersonal style. The types of leaders we will note shortly may well get results, but they tend towards the authoritarian, dominator, aggressive, anti-social leadership style. I will refer to these collectively as anti-social because their style can have very negative effects on and for others.

Anti-social leaders tend to come from insecure backgrounds with a history of abusive, emotionally cold, rigid/authoritarian or neglectful parenting which leads them to develop various mixtures of the above mentioned traits. Judged through the lens of the last two chapters we could see these individuals as being highly shame prone, sensitive to humiliation, extraordinarily status conscious, and in need of defending against humiliation at all costs. The way this is done, as in the Hitler complex, is not just via defence of self but an active promotion of one's superiority - in other words heightened activity of a primitive up-rank, archetypal mentality. To be superior promises the power to defeat any who would make claims on one's status or position. Although one can certainly link such psychologies to reproductive strategies - and genes - these distal explanations do not always help us understand the complex of forces which bring these archetypes to such prominence within any one person at a point in history. Thus we should always consider family background and social context. Anti-social leaders have particular philosophies, motives and tendencies which include: A perception of the world as competitive and the strongest wins; a belief in the superiority of one's social group, often with a fear, dislike or even contempt for outsiders; a belief in the importance of strength and pride; a belief in the importance of close ingroup loyalties as a protection against external badness (us against them); a need for control and power over others; a fear of losing status; a belief that their own way (vision) is superior; a simple right versus wrong moral system or no moral system at all; a tendency to use people to met their own ends; and often a lack of care for others.

Prosocial leaders tend to have very different backgrounds, coming from a secure and warm family life and have developed the archetypal abilities to empathise and care for others. This there are far more altruistic strategies in their styles. Compared to anti-social leaders they have different philosophies, motives and tendencies which include: A preference for cooperative over competitive behaviour; a preference for partnership and peaceful solutions to conflicts rather than winning; a belief in the importance of valuing and nurturing others as people rather than as means to an end; a complex moral system; an opening up of groups and dissolving boundaries (we are all the same under the skin); and a sardonic sense of the heroic.

These are dimensions rather than absolute categories. One could compare (say) Nelson Mandala with Hitler to get a feel of the differences. But, in general, it is probably preferable to think of style rather than 'the individual' because at times a person may show one face of leadership but at other times another. They may have mild tendencies towards either prosocial or anti-social styles or these styles may be marked and rigid. They may appear highly prosocial to ingroup members who show allegiance but anti-social to outsiders and defectors.

They may be intuitively inclined towards (say) prosocial leadership but the social group (electorate) which supports them demands another style, and invalidates their prosocial efforts - telling them they need to be tough-minded. The ease (and degree) by which a leader will compromise their own values in order to get elected or chosen suggests that for some, gaining leadership roles is more important that pursuing personal principles. Personal principles can be too costly. On the other hand, the group might encourage an amplification of a preferred personal style. Some who are mildly aggressive become more so with being encouraged to go further and be more ruthless. As we noted above insecurity can effect style, but this insecurity may come from stresses in the environment.

People who are groomed for leadership by virtue of their families' social position, ie., they are placed in leadership positions, need not be socially skilled. However, some anti-social leaders are highly socially skilled, good orators and good at manipulating the values and (usually) needs for superiority, certainty, and strength in their followers.

Trepidation Based Patterns

Sometimes those with anti-social leadership styles can inspire devotion. At other times, as in China and the old USSR, they bring to life social patterns of fear and suspicion. Such regimes usually only survive with the support of a hidden class of 'secret police' who are ruthless and vicious and can create the fear of 'the knock on the door in the middle of the night'. Societies never seem to have had much problem in finding such folk and such 'police forces' can include a fair number of both narcissistic and sadistic personalities, who colour the whole police force. Anti-social leaders, protected by the young men of the secret police and other arms of enforcement, may slowly age and can in fact be quite old before they are deposed or simply die in post. China and the USSR were classic examples of this.

For some supporters, appeasement and compliance is used to reduce the potential aggression of the leader(s) and/or his/her supporters. That is, the primary internal psychological organisation in both leaders and subordinates is defensive rather than relaxed and open. The fear based anti-social leadership style and its effects are the most easily detected. Even if the leader appears friendly, fear and apprehension can be common experiences. The psychology of subordinate, is to make sure they know where the threat might be (and for what), and avoiding it, or at least taking necessary steps to reduce it. Behaviourists would call this 'punishment' based control. The ethologist Michael Chance called this pattern of social behaviour agonic - meaning that the defensive aspects of fight/threaten (in the dominant) and appeasement/submit or flight/escape (in the subordinate) are primed. This leads to constrictions on the patterns of attention, reduces open exploration and may reduce the development of compassionate values.

If you watch members of a group interact when the leader is out of the room and compare this to when he/she is present you can sometimes have a feel for whether an anti-social style is operating. When an anti-social leader enters, the previous fun and jokey exchanges may cease, as does the free exploration of ideas. There is a switch in attention. Everyone watches their backs to ensure they are not the next to be attacked and they are preoccupied with the mood the leader is in. Bad moods signal hard times and times to watch yourself. Every thing is done to avoid putting the leader in a bad mood - even withholding important information about 'bad news' or mistakes. The poor folk who do put the leader in a bad mood can be blamed by other subordinates for causing them a hard time. At one meeting a subordinate said to another "why did you say that. You know what he's like. Now we are all going to suffer. Why couldn't just keep your mouth shut." My housemaster at school was very much like this and it was well known that the other masters (we called them master then not teachers) were wary, if not frightened, of him. He was a cane happy sod.

Of course, at times anti-social styles are unintended and reflect poor social skills, or stress, but at other times anti-social leaders enjoy the idea that others are apprehensive of them and believe this ensures them respect. Indeed, a belief in, and even admiration of, fear based respect probably marks the anti-social leader.

Industry is just beginning to recognise that some leadership styles are disastrous; that there is a dark side to charisma. Perhaps in our modern age there is a gradual fading in the valuing of tough leadership (but it is gradual and at times I doubt it). Those who do well at interview and present themselves with confidence, keenness and are socially skilled (often being male helps too) have often appeared the preferable people to place in positions of power and leadership. However, unless you observe them working with their team you have little idea how they will perform as leaders. Some turn out to be narcissistic, who value themselves but not others, are competitive with subordinates and shaming. They create such poor morale and inhibit other's creativity that they can cost an organisation dearly. Nearly all of us will have had some experience of having to work with these characters. So management training is all the vogue right now, teaching how to be socially rewarding and supportive, able to appreciate subordinate feedback and build a cooperative-friendly team spirit.

The thing to watch out for is those who can mimic such behaviours in 'training workshops' but do not really (privately) value these behaviours. So there can be slippage in their non-verbal behaviour and style. They may say 'the right things' but not feel or act friendly. At the slightest conflict they become aggressive/shaming, threatening to escalate conflict unless the other backs-down. Non-verbal behaviour is so important, I believe, because it taps right into the reptilian brain, and this, in interpersonal interactions, is what can set the emotional tone of the relationship(s). Indeed, we know that people monitor non-verbal communication at least as much as verbal. The way leaders deal with conflicts (of interest) both verbally and non-verbally is crucial to the skill of a leader. Good prosocial leaders have the ability to keep conflicts serious but also playful. People don't feel personally attacked; they play the ball not the player. Leaders like the Dalai Lama, Nelson Mandela and Gandhi are well known for such abilities.

Prosocial leaders are rarely feared. They encourage free exploration and affiliative styles. They are easy to approach and open to the opinions of others. Subordinates do not fear them because as leaders they do not use shame and humilation as a means of control. Generally, subordinates enjoy working with and for them and do not feel patronised or looked down on. Prosocials are concerned to see others mature, grow and pass on. They are not envious of others success. Their dark side is that they may not perform well in conflict situations - or at least can be very stressed by it and indecisive. Their needs for affiliation can interfere with tough decision making.

Leadership and Deception

A prosocial style can be superficial - it is a con and deception devised to be attractive to others. It is seen most commonly in cults, but not uncommonly in politics where self-presentation to win votes may hide a dark, scheming and manipulative style. That the prosocial style is a deception is revealed at times of conflicts of view, doubt, or if a member of the group desires to leave the group and defect. Everything changes for the potential defector. Where before they were wanted and esteemed now they are degraded (*e.g.*, called scab, traitor, heretic, weak, or made fun of etc.).

They can be threatened with fear of permanent expulsion, loss of status and prestige, loss of support, or outright persecution from the previously supportive group and its leader. To put this another way when a subordinate looks for the exit they find they are trapped - it is hard to leave, or if they do, impossible to return. Many religions use this threat of course. No-one can love you like God can love you - if you leave the clan, the religion, you will put yourself beyond God and his love. Don't defect.

So the superficial prosocial leader knows how to play the game. They can stay prosocial as long as they receive sufficient subordinate, compliant, loving, or devotional signals.

As we shall see later, Jim Jones was almost certainly one of these types. They are among the most dangerous because of their skilful manipulation of needs for love, acceptance and conformity in subordinates, and their ability to create a sense of protection and belonging for ingroup members, with subtle (and sometimes not so subtle) undercurrents of fear.

Most of our history has not been shaped by leaders who have been on management training courses. It is alarming how much human history, not to mention our value systems, have been shaped by people who, at least from our position, seem rather crazy and certainly anti-social. Our civilization, culture and even our self-identities have been significantly shaped by our leaders and the mimicry of their values. Even now we don't take nearly enough care in choosing our leaders. But through most of our history we have not had that much choice.

Recent Leaders

Although we now live in a democracy, it is in the very nature of the manipulation of power that democracy often fails to provide prosocial leaders. Hugh Freeman, who was president of the Royal College of Psychiatrists, has given a powerful and frightening review of how psychological and physical health problems have plagued many of our recent leaders in Europe and America. His review highlights many concerns, some of which are noted here. Woodrow Wilson suffered a number of mini-strokes that led to a personality change. In 1945, at the time of the Yalta conference Roosevelt was so terminally ill he may not have really understood what was going on. J.F. Kennedy used amphetamine and steroids, both of which could have affected his judgement. Lyndon Johnson has been described as highly narcissistic with feelings of insecurity and grandiosity.

In 1966-67, when the Vietnam war was becoming preoccupied with carpet bombing and defoliation, Johnson viewed his critics as 'enemies and traitors'. Nixon was known to have many narcissistic traits, to be exploitative and untrustworthy. At the time of the Watergate scandal he was drinking to such an extent, "that his aids thought him incapable of dealing with any business - however urgent- at these times."(p. 24) Ronald Reagan, towards the end, was known to be suffering from dementia, now sadly well advanced. Yet it was believed that if he could have stood again he would have won. It is true of course that the personalities of leaders do not exclude them from bringing social advances. Johnson did introduce important polices of social reform and a "new deal." But the pressures of modern leadership can still play havoc with a person and while they may be helpful to insiders they can be highly destructive to outsiders.

In Britain, Anthony Eden, at the time of the Suez crisis, was abusing drugs and alcohol and was described by some to be, "quite simply mad". As the history books are written on Margaret Thatcher and the up-surgence of the right in the 1980's, we get clear evidence of the autocratic leadership style. Ian Gilmour's book `Dancing with Dogma' leaves little doubt that at least some of the elements that go to making an autocrat were present in Thatcher's style. For example, Gilmour (who was one of her ministers in the early years) writes:

Mrs Thatcher regarded her first cabinet not as an aid to good government but as an obstacle to be surmounted. Her belief that dialogue was a waste of time rather than a means of arriving at an agreed course of action was a part of her rejection of consensus politics. Consensus, the Prime Minster later proclaimed, was achieved only by 'abandoning all beliefs, principles and values. Whoever won a battle,' she asked, 'under the banner of, "I stand for consensus"?' In her mind, of course, 'conviction' was diametrically opposed to consensus."

As the years passed and more and more cabinet colleagues defected, speaking of her autocratic treatment of them, we began to get more insight into the psychology that controlled her. Rank and dominance and the need for greatness were written everywhere. And for whom was this greatness desired? Not for the poor who became poorer still, but for an elite; for an ideal of being British. Her obsession with enemies was revealed clearly when she said at the time of the miners strike in 1984, "We had to fight the enemy without in the Falklands. We always have to be aware of the enemy within, which is more difficult to fight and more dangerous to liberty." (Quoted by Gilmour). So the miners were not just ordinary people fighting, often violently, for their jobs (manipulated by their own leader to a degree) but were potential enemies of the cause. This was a time when a Prime Minister openly talked about ninnies and wimps, and efforts at shaming. It was a time that ideology and causes matter more than people. It was a time when there was no such thing as society only a collection of individuals, until that is, Brussels threatened British interests, then the idea of Britishness made a come back.

When her end came it was shabby, marred by back-stabbing and retribution for the failures in the courage and loyalty of her subordinates (colleagues). Such an old story and somewhat typical of a person who has little ability to reflect on the self and see the sources of her difficulties as coming from within. To be fair to Thatcher though, it is less clear how much she was motivated by a personal ambition to be great, or more to rescue an identity for family and country. Certainly, her stated intent was to free people from government control, although in this quango-ised state of ours even this is doubtful. It is now estimated there are 7,700 quangos of various sorts, often staffed by conservative appointees and costly the state £54 billion. She was certainly a strong leader and enjoyed the title the 'Iron Lady'. We must leave it to the historians to decide. She changed Britain significantly. Who knows what we may now be like without her. But it is her style that marks her as being the autocratic type.

So we can see that anti-social leaders have a number of qualities. A need for power; a belief in their own way, a focus on the importance of strength, a tendency to talk in terms of fighting, conquering, pride and becoming great, a need to stress the importance of being more powerful than competitors, paranoid or contemptuous attitudes to those who are not ingroup members, a preparedness to subdue subordinates not with argument but with fear or shame - the language of wimps and ninnies. In whatever context leadership arises, the lack of compassion for followers and subordinates can lead to appalling abuses of power; the first world war being a most tragic example. As Dixon makes clear, at times military leaders have seen their subordinates as no more than cannon-fodder. But even democratically elected leaders can show a complete lack of interest in certain sections of the groups they lead, except to keep them in check. Many leaders in the West appear to have a view of the "workers" as manoeuvrable production units whose value depends on whether they can be fitted in with wealth creating—*i.e.*, production fodder. Rebellion can be ruthlessly put down.

If we are becoming increasing cynical about our leaders, religious and political, and even democracy, we might remember our history and what has gone before. There is no way to avoid leadership. Sure, some will try to manipulate us to get our vote and sure they will have the various human failings, like sexual ones, but we can still insist on compassionate values once we sort out in our own minds the issue of how we want the world to look for our grandchildren. Do we want them to live in a polluted, highly competitive, 'dump the losers', world?

We don't have to go with the message of a need to be special or great or if we do we can be great for other reasons apart from beating opponents or competitors. We may need strong leaders but they need to be chosen by us to tell the truth and advise us of the reality - a reality that in our hearts we all know.

As Freeman makes clear some of our problems with leadership arise because our jerry built brains were never designed to cope with the leadership of the mega-groups we now live within, nor the mass of information leaders have to cope with, nor the uncertainties of positions that can change rapidly, nor the complexity of the competing interests of all the subgroups that exist within the modern state, nor indeed with the grandiosity and scale of power that is so much part of a modern nation state. To say that political leadership, with its hands on nuclear buttons and the arms trade, is in crisis, is an understatement.

5

Leadership and Management

Management develops the capacity to achieve its plan by organising and staffing – creating an organisational structure and a set of jobs for accomplishing the plan. The equivalent leadership activity, however, is aligning people: this means communicating a new direction to those who can create coalitions and who both understand the vision and are committed to its achievement.

In addition, management ensures plan accomplishment by controlling and problem solving (monitoring the results versus the plan in some detail (both formally and informally) by means of reports, meetings and other tools; identifying deviations; and then planning and organising to solve the problems). But for leadership, achieving a vision requires motivating and inspiring – despite major obstacles to change – by appealing to the basic, but often untapped, human needs, values and emotions. More than anything else, however, the difference between the leader and the manger rests with the status quo: managers are willing to live with it and leaders are not.

In summary, then, perhaps the best way to explain the difference between leadership and management.

The Manager	The Leader
The manager administers	The leader innovates.
The manager is a copy	The leader is an original.
The manager maintains	The leader develops.
The manager controls	The leader inspires trust.
The manager has a short-range view perspective.	The leader has a long-range
The manager asks how and when	The leader asks what and why.
The manager has his or her eye on	The leader has his or her eye on the the bottom line horizon.
The manager is the classic good soldier	The leader is his or her own person.
The manager does things right	The leader does the right thing.

LEADERSHIP AND COMMAND

Leadership and 'headship' are uniquely different and it is always important to focus on the leader as a person, and not those who merely serve as heads ('commanders') in positions of leadership. While many people regard 'command' and 'leadership' as much the same thing, it is more helpful to treat them as 2 separate but related functions. Successful leaders persuade people willingly to endure hardships (usually prolonged) and incur dangers (usually acute) that if left to themselves, they would do their utmost to avoid. Leadership is, therefore, concerned with inspiration and motivation. Command, by contrast, is the direction, coordination and effective use of military force."

LEADERSHIP

Lindholm notes, in his study of charisma, that we do not always behave in our own genetic self-interest when it comes to following leaders. There has been more than one leader who has taken us on a trip into mass destruction. In 1978 the world was shocked by the Jones Town suicide of men, women and children. Some, who were not present at the time, killed themselves later. And this was not the first, nor will it be the last, time that followers have killed others and themselves in devotion to a cause, manipulated by a leader. It is our rank psychology that courts so much craziness. So in this chapter we explore some facets of leadership.

Leaders vary in style and basic psychology (*e.g.*, in terms of their charisma, skills/knowledge, tendency to punish or reward). But they are also shaped and given access to leadership positions/roles via their cultures and social relationships. Some leaders are elected by those they will lead, others are imposed (as in the military) by superiors. Some leaders are encouraged to adopt certain styles and do certain things because of what is expected of (and projected onto) them. We noted how George Orwell had to shoot the elephant, not from any personal desire to do so, but because of the expectations of the crowd and his concern to maintain his image of himself and of his "white-man" group. In his book, `On the Psychology of Military Incompetence', Norman Dixon notes that preferred leadership style varies according to the context. For example, in low stress times soldiers prefer democratic leaders, but in stressful situations, like war, they prefer autocratic, strong leadership on whom they can depend. Thus, subordinate preferences for styles of leaders are effected by personal and social stresses and the potentially saving, protective qualities the leader seems to provide. Given this, some individuals are able to manipulate group values for their own ends and farm support. Authoritarian leaders can, for example, exaggerate threats, especially from outsiders and thus increase their appeal by offering themselves as strong, protective and decisive leaders. In low stress times leaders may rely more on their intelligence and less on experience but the reverse is the case in stressful times.Thus, there is a complex interaction between leadership behaviour, the psychology of followers, and social context which allows, encourages or even demands certain actions.

Leadership behaviours can be expressed in many contexts and at many different social positions. It involves various combinations of power such as directing the attention of others, and the ability/power to control, guide, influence, encourage or coerce the behaviour and values of others. Nearly all humans have the ability to adopt leadership behaviours. Even in simple two-some's one may be more the leader than the other, although they may swap roles from time to time. Thus, leadership behaviours can emerge in just about any social relationship; *e.g.*, playground, street gang, terrorist group, church fete society, local cricket team, the hospital ward, business organisation, and government. Leadership research also makes the distinction between task orientated leadership and person orientated leadership. The person orientated leader will attempt to manipulate the values and emotions of subordinates, getting them 'devoted to the cause' that they will lead.

Although leader-follower relationships are to some degree archetypal potentials (and this is what can give them their passion and emotion distorting qualities) we should note that our first experiences of 'leaders' are our parents.

The Family

Family structures are also authority, hierarchical structures. Human family relationships, however, are highly contextualised within their cultures. Cultures legitimise the use of power within the family. They may not only amplify gender differences in the power exercised within families (men as head of the household) but bestow rights. In many societies men are (more or less) bestowed the right of sexual access to their wives and even today there are issues around whether rape can occur inside marriage. In the middle ages, wife beating was allowed, provided the stick was no thicker than a thumb. In modern societies, noted for their highly segregated and privatised families, power is exercised by the limitation of freedom of choice and rights. Thus, for example, women and children who are locked into abusive relationships may lack the resources or opportunities to move away. Male dominance of the family is thus encased in socially bestowed privileges and values.

For all animals, parents are automatically positioned to control the behaviour of their offspring. Thus, the parent-child relationship is also a dominant-subordinate one. In childhood, the experience of being subordinate to one's parents is also associated with enormous needs for care and acceptance from them. This combination of care eliciting and care giving with subordination, has the effect of blending different archetypal potentials together. It is not surprising, therefore, that humans can learn and develop their attitudes and emotional sensitivity 'to authority' from the experiences they have with, and of, their parents. So parenting is, in many ways, a leadership role because it involves differences in power and demands for obedience. And our attitudes to leadership and authority (seeking it, subordinating ourselves to it, or hating it) can be shaped during our formative years.

Society bestows and accepts the rights of parents to behave in certain ways to their children. Children are automatically assumed to come under the power and control of their parents. The use of physical punishment (and types of punishment in general), religious indoctrination, diet, indeed the right to impose various forms of life style are seen as parental rights. The state may intervene at times, as with laws on education, and there can be conflicts over the exact limits of power that can be exercised with families, *e.g.*, the state intervenes in cases of sexual abuse or if parents refuse blood transfusions on religious grounds. Generally though, children are indoctrinated to adopt the prevailing attitudes and values of their group be these religious, political, or gender. Young children can be taken on political marches, made to read the Bible or Koran, to view history through a particular lens and so forth. If any of these practices are crazy then we can easily pass them on.

Leadership Roles

Once out of the family there are other groups and social relationships in which we must find our place. Leadership roles can be ascribed and defined by social groups and one passes some entrance test or exam to enter them (*e.g.*, lawyer, doctor) which legitimises the use of power. In some societies obtaining the recognition of manhood legitimises the use of certain types of power and authority (*e.g.*, over women). Historically, leaders could be given their roles 'as of right' (*e.g.* by an institutionalised class or caste system). In fact many leadership positions (Kings, Emperors, and so forth) were family determined. Even today the family of origin and the social rank of the family can significantly influence a person's chances and aspirations to leadership positions. Top leaders of social institutions are rarely those who have risen through the ranks, but usually begin their claims from class-bestowed privileged positions. But the importance of the rank of one's family is also noted in many non-human primates. Females especially, usually obtain their rank from their mother's and aunt's rank. As it has been for millions of years, we leave the family and emerge into the social world where rank is everywhere.

Secure and Insecure Dominance

Styles of leadership have been studied in animals as styles of dominance. In most non-human primate studies to date, subordinates show greater activation of stress hormones than dominant animals, especially higher levels of circulating cortisol.

However, in unstable groups dominant animals can show almost as high levels as subordinates. The work of Sapolsky, who has studied free ranging baboon's in Africa, suggests that secure, dominant baboons in stable groups have: Low stress cortisol levels, they differentiate well between a threatening rival and other animals; when threatened they escalate fights and usually win;

if they lose they displace aggression on to a third party; they have high levels of non-sexual interactions with infants and females and are generally relaxed and affiliative.

High ranking but insecure baboons (especially if the group is unstable) have: High levels of stress hormones, tend to be more aggressive (generally and sexually), are more likely to pick fights (rather than just respond to threats), appear more suspicious, and are generally less relaxed and less affiliative. While these differences in leadership/dominance style reflect the stability of the group they also reflect individual differences.

Thus, we see that security of the position may be important for the kinds of behaviour that dominant's express. This leads us to the idea of differences between secure and insecure dominance. Some human leaders certainly seem to show forms of insecure dominance.

This insecurity is mediated through both the social context and personality. It is possible that in humans insecurity may be, in part, a general personality trait (as it seems to be for baboons and chimpanzees). The combination of strong needs for power in humans (to control others) compensates, perhaps, for basic personal insecurities, quite possibly of an insecure, avoidant attachment style. In fact many researchers have argued that aggressive leaders have had disturbed backgrounds with low parental warmth. There is a basic view in psychotherapy that 'where love was not there shall be a power and fear.'

We noted many researchers draw distinctions between threat/aggression based dominance and affiliation based dominance styles. Insecure dominance, we can suggest, shows itself in the readiness to adopt threat based leadership styles; that is leadership is primarily organised via the defence system. In humans the interaction between threat and affiliation is complex because humans can be far more manipulative of their social-presentation and image, *i.e.*, presenting themselves as affiliative when in fact they are not. As we shall now see, insecure patterns of dominance show up quite commonly in leadership styles.

Personality

Although this book has tried to veer away from being overly focused on traits within individuals (and research on leadership suggests that personality is only one facet of leadership for it is always the interaction that is important), our exploration of leadership does require some consideration of personality.

It seems to be the case that some leaders are more likely to have particular traits and personality styles which reflect quite serious insecurities. These may include: Narcissistic, obsessional, autocratic, authoritarian, psychopathic and hypomanic (or manic-depressive). The definition of narcissistic, which underpins many of them, is captured by Adler (1986).

These patients tend to be extremely self-centred, often needing praise and constant recognition in order to feel momentarily good about themselves. Rather than feeling a sense of their own worth or value, they require repeated bolstering from the outside. In their relationships with people, they tend to be exploitative and insensitive to the feelings and needs of others. Their behaviour can be superficially charming on the one hand and arrogant on the other. They expect special privileges from those around them without giving anything in return, yet they can feel easily humiliated or shamed and respond with rage at what they perceive to be criticisms or failure of people to react in the way they wish Many can elaborate active fantasies about magnificent success in love, sex, beauty, wealth or power. They often devalue people they have previously idolised and tend to split, *i.e.* see people as either all good or all bad, or alternate between these extremes.

Adler's description highlights status evaluative and powerhostility components, the use of others for selfvaluing purposes, exploitativeness and sense of entitlement, and a comparative lack of the more prosocial aspects of human nature such as empathy, moral thinking, and care giving. They can have the motto 'if you're not with us you're against us'. They can be strident in emphasising the importance of their own vision and truck little disagreement. They can be envious, grandiose and expect allegiance. They can maintain this allegiance by a mixture of threats, shaming and offering favours and prestige to allies and followers. Yet for all this at times their style may inspire devotion.

The psychopathic person has many narcissistic traits but in addition is generally more callous, sadistic, distrustful, amoral, exploitative, ruthless and easily activated into violent fights. Their compassion for others is notable by its absence.

Autocratic and authoritarian personalities are similar to the narcissist but they are extremely ranked focused. Norman Dixonused psychoanalytic theory to argue that these personality styles are a defence against uncertainty and anxiety; *i.e.*, insecurity. They must know their place and can be incredibly deferential and submissive to those ranking above them and controlling of those ranking below. They have strong beliefs in the value of the ranked authority system, the importance of obeying orders and are not so keen on democracy.

The manic-depressive traits, from which some leaders suffer, are believed to relate more to a mood disorder. Winston Churchill was a classic example. This leads them to swing between grandiose ideas about their self-importance, have marked needs for power, low frustration tolerance but they have high energy, are charismatic, take risks and are creative. However, when depressed they are riddled with self-doubt and feelings of worthlessness, with a tendency to hide away and feel suicidal. They usually lack the sadistic and callousness of the psychopath but can be paranoid to some degree and are very sensitive to threats and challenges to their own (and their group's) status. People with narcissistic traits (and these can be present in any of the above types) may not have full blown manic-depressive illnesses, but non-etheless they can show marked swings of mood and confidence.

Although these are usually regarded as personality or mood disorders, it is quite wrong to think that having a disorder consigns one to the backstreets of history. Indeed, some are not satisfied with simply being psychopathic and narcissistic in their own limited social domains. Their drive for leadership and greatness marks them out from other less leadership focused personalities. In such a pursuit these traits can be a positive advantage in making it big. Unfortunately, in the past and to some degree still, these individuals can take hold of whole cultures, societies, groups and organisations with a terrible cost. More worryingly, once in power their poor emotional and/or physical health can have very serious consequences.

LEADERSHIP, MANAGEMENT AND COMMAND RELATED TO EACH OTHER

Leadership, management and command are 3 distinctive and complementary systems of action and the precise activities—and the characteristics required—of each system are intensely human matters. Critically, leadership, management and command (as individual components, and as a trinity) are necessary for success in an increasingly complex and volatile military environment.

The simple model of leadership, management and command. The main difference between leadership is now the dominant component of the trinity.

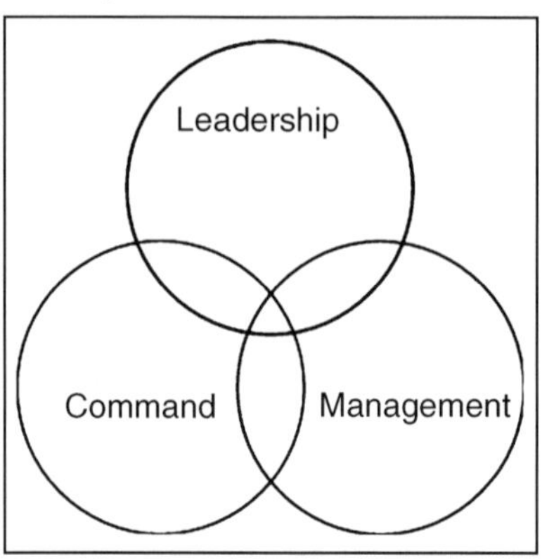

Fig. A Revised Model of Leadership, Management and Command

Part of the reason leadership has become so important (and therefore, the dominant component of the trinity) in recent years, is that the macro-environment (consisting of political, economic, socio-cultural and technological dimensions) has become more competitive and more volatile. The net result is that doing what was done yesterday – or even doing it 5 per cent better – is no longer a formula for success. For example, consider a simple military analogy: a peacetime Air Force can usually survive with good command and management procedures up and down the hierarchy, coupled with good leadership at the very top. A wartime Air Force, however, needs competent leadership at all levels. No one yet has figured out how to manage people effectively into battle; they must be led! Indeed, in times of rapid change, there is no substitute for leadership.

Unfortunately, most organisations are still based on the old-fashioned form of bureaucracy: the mind-set of control, order and predict. Those are the things of command and management. If we existed in an environment where we could control order and 'predict', a manager and commander would be a terrific thing and bureaucracy in a stable environment – as in the Victorian era – would be a great social invention.

But today, organisations have become 'unhinged': they are confusing, rapidly changing, unpredictable and full of surprises. This is why leadership is now critical: it (leadership) moves people into the arena of creative solutions, by first breaking barriers that inhibit fresh and new 'unthinked' thinking. Indeed, preparing airmen for future (rather than past wars) involves constant encouragement of open-minded thinking to ensure intellectual growth. Thus the art of leadership involves moving people forward towards a goal and inspiring them to perform and succeed for the greater goal.

In this sense, leadership cannot be bestowed upon a person by higher authority.

Therefore, it is misleading to think that leadership is only a characteristic of senior ranks or specific positions. Leadership is needed and must be practiced at every level of an organisation: great leaders understand that to achieve their vision and gain respect and authority, they must be willing to give power (command authority) to others; they delegate responsibility to other individuals and give those individuals the knowledge and resources to succeed.

MANAGEMENT

Management is defined as the allocation and control of resources (human, material and financial) to achieve the goals and objectives of the organisation and the measure of good management is the ability to achieve the right balance: neither an over-abundance nor a shortage of resources, either of which would undermine the concentration of effort on the main objective, whatever that may be.

UNDERSTANDING THE ROLES OF THE MANAGER

Mintzberg analysed a managers' job in terms of roles and identified 10 managerial roles clustered around 3 main categories (interpersonal, informational and decisional).

Table. The Roles of the Manager The Manager's Role

Interpersonal	Informational	Decisional
Figurehead	Monitor: scans for information.	Entrepreneur: seeks change.
Leader	Disseminator: shares information with other people.	Disturbance handler: responds to pressures and crisis.
Liaison	Spokesperson: shares information with outsiders.	Resource allocator: gives resources to others.
	Negotiator: reaches agreement.	

Management practices and procedures are largely a response to one of the most significant developments of the 20th Century: the emergence of large organisations. Without good management, complex enterprises in a fast-moving and dynamic environment tend to become chaotic in ways that threaten their very existence and effective management, therefore, brings a degree of order and consistency to the key decisions made by managers.

WHAT ACCURATELY IS COMMAND

So what exactly is command then? In the military literature, there are a vast amount of definitions of command. Indeed, one-third of the United Kingdom Doctrine for Joint and Multinational Operations is dedicated to Command. Furthermore, in the Queen's Regulations for the RAF, the concept and act of commanding is explained at length; however, no formal definition for command exists. Moreover, command is also different at each level of war and this task becomes all the more difficult in joint and multi-national operations, where senior commanders may have to impose their will, in an atmosphere of political, legal and even moral confusion.

Lawful and Process

Firstly, command has a legal and constitutional status, as codified in the Queen's Regulations. In the Queen's Regulations for the RAF, it states that at the highest level: "The government and command of each of the Services is vested in Her Majesty the Queen, who has charged the Secretary of State with general responsibility for the defence of the Realm and established a Defence Council having command and administration over Her Armed Forces;" and, in turn, Commanders in Chiefs who: "in conjunction with other duties are operationally responsible to the Defence Council for command of personnel in their area". Therefore, command is vested in a commander by higher authority and gives him direction (often encapsulated in a mission) that assigns forces to him, to accomplish that mission.

The concept of authority requires further definition: traditionalists define authority as 'the right to command and to induce compliance.' They regard authority as a central feature of the structure of formal organisations that 'prescribe expectations that certain individuals should exert control and direction over others within defined areas of competence.' In this context, authority involves the right and freedom to use the 'power of command' and ultimately to enforce obedience; whilst a commander can devolve specific authority to subordinates to decide and to act within their own areas of delegated responsibility, a commander retains overall responsibility for his command.

PERSONALITY COMMAND

Secondly, 'the exercise of command' includes the process by which a commander makes decisions, impresses his will upon, and transmits (*i.e.* tells) his intention to his subordinates. It, therefore, encompasses the authority, responsibility and duty to act. Therefore, individual command – at all levels – is defined as the art of decision-making, motivating and directing all ranks into actions to accomplish missions, whilst at the same time maintaining accountability and control.

The accountability and control require further analysis. Accountability is a corollary to both responsibility and authority; it involves a liability and obligation to answer to a superior for the proper user of delegated responsibility, authority and resources. Thus, he who delegates responsibility should grant sufficient authority to a subordinate for him to carry out his task; the subordinate, meanwhile, remains accountable to his superior for its execution.

In addition, Armed Forces often use the acronym C3I (command, control, communication and intelligence) and the addition of 'computers' to the list of Cs to produce C4. These definitions apply to command at every level: grand strategic, military strategic, operational and tactical. The German sociologist Max Weber (1864-1920) was one of the most prolific and influential sociologists of the 20th Century and he was the first person to coin the phrase 'command and control'. Three words describe his bureaucratic model: control, order and predict. Therefore, control is the process through which the commander—assisted by his staff—organizes, directs and co-ordinates his activities of the forces allocated to him. To achieve this, he and his staff employ a common doctrine for command and use standardized procedures for control in conjunction with the equipment, communication and information systems available. Command and control are thus inextricably linked with commanders requiring an understanding of both and the roles of each other if they are to perform their duties effectively. Command and control, however, are not 'equal partners' as control is merely one aspect of command.

In essence, command requires a vision of the desired result; an understanding of the concepts, missions, priorities and the allocation of resources; an ability to assess people and risks; and a continual process of re-evaluating the situation. A commander requires – above all – to decide on a course of action and to lead his command. Broadly speaking then, there are 2 styles of individual command: Befehlstaktik is an inflexible, authoritarian form of 'top-down' command in which subordinates receive rigid orders, that leave little or no scope to exercise low-level initiative. By contrast, Auftragstaktik emphasizes mission-type orders; the superior commander sets broad objectives, but then allows subordinates to use their initiative to achieve their part of the plan in the way that they think best. The BAFs version of Auftragstaktik is known as 'Mission Command.' Befehlstaktik dictates not just what is to be done, but how it is to be done and can be represented by the extreme left-end of the command circle in Figure 2.0 (*i.e.* 'tells'). Auftragstaktik can be represented by the right end of the command circle (*i.e.* shares the information).

Although BDD currently adopt Mission Command (the commander defines the limits of the operation and then lets the subordinates take the appropriate action at the coal-face), Befehlstaktik is wholly appropriate in certain circumstances; in times of crisis/emergency, a one-way, directional and autocratic approach to command must always be used. In this context, 'command-by-direction' is a description of the method used by commanders who directly command subordinates before and during battle; the commander feels he has positive control over each element. Van Creveld describes this as a method, which prioritises uncertainty; the commander, accepting that he will never have perfect information, nevertheless brings all uncertainty to himself and deals with whichever uncertainty assails him most at each moment.

Managerial Command

Thirdly, organisational command is related to organisational design: human beings profit from living in structured groups and irrespective of the organisational design (for example hierarchical, network/cellular or indeed a combination of the both – the matrix), organisations require a structure so that work can be divided to achieve coordination among its various work activities.

Organisational command, therefore, centres on the issues of:

- Division of labour.
- Allocation of authority.
- Departmentalisation.
- Span of control.

In addition, Burns and Stalker, 2 British Social Scientists, labelled organisations as either mechanistic or organic. The RAF employs (at present) a mechanistic organisational structure, which could be argued consists of tight rules and policies; limited individual job discretion; and coordination, which is both formal and written. In addition, mechanistic organisations also posses:

- High divisions of labour.
- Low delegation of authority.
- Departments with great uniformity of work activities.
- Narrow spans of control.

At the organisational level then, senior commanders make countless decision about the division of labour, delegation of authority, departmentalisation and span of control. Over time, these decisions result in the elaboration of the organisations structure. Therefore, organisational command is defined as the arrangement of roles and reporting relationships, which govern employee behaviour with two primary components of organisational structure, namely centralization and co-ordination.

UNDERSTANDING ORGANISATIONS, LEADERSHIP AND MANAGEMENT

To really understand organisational change and begin guiding successful change efforts, the change agent should have at least a broad understanding of the context of the change effort. This includes understanding the basic systems and structures in organisations, including their typical terms and roles. This requirement applies to the understanding of leadership and management of the organisations, as well. That is why graduate courses in business often initially include a course or some discussion on organisational theory. Organisational change should not be conducted for the sake of change. Organisational change efforts should be geared to improve the performance of organisations and the people in those organisations. Therefore, it's useful to have some understanding of what is meant by "performance" and the various methods to manage performance in organisations.

SYSTEMS THINKING

The past few decades have seen an explosion in the number of very useful tools to help change agents to effectively explore, understand and communicate about organisations, as well as to guide successful change in those organisations. Tools from systems theory and systems thinking especially are a major breakthrough. Even if the change agent is not an expert about systems theory and thinking, even a basic understanding can cultivate an entire new way of working.

The field of Organisation Development is focused on improving the effectiveness of organisations and the people in those organisations. OD has a rich history of research and practice regarding change in organisations. Why not learn from that history? Your nature and the way you choose to work has significant impact on your client's organisation, whether you know it or not. You cannot separate yourself from your client's organisation, as if you are some kind of detached observer. You quickly become part of your client's system — the way the people and processes in the organisation work with each other on a recurring basis. Thus, it is critical that you have a good understanding of yourself, including your biases (we all have them), how you manage feedback and conflict, how you like to make decisions and solve problems, how you naturally view organisations, your skills as a consultant, etc.

Nowadays, with the complex challenges faced by organisations and the broad diversity of values, perspectives and opinions among the members of those organisations, it's vital that change agents work from a strong set of principles to ensure they operate in a highly effective and ethical manner.

CHANGE MANAGEMENT

There are several phrases regarding organisational change and development that look and sound a lot alike, but have different meanings. As a result of the prominence of the topic, there seems to be increasingly different interpretations of some of these phrases, while others are used interchangeably. Without at least some sense of the differences between these phrases, communications about organisational change and development can be increasingly vague, confusing and frustrating.

There are different overall types of organisational change, including planned versus unplanned, organisation-wide versus change primarily to one part of the organisation, incremental (slow, gradual change) versus transformational (radical, fundamental), etc.. Knowing which types of change you are doing helps all participants to retain scope and perspective during the many complexities and frequent frustrations during change.

Successful change efforts often include several key roles, including the initiator, champion, change agent, sponsor and leaders. Organisation-wide change in corporations should involve the Board of Directors. Whether their members are closely involved in the change or not, they should at least be aware of the change project and monitor if the results are being achieved or not.

As the change agent, you might be performing different roles during the project.

Appreciative Inquiry is a recent and powerful breakthrough in organisational change and development. It's based on the philosophy that "problems" are often caused as much by our perception of them as problems as by other influencing factors. The philosophy has spawned a strong movement that, in turn, has generated an increasing number of models, tools and tips, most of which seem to build from the positive perceptions (visions, fantasies, wishes and stories) of those involved in the change effort.

There are numerous well-organized approaches (or models) from which to manage a change effort. Some of the approaches have been around for many years — we just haven't thought of them as such. For example, many organisations undertake strategic planning. The implementation of strategic planning, when done in a systematic, cyclical and explicit approach, is strategic management. Strategic management is also one model for ensuring the success of a change effort. There are numerous, major methods and movements to regularly increase the performance of organisations. Each includes regular recurring activities to establish organisational goals, monitor progress towards the goals, and make adjustments to achieve those goals more effectively and efficiently.

Any or all of the following approaches will improve organisational performance depending on if they are implemented comprehensively and remain focused on organisational results. Some of the following, *e.g.*, organisational learning and knowledge management, might be interpreted more as movements than organisation performance strategies because there are wide interpretations of the concepts, not all of which include focusing on achieving top-level organisational results. However, if these two concepts are instilled across the organisation and focus on organisational results, they contribute strongly to organisational performance. On the other hand, the Balanced Scorecard, which is deliberately designed to be comprehensive and focused on organisational results, will not improve performance if not implemented from a strong design.

STRATEGIC PLANNING IN HOTEL MANAGEMENT

Strategic planning involves defining objectives and developing strategies to reach those objectives. It may employ methods like SWOT analysis to help clarify objectives and strategies. Strategic planning uses "the big picture" to pursue large scale, long term objectives. This is in contradistinction to "tactical" planning, which has to focuss on short term, smaller objectives. "Long range" planning typically projects current activities and programmes onto a model of the external world, thereby predicting likely results. "Strategic" planning tries to "create" more desirable future results by (a) influencing the outside world or (b) adapting current programmes and actions so as to have more favourable outcomes in the external environment.

Within business, strategic planning may provide overall direction strategic management to a company or give specific direction in such areas as:

- Financial strategies
- Human resource/organisational development strategies
- Information technology deployments
- Marketing strategy

We want to do Strategic Planning to:

- Have the capability to obtain the desired objective
- Fit well both with the external environment and with an organisation's resources and core competencies - it should appear feasible and appropriate
- Have the capability of providing an organisation with a sustainable competitive advantage - ideally through uniqueness and sustainability
- Prove dynamic, flexible, and able to adapt to changing situations
- Suffice on its own - specifically providing favorable outcomes without the need for cross-subsidization

Most strategic planning methodologies depend on a three-step process (sometimes called the STP process):

- Situation - evaluate the current situation and how it came about
- Target - define goals and/or objectives (sometimes called ideal state)
- Path - map a possible route to the goals/objectives

An alternative approach is called Draw-See-Think

- Draw - what is the ideal image or the desired end state?
- See - what is today's situation? What is the gap from ideal and why?
- Think - what specific actions must be taken to close the gap between today's situation and the ideal state?
- Plan - what resources are required to execute the activities?

In general terms, strategic planning can proceed incrementally or revolutionarily.

Strategic planning as a set of logical and creative steps

1. Clarification of objective (end-state) to be pursued. The following terms have been used in the literature: desired end states, plans, policies, goals, objectives, strategies, tactics and actions. Definitions vary, overlap and fail to achieve clarity. The following concept has been found useful. The items listed above may be organized in a hierarchy of means and ends and numbered as follows: Top Rank Objective (TRO), Second Rank Objective, Third Rank Objective, etc. From any rank, the objective in a lower rank answers to the question "How?" and the objective in a higher rank answers to the question "Why?" The exception is the Top Rank Objective (TRO): there is no answer to the "Why?" question. That is how the TRO is defined. An example may help to clarify the concept presented above.
2. Information gathering and analysis. This includes an external assessment (such as environmental scanning), and an internal resource assessment. Morphological analysis may be applied to both internal resource assessments and external assessments. SWOT (Strengths, Weaknesses, Opportunities, Threats) Analysis may be used to assess those aspects of the organisation and the environment that are important to achieving the objective of the strategic plan.
3. Evaluation of the feasibility of the objective in view of the SWOTs.
4. Strategy-development. This is a creative step that answers these four questions: How can we use the Strengths, stop the Weaknesses, exploit the Opportunities and defend against the Threats in pursuit of the selected objetive.
5. Developing Action Programmes for the more attractive strategies, covering: Name of the strategy, Benefits to be expected from implementing this programme, Actions: What will be done? Responsible persons: Who will be in charge of the programme?

Timing: When will the programme start? When will it be completed? Location(s): Where will the programme be implemented? Resources: What will be needed: people, money, information, other resources? Control System: How will progress be measured and reported? Rewards for performance, if any. Contingency plans: What will be done if results fall short?

STRATEGY AS REVOLUTION

- Identify the unquestioned beliefs in the organisation and challenge them - look for opportunities to re-write the rules of the environment
- Look for major discontinuities in technology, and embrace such changes wholeheartedly - do not waste time making small incremental adjustments - stand by to create a completely new business model at any time
  — More a mind-set than a formal technique
  — Not rule or ritual-oriented, not reductionist, not reactive, not autocratic

Theorists frequently make the distinction between strategy and tactics. Strategy involves planning how to get where one wants to go. Tactics can potentially comprise the implementation of such over-arching plans. They deal with specific actions by particular people or by particular groups. Some theorists see it as a mistake to separate strategy and tactics. Constantinos Markides describes strategy formation and implementation (tactics) as an on-going, never-ending, integrated process requiring continuous re-assessment and reformation. He sees strategic planning as both planned and emergent - dynamic and interactive. J. Moncrieff also stresses strategy dynamics - he recognizes strategy as partially deliberate and partially unplanned.

The unplanned element comes from two sources:

1. Emergent strategies - resulting from the emergence of opportunities and threats in the environment
2. Strategies in action - ad hoc actions by many people from all parts of an organisation

Strategic plans typically look 5 or more years into the future. They differ in this respect from tactical plans (sometimes referred to as functional plans), which look 2 to 4 years into the future; and from operational plans [such as budgets] which have an annual scope.

Finally, strategic planning is not what you think you want to do but a thing that you have to do.

SITUATIONAL ANALYSIS

When developing Corporate strategies, analysis of the company and environment as it is at the moment and how it will be in the future, is very necessary, this is called the analysis phase of strategic planning. The analysis has to be executed at an internal level as well as an external level to identify all opportunities and threats of the new strategy.

One aspect of internal analysis that has been underestimated through the last decades in developing corporate strategies is the field of corporate cultures. Consultants, when developing corporate strategies, are mostly focused on tangible internal and external factors when analysing the company and did not really take the cultural, often intangible and invisible, aspects into account.

IDENTIFYING CULTURES

When creating new corporate strategies, or adjusting existing ones, as said in the introduction, the business consultant most generally starts by analysing the following aspects of an organisation:

1. Visionary aspects such as goals and objectives.
2. Situational aspects such as financial information, company structure and systems and the business which the company is operating in.
3. External aspects concerning the environment, market findings, competitors and rules and legislations that apply to the region the company is in.
4. Technical aspects that concern the amount of risk involved in the new strategy, the time span the strategy has to be enrolled in and resources and inputs required.

The one aspect that is not often thought of is the cultural aspect of a company. With culture we mean:

"Culture is a series of values, standard interpretations, insights and ways of thinking that is shared by members of an organisation and is passed on to new members of this organisation."

This is hardly plausible when thinking of the resistance and problems a group of employees can cause if they oppose to-be-employed or already-employed strategies. The relation between culture and strategy has been described thoroughly by Kono :

"The product-market strategy defines the work which employees have to do. If the work requires a high level of competence and new skills, this revitalizes the culture. The strategy also affects the financial performance and the level of salaries and incentives which are available to employees. On the other hand, the effective implementation of new strategies depends on the creativity of the employees and their willingness to change."

Kono precisely describes the relation that the company culture and the company strategy have with each other, they are interdependent. So it is key to analyze the company culture as well as possible, to be able to adjust the 'to be developed' strategy the best way possible to avoid conflicts and maximize compatibility.

PERSPECTIVES

To analyze the culture of a company, one has to use some kind of perspective to look at the artifacts (visible or not) that are active within the company and describe its culture. Basically two important schools with their perspectives can be distinguished:

- Ethnographical versus clinical analysis
- Functionalistic versus Interpretionistic analysis

This approach towards analysing corporate cultures has been developed by Schein and makes the distinction between the following two ways of looking at artifacts within a company:

- Ethnographical – Focused on concrete data to understand the culture, which is mostly used for scientific research. Researchers who use this ethnographical way of analysis start with some predefined assumptions and try to find proof for these assumptions when investigating the organisation.
- Clinical – Focused on cultural processes that are active within the organisation and how these processes can be adjusted or modified to achieve a certain goal. Hereby looking at indicators such as artifacts, values and assumptions.

FUNCTIONALISTIC VERSUS INTERPRETIONISTIC APPROACH

- The functionalistic approach towards analysing culture is concerned with merely the same aspects as the clinical approach and is aimed at analysing current cultural signals that can possibly be extracted to be used in other organisations
- The interpretionistic approach is more interested in the processes that form the coherence between employees in the same company. The interpretionistic approach thus is more aimed at communicational processes between employees in contrary to the more 'describing' way of the functionalistic approach.

VISIBLE ARTIFACTS

Visible artifacts include the following and can be experienced and analysed fairly easy because of the extrovert character they have. Visible artifacts include:

- Rituals and ceremonies
- Organisation Stories
- Symbols
- Business Language

The business language of a company is the use of language employees speak, common used words and textual expressions that characterize the companies culture.

INVISIBLE ARTIFACTS

Next to visible artifacts, a company's culture also thrives on processes and events that are not that easily seen by outside consultants or even in-house employees.

These include:

- Value (personal and cultural)
- Assumptions
- Perspectives
- Attitudes
- Feelings

When looking at these invisible artifacts, one can state that these are of great value when creating a new corporate strategy, the attitudes and feelings that employees have towards for example radical changes can make or break your corporate strategy. The company's strategy also depends on the external / internal focus and needs from the environment of the company.

CULTURE TYPES

When setting the external versus internal strategic focus against the environmental needs (flexibility versus stability) The following figure emerges: to be very externally oriented when it comes to the strategic focus. Companies that hold this culture are flexible and able to respond to outside needs and changes fast and adequately. Employees are stimulated to be innovative. Examples of these companies today are mainly in the services-sector such as online marketplaces like eBay or online communities such as Hyves in the Netherlands.

- Mission Culture: The mission culture is externally oriented like the adjustment based entrepreneurial culture, but is not subject to quick environmental and external changes. Companies that have the mission culture are focused on reaching targets that have been set earlier in order to be competitive. A company such as Iriver (Korea), which is a company that produces mp3 players, is a good example. Iriver is very externally focused, and copies existing mp3 player models like the Apple iPod, but is also very focused on internal targets to guarantee low prices.
- Clan Culture: The clan culture is focused at flexibility when it comes to external needs, but this is reached through excellence of the employees, which makes the strategic focus internally focused. Examples of companies who fit the clan culture are Baan and IBM who are mainly considering the wellbeing of their employees as top priority and have the intention not to fire a single employee from the company perspective.

- Bureaucratic Culture: The bureaucratic culture is internally focused and operates in a market that is not demanding high flexibility. Examples are some government institutions or insurance companies. When a company's culture is analyzed, by using one of the perspectives used before, artifacts will make clear in what part of the quadrant (or very possibly also a combination of more than one) a company is in according to their culture. This information can be valuable to adjust the corporate strategy too but it can also be valuable to identify the current culture and change it according to for example changing needs from the external environment.

6

The Functional Approach to Leadership

INTRODUCTION

The functional approach to leadership first appeared at about the same period of time that scientists began questioning the trait and style approaches. Some scientists responded to the problems with the trait and style approaches by adopting the situational and contingency perspectives.

As you recall, each of these approaches has a unique perspective on leadership. For instance, the trait approach is concerned with the permanent characteristics of a leader. The style point of view maintains that the method a leader uses is most important. The situational perspective looks for differences in leadership style across different circumstances. Finally, the contingency approach examines leadership by looking at the association of trait and situation. These four points of view all have one thing in common, however. All of them, in the end, are concerned with a particular person in a leadership role.

The functional perspective, in contrast, in concerned with the behaviours of a group. Specifically, the functional approach examines the behaviours that allow the group to reach its goals. We discussed how behaviours serve functions that help a group solve its task and maintenance problems. Certain behaviours serve as leadership functions. For instance, leadership functions include actions that serve to help the group perform its task and clarify the group's goals. They also include behaviours that help the group interact effectively and give members social support.

The functional approach maintains that a group need not have only one particular member who performs these leadership functions. Any group member can perform them. This means that any member can lead. If we accept the functional perspective, we have the potential to uncover which behaviours help lead a group towards its goals. These behaviours help the group if at least one member performs them.

THE TRAIT APPROACH TO LEADERSHIP

The first time that researchers attempted to use a scientific method to study leadership was in the 1920s. Taken as a group, these early scientists worked with a basic hypothesis regarding who leaders were. They assumed that leaders were people with personal characteristics, or traits, that set them above and apart from non-leaders. This assumption was consistent with a philosophical view that was popular in the nineteenth century.

The "Great Man Theory"

The 1800s philosophical outlook that created the trait approach is known as the "Great Man Theory of Leadership." The theory states that certain people are born to be leaders. They have a special quality that sets them apart from "common" folk. The idea is that the great leaders of the world would have assumed a leadership role at any place or time in history. Thus, Julius Caesar or Napoleon would have been influential figures anywhere, at any time. Note that the "Great Man" title reflects the thinking of the times. Back then, most people did not consider women capable of possessing leadership qualities. We use the title here only because it is historically correct.

THE EARLY SCIENTIFIC APPROACH

Literal Approach

In the 1920s, various leadership researchers occasionally took the "Great Man" hypothesis literally. They searched for characteristics that differentiated between leaders and followers. They thought that there were certain qualities that only a leader could possess, such as charisma. Usually, however, the scientists looked at the characteristics that all people possess to some degree. They then would cautiously attempt to discover which traits were particularly evident in leaders. It was true that the idea that certain people would always be leaders, no matter what, intrigued researchers. However, it was not just the nineteenth century "Great Man" theory that caused scientists to examine leadership. In the 1930s, fascist governments in Europe and Asia grew increasingly belligerent. As they did so, the democracies of Europe and North America became fearful of impending war. In times of war, nations need leaders. They also need to find them quickly. Hence, these early scientists wanted to devise a psychological test that would allow them to recognize good leaders easily. If they could create such a test, countries could use it during the impending years of crisis. A leadership test would make it a relatively simple task for a country to place gifted people into the necessary leadership roles.

Early scientists created various types of leadership tests that they hoped would fulfill this need. Each test attempted to create a method to predict who would be a leader and who would not be. Before we describe the results of these tests, it is useful for us to discuss how the researchers performed their studies.

Methodology

These early researchers were interested in discovering which traits contributed to a person's degree of leadership. To do this, they decided to compare measurements of leadership scores with measurements of other traits. The scientists used a particular method to compare various measurements. This technique allowed the researchers to discover how the different measurements were related. We shall discuss their methodology step by step.

METHOD FOR ASSUMING LEADERSHIP

They wanted to know whether there are differences between groups whose leaders get their position in different ways. Does it matter whether leaders are assigned from the outside, elected by the members, or allowed to emerge from group discussion? Contrasting hypotheses could be proposed concerning this issue. It could be that groups with assigned or elected leaders perform better than groups with emergent leaders because emergent-led groups begin discussion without knowing who is in charge. It also could be that groups with emergent or elected leaders perform better than groups with assigned leaders because assigned-leader groups are not involved in the choice of leader and as a consequence are less satisfied with their leadership. Several studies have been performed that are relevant to this issue.

Mortensen study. Mortensen (1966) analyzed the leadership emergence process in six groups that met three times. Three of the groups had assigned leaders, and three did not.

The three assigned leaders performed the most leadership actions during the first group meeting. However, by the third meeting, only one on the three was still leading his or her group. In the other two, the assigned leader had been supplanted by another member to whom the group had responded more positively.

Mortensen concluded that the group's approval of an assigned leader is important. Assigned leadership can help a person quickly assume the leadership role, but only if the group approves of him or her. In contrast, assigning a leader can slow down a group and make it difficult for a leader to emerge if the group disapproves of the assignment. In this case, leadership emergence would have been faster if there had been no leadership assignment.

Goldman and Fraas study. Goldman and Fraas (1965) found that the way in which a group acquires its leaders is important to the group's performance. They assigned leaders to groups through four methods. One way was that the group elected a leader by vote. The second method was that the experimenters selected a leader based on the person's ability. The third way was that the scientists arbitrarily chose a leader, and the last method involved groups that had no assigned leader.

The researchers then had the groups play "Twenty Questions." They compared the success rates of each group. The researchers found that groups with elected leaders performed the best. The performance of groups that had leaders appointed based on ability was close to the best success rate. Leaderless groups were a distant third. The groups with the worst scores were the ones with arbitrarily appointed leaders.

Hollander and Julian study. Hollander and Julian (1970) decided to compare the performance of elected and appointed leaders. The researchers told groups and the leaders of the groups that one of two criteria had determined leadership. They led their participants to believe that either the group had elected the leader or the experimenters had appointed him or her. In either case, the leader supposedly had important abilities for the position.

Hollander and Julian found that "elected" leaders had slightly more influence on their group's opinions than "appointed" leaders. They also were far more willing to deviate from their group's ideas. However, their position was far more precarious. Members lost confidence in "elected" leaders if they failed or if the group considered them incompetent at their task. In contrast, "appointed" leaders had to both fail and have the group consider them incompetent before the group would reject them.

Larson study. Larson (1971) compared nine groups whose members agreed on whom they felt had emerged as leader with five other groups whose members did not agree on who led the groups. Larson called the first nine groups "stable leadership" groups and the other five "unstable leadership" groups. The stable leadership groups spent more time on substantive issues and less time on procedural and irrelevant topics than the unstable groups. Further, the leader initiated the most substantive ideas in the stable groups. In addition, the stable groups spent more discussion time, per idea, on the topic that the leader had initiated, in comparison with topics the other members initiated. Thus, it appears that groups with stable leadership were more prepared to take on the their task than groups with unstable leadership.

Looking at these studies as a whole, it appears that competence and group acceptance are the most important factors in how a group will behave with a certain leader. It does not necessarily matter whether a leader is elected, emergent, or appointed. A group can behave well and be successful under any of these conditions. As long as the group accepts the leader and he or she is competent, the group can function well with the leader.

LEWIN'S RESEARCH

Methodology

In the late 1930s, Lewin and his students Lippitt and White performed a landmark study of the three leadership styles. They wanted to determine how each style would affect a group. The groups they chose to study were made up of 10-year-old boys. There were four groups with five members in each. The boys met to participate in arts and crafts activities or in similar hobbies. The groups experienced a succession of various adult leaders. These leaders were Lippitt, White, and two other coworkers. Each adult assumed a different leadership style. The study defined these styles in the following ways:

- Authoritarian leaders
  - These leaders determined all policies for the group members. They told the boys which projects to do.
  - They also dictated the methods and stages of goal attainment one step at a time. The adults would give instructions for a subsequent step only after the boys had completed the previous step. They did not give them all of the instructions at once at the beginning of a project. The researchers reasoned that the boys would have little understanding of the project as a whole if the leaders gave them instructions in this step-by-step manner. Without an understanding of the whole project, the boys would have little ability to make their own creative contributions to the assignment. This meant that the leader would have increased control over their activities. Remember that according to Lewin, the authoritarian leader wants group members to reach the leader's goals, not their own.
  - The authoritarian leaders also assigned work companions. They told the boys with whom they could work on their projects.
  - They further evaluated the boys individually. They did not judge the group as a whole. They expected that the approach would cause the boys to be concerned with their own tasks rather than with the work of the group as a whole.
- Democratic leaders
  - These leaders encouraged the group to make its own policy. They asked the boys which projects they wanted to do.
  - They also explained the stages of the project, along with the methods of goal attainment, in advance. This gave the boys the knowledge that they needed to take the initiative concerning how the group would perform its task. Remember that the democratic leader wants to help group members reach their own goals.
  - They further allowed the boys to choose their own work companions.
  - The democratic leaders evaluated the work of the group as a whole. They did not judge members separately. They expected that this method would influence the boys to be concerned with the whole group's efforts rather than with only their own work.

- Laissez faire leaders
  - Laissez faire leaders refused to help the group choose its policy.
  - They also never volunteered information on the stages and methods necessary to attain the group's goals.
  - Further, these leaders refused to help the boys choose their work companions.
  - They also did not evaluate any work. The laissez faire leaders only answered questions and provided work materials.

THE TRAIT APPROACH TO LEADERSHIP

The Trait Approach arose from the "Great Man" theory as a way of identifying the key characteristics of successful leaders. It was believed that through this approach critical leadership traits could be isolated and that people with such traits could then be recruited, selected, and installed into leadership positions. This approach was common in the military and is still used as a set of criteria to select candidates for commissions. The problem with the trait approach lies in the fact that almost as many traits as studies undertaken were identified.

After several years of such research, it became apparent that no consistent traits could be identified. Although some traits were found in a considerable number of studies, the results were generally inconclusive. Some leaders might have possessed certain traits but the absence of them did not necessarily mean that the person was not a leader. Although there was little consistency in the results of the various trait studies, however, some traits did appear more frequently than others, including: technical skill, friendliness, task motivation, application to task, group task supportiveness, social skill, emotional control, administrative skill, general charisma, and intelligence. Of these, the most widely explored has tended to be "charisma".

THE BEHAVIOURAL SCHOOL

The results of the trait studies were inconclusive. Traits, amongst other things, were hard to measure. How, for example, do we measure traits such as honesty, integrity, loyalty, or diligence? Another approach in the study of leadership had to be found. After the publication of the late Douglas McGregor's classic book The Human Side of Enterprise in 1960, attention shifted to 'behavioural theories'. McGregor was a teacher, researcher, and consultant whose work was considered to be "on the cutting edge" of managing people. He influenced all the behavioural theories, which emphasize focusing on human relationships, along with output and performance.

McGregor's Theory X and Theory Y Managers

Although not strictly speaking a theory of leadership, the leadership strategy of effectively-used participative management proposed in Douglas

McGregor's book has had a tremendous impact on managers. The most publicized concept is McGregor's thesis that leadership strategies are influenced by a leader's assumptions about human nature. As a result of his experience as a consultant, McGregor summarised two contrasting sets of assumptions made by managers in industry.

Theory X and Y Managers:

- Theory X managers believe that:
  a. The average human being has an inherent dislike of work and will avoid it if possible.
  b. Because of this human characteristic, most people must be coerced, controlled, directed, or threatened with punishment to get them to put forth adequate effort to achieve organisational objectives.
  c. The average human being prefers to be directed, wishes to avoid responsibility, has relatively little ambition, and wants security above all else.
- Theory Y managers believe that:
  d. The expenditure of physical and mental effort in work is as natural as play or rest, and the average human being, under proper conditions, learns not only to accept but to seek responsibility.
  e. People will exercise self-direction and self-control to achieve objectives to which they are committed.
  f. The capacity to exercise a relatively high level of imagination, ingenuity, and creativity in the solution of organisational problems is widely, not narrowly, distributed in the population, and the intellectual potentialities of the average human being are only partially utilized under the conditions of modern industrial life.

It can therefore be seen that a leader holding Theory X assumptions would prefer an autocratic style, whereas one holding Theory Y assumptions would prefer a more participative style.

BLAKE AND MOUTON'S MANAGERIAL GRID

The Managerial Grid developed by Robert Blake and Jane Mouton focuses on task and employee orientations of managers, as well as combinations of concerns between the two extremes. A grid with concern for production on the horizontal axis and concern for people on the vertical axis and plots five basic leadership styles.

The first number refers to a leader's production or task orientation; the second, to people or employee orientation. Blake and Mouton propose that "Team Management" - a high concern for both employees and production - is the most effective type of leadership behaviour.

THE CONTINGENCY OR SITUATIONAL SCHOOL

Whilst behavioural theories may help managers develop particular leadership behaviours they give little guidance as to what constitutes effective leadership in different situations. Indeed, most researchers today conclude that no one leadership style is right for every manager under all circumstances. Instead, contingency-situational theories were developed to indicate that the style to be used is contingent upon such factors as the situation, the people, the task, the organisation, and other environmental variables.

Fiedler's Contingency Model

Fiedler's contingency theory postulates that there is no single best way for managers to lead. Situations will create different leadership style requirements for a manager. The solution to a managerial situation is contingent on the factors that impinge on the situation. For example, in a highly routine environment where repetitive tasks are the norm, a relatively directive leadership style may result in the best performance, however, in a dynamic environment a more flexible, participative style may be required. Fiedler looked at three situations that could define the condition of a managerial task:

- Leader member relations: How well do the manager and the employees get along?
- Task structure: Is the job highly structured, fairly unstructured, or somewhere in between?
- Position power: How much authority does the manager possess?

Managers were rated as to whether they were relationship oriented or task oriented. Task oriented managers tend to do better in situations that have good leader-member relationships, structured tasks, and either weak or strong position power. They do well when the task is unstructured but position power is strong. Also, they did well at the other end of the spectrum when the leader member relations were moderate to poor and the task was unstructured. Relationship oriented managers do better in all other situations.

Thus, a given situation might call for a manager with a different style or a manager who could take on a different style for a different situation. These environmental variables are combined in a weighted sum that is termed "favourable" at one end and "unfavourable" at the other. Task oriented style is preferable at the clearly defined extremes of "favourable" and "unfavourable" environments, but relationship orientation excels in the middle ground. Managers could attempt to reshape the environment variables to match their style.

Another aspect of the contingency model theory is that the leader-member relations, task structure, and position power dictate a leader's situational control. Leader-member relations are the amount of loyalty, dependability, and support that the leader receives from employees. It is a measure of how the manager perceives he or she and the group of employees is getting along together. In a favourable relationship the manager has a high task structure and is able to reward and or punish employees without any problems. In an unfavourable relationship the task is usually unstructured and the leader possesses limited authority. The spelling out in detail of what is required of subordinates affects task structure. Positioning power measures the amount of power or authority the manager perceives the organisation has given him or her for the purpose of directing, rewarding, and punishing subordinates. Positioning power of managers depends on the taking away or increasing the decision-making power of employees.

The task-motivated style leader experiences pride and satisfaction in the task accomplishment for the organisation, while the relationship-motivated style seeks to build interpersonal relations and extend extra help for the team development in the organisation.

There is no good or bad leadership style. Each person has his or her own preferences for leadership. Task-motivated leaders are at their best when the group performs successfully such as achieving a new sales record or outperforming the major competitor. Relationship-oriented leaders are at their best when greater customer satisfaction is gained and a positive company image is established.

The Hersey-Blanchard Model of Leadership

The Hersey-Blanchard Leadership Model also takes a situational perspective of leadership. This model posits that the developmental levels of a leader's subordinates play the greatest role in determining which leadership styles are most appropriate. Their theory is based on the amount of direction and socio-emotional support a leader must provide given the situation and the "level of maturity" of the followers.

- Task behaviour is the extent to which the leader engages in spelling out the duties and responsibilities to an individual or group. This behaviour includes telling people what to do, how to do it, when to do it, where to do it, and who's to do it. In task behaviour the leader engages in oneway communication.
- Relationship behaviour is the extent to which the leader engages in two-way or multi-way communications. This includes listening, facilitating, and supportive behaviours. In relationship behaviour the leader engages in two-way communication by providing socio-emotional support.
- Maturity is the willingness and ability of a person to take responsibility for directing his or her own behaviour. People tend to have varying degrees of maturity, depending on the specific task, function, or objective that a leader is attempting to accomplish through their efforts.

In summary therefore leader behaviours fall along two continua:

- Directive Behaviour
    g. One-Way Communication
    h. Followers' Roles Clearly Communicated
    i. Close Supervision of Performance
- Supportive Behaviour
    j. Two-Way Communication
    k. Listening, providing support and encoura-gement
    l. Facilitate interaction Involve follower in decision-making

For Blanchard the key situational variable, when determining the appropriate leadership style, is the readiness or developmental level of the subordinate. As a result, four leadership styles result:

- Directing: The leader provides clear instructions and specific direction. This style is best matched with a low follower readiness level.
- Coaching: The leader encourages two-way communication and helps build confidence and motivation on the part of the employee, although the leader still has responsibility and controls decision making. Selling style is best matched with a moderate follower readiness level.
- Supporting: With this style, the leader and followers share decision making and no longer need or expect the relationship to be directive. Participating style is best matched with a moderate follower readiness level.
- Delegating: This style is appropriate for leaders whose followers are ready to accomplish a particular task and are both competent and motivated to take full responsibility. Delegating style is best matched with a high follower readiness level.

To determine the appropriate leadership style to use in a given situation, the leader must first determine the maturity level of the followers in relation to the specific task that the leader is attempting to accomplish through the effort of the followers. As the level of followers' maturity increases, the leader should begin to reduce his or her task behaviour and increase relationship behaviour until the followers reach a moderate level of maturity. As the followers begin to move into an above average level of maturity, the leader should decrease not only task behaviour but also relationship behaviour. Once the maturity level is identified, the appropriate leadership style can be determined.

Tannenbaum and Schmidt's Leadership Continuum

One criticism of early work on leadership styles is that they looked at styles too much in black and white terms. The autocratic and democratic styles or task-oriented and relationship-oriented styles which they described are extremes, whereas in practice the behaviour of many, perhaps most, leaders in business will be somewhere between the two. Contingency theorists Tannenbaum and Schmidt suggested the idea that leadership behaviour varies along a continuum and that as one moves away from the autocratic extreme the amount of subordinate participation and involvement in decision taking increases.

They also suggested that the kind of leadership represented by the democratic extreme of the continuum will be rarely encountered in formal organisations. Four main leadership styles can be located at points along such a continuum:

- Autocratic: The leader takes the decisions and announces them, expecting subordinates to carry them out without question.
- Persuasive: At this point on the scale the leader also takes all the decisions for the group without discussion or consultation but believes that people will be better motivated if they are persuaded that the decisions are good ones. He or she does a lot of explaining and 'selling' in order to overcome any possible resistance to what he or she wants to do. The leader also puts a lot of energy into creating enthusiasm for the goals he or she has set for the group.
- Consultative: In this style the leader confers with the group members before taking decisions and, in fact, considers their advice and their feelings when framing decisions. He or she may, of course, not always accept the subordinates' advice but they are likely to feel that they can have some influence. Under this leadership style the decision and the full responsibility for it remain with the leader but the degree of involvement by subordinates in decision taking is very much greater than telling or selling styles.
- Democratic: Using this style the leader would characteristically lay the problem before his or her subordinates and invite discussion. The leader's role is that of conference leader, or chair, rather than that of decision taker. He or she will allow the decision to emerge out of the process of group discussion, instead of imposing it on the group as its boss.

What distinguishes this approach from previous discussions of leadership style is that there will be some situations in which each of the above styles is likely to be more appropriate than the others.

- Telling: In an emergency, a telling style may be most appropriate and would normally be considered justified by the group.
- Selling: The selling style would tend to fit situations in which the group leader, and he or she alone, possesses all the information on which the decision must be based and which at the same time calls for a very high level of commitment and enthusiasm on the part of group members if the task is to be carried through successfully.

- Consulting: The consulting style is likely to be most appropriate when there is time in which to reach a considered decision and when the information on which the decision needs to be based lies among the members of the group.
- Joining: The joining style is appropriate under similar conditions, with the important exception that this is likely to be appropriate only in those instances where the nature of the responsibility associated with the decision is such that group members are willing to share it with their leader, or alternatively the leader is willing to accept responsibility for decisions which he or she has not made personally.

Adair's Action-Centred Leadership Model

John Adair has a long pedigree in the world of leadership. The Adair model is that the action-centred leader gets the job done through the work team and relationships with fellow managers and staff. According to Adair's explanation an action-centred leader must:

- Direct the job to be done
- Support and review the individual people doing it
- Co-ordinate and foster the work team as a whole

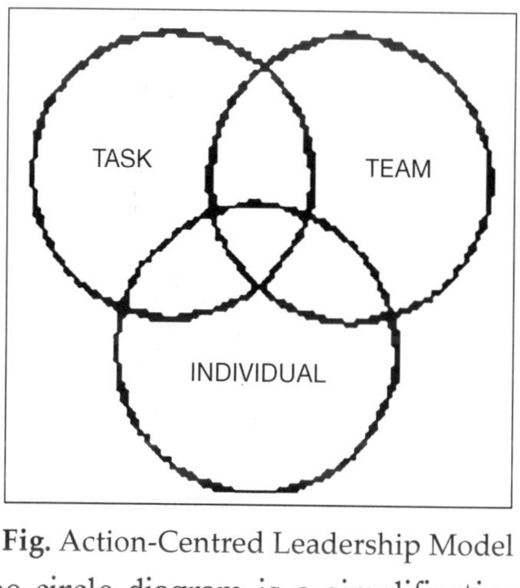

Fig. Action-Centred Leadership Model

His famous three circle diagram is a simplification of the variability of human interaction, but is a useful tool for thinking about what constitutes an effective leader/manager in relation to the job he/she has to do. The effective leader/manager carries out the functions and exhibits the behaviours depicted by the three circles. Situational and contingent elements call for different responses by the leader. Hence imagine that the various circles may be bigger or smaller as the situation varies *i.e.* the leader will give more or less emphasis to the functionally-oriented behaviours according to what the actual situation involves. The challenge for the leader is to manage all sectors of the diagram:

- Task:
  m. define the task
  n. make the plan
  o. allocate work and resources
  p. control quality and rate of work
  q. check performance against plan
  r. adjust the plan
- Team:
  s. maintain discipline
  t. build team spirit
  u. encourage, motivate, give a sense of purpose
  v. appoint sub-leaders
  w. ensure communication within group
  x. develop the group
- Individual:
  - attend to personal problems
  - praise individuals
  - give status
  - recognise and use individual abilities
- Develop the individual

LEADERS AND FOLLOWERS

The models discussed so far have dwelt on the leader as some frontal figure who stands out from the rest as being somehow different and "leading" the rest of the people. The discussion now moves to recognition of the importance of the leaders' relationship with his/her followers and an interdependency of roles. No longer the hero or solo leader but the team leader. Not the leader always out in front but the leader who has the capacity to follow. Not the master, but the servant.

Servant Leadership

The notion of "Servant Leadership" emphasises the leaders' duty to serve his/her followers - leadership thus arises out of a desire to serve rather than a desire to lead Robert Greenleaf, founder of the Center for Servant Leadership describes it as follows:

- "The servant-leader is servant first… It begins with the natural feeling that one wants to serve, to serve first. Then conscious choice brings one to aspire to lead. He or she is sharply different from the person who is leader first, perhaps because of the need to assuage an unusual power drive or to acquire material possessions. For such it will be a later choice to serve – after leadership is established. The leader-first and the servant-first are two extreme types. Between them there are shadings and blends that are part of the infinite variety of human nature.

- The difference manifest itself in the care taken by the servant-first to make sure that other people's highest priority needs are being served. The best test, and difficult to administer, is: do those served grow as persons; do they, while being served, become healthier, wiser, freer, more autonomous, more likely themselves to become servants? And, what is the effect on the least privileged in society; will they benefit, or, at least, will they not be further deprived?"

Characteristics of Servant Leaders are as follows:

- "Servant-Leadership is a practical philosophy which supports people who choose to serve first, and then lead as a way of expanding service to individuals and institutions. Servantleaders may or may not hold formal leadership positions. Servant-leadership encourages collaboration, trust, foresight, listening, and the ethical use of power and empowerment."

The emphasis on serving a higher purpose has made this model popular within the Church and other religious institutions.

The Following Part of Leading

Katzenbach and Smith, authors of 'The Wisdom of Teams' talk of the "following part of leading", saying that the critical behaviours of leaders are:

- Key Behaviours of Leaders:
  - Asking questions instead of giving answers: By asking such questions such as "What do you think we should do?" or "How do you suggest we proceed?" you take a step behind another person. Whether you stay behind, of course, depends on your intention to actually follow the suggestion or answer of that other person.
  - Providing opportunities for others to lead you: This goes beyond the traditional notion of looking for growth opportunities for other people. Unless the opportunity in question bears a real risk for your personal performance outcome, you are not actually positioning yourself as a follower.
  - Doing real work in support of others instead of only the reverse: Rolling up your sleeves and contributing "sweat equity" to the efforts and outcomes of other people earns you their appreciation as someone upon whom they can depend, regardless of the relative hierarchical or functional position each of you holds.
  - Becoming a matchmaker instead of a "central switch": In addition to following other people yourself, you must learn to help them follow each other. This requires you to get beyond considering

yourself the "central switch" through which all decisions flow. Instead, you need to look for every possible chance to help people find their best collaborators. "Have you asked Sally or Rasheed what they think?" is often the only input required to facilitate the effort at hand, although you then must submit your effort and support to whatever the people in question suggest.

- Seeking common understanding instead of consensus: The pejorative meaning associated with consensus management has nothing to do with either effective leading or effective following. Leaders who know when and how to follow build deep common understanding, not superficial consensus, around the purpose, goals, and approach at hand. They submit themselves and others to the discipline of ensuring that all sides to any disagreement are fully understood by everyone, recognising that mutual understanding is far more powerful than any particular decision to choose path A over path B. All people will follow strong, commonly understood purposes and goals more easily than the "put-up jobs" associated with consensus.

They go on to say that the indicators of when a leader must follow are:

- When a leader must follow Leaders:
  - Individual performance: As a leader, you must follow another individual, regardless of hierarchy, if:
    i. That individual, through experience, skill, and judgement, knows best.
    ii. That individual's growth demands that you invest more in his or her skill and self-confidence than in your own.
    iii. Only that individual, not you, has the capacity to "get it done"
  - Team performance: As a leader, you must follow the team if:
    i. The team's purpose and performance goals demand it
    ii. The team, not you, must develop skills and self-confidence
    iii. The team's agreed-upon working approach requires you, like all the others, to do real work
  - Organisational performance: As a leader, you must follow others, regardless of hierarchy, if:
    i. The organisation's purpose and performance goals demand it
    ii. The need for expanding the leadership capacity of others in the organisation requires it
    iii. "Living" the vision and values enjoins you to do so

Team Leadership

In the late 1970's Meredith Belbin conducted a study of teams focusing on the factors separating successful and unsuccessful teams via a college business game at Henley a feature of which was shared leadership. Through the game Belbin found that the composition of the team was important and that individual differences in style, role and contribution far from underlining personal weaknesses, were a source of potential team strength. Balanced teams comprised of such individuals who engaged in complementary role behaviour performed better than unbalanced teams. Nine distinctive roles were identified in the study, with most people being found to embrace a mix of two or three roles whilst also avoiding others with which they were uncomfortable. Where there was an individual with clear, useful and appreciated attributes they would fit into a team on the basis of the strengths they brought.

These people would also have weaknesses that belonged to the same cluster of characteristics as the strength itself. These potential deficiencies were considered the price that has to be paid for a particular strength, a price that is worth paying, and were referred to as 'allowable weaknesses. Belbin found no 'ideal' team member, individual who could perform all of the roles. From this work, Belbin drew the distinction between the "Solo" and the "Team" leader. He suggests that "leaders are not notable for admitting their weaknesses, whether allowable or not. They act as though they have no weaknesses".

To many people the image of the leader - a person heading up a team of followers, ever ready to take on any role and assuming any responsibility - is very familiar to us for it is the one based upon our past experiences and beliefs. Belbin classified such leaders as 'Solo leaders' and in the workplace this type of behaviour may have great advantages, for internal barriers can be overcome and decisions, especially those of an urgent nature, can be made and put into effect with little or no delay. The increasing complexity and the discontinuous nature of modern work however, poses greater problems where Solo leadership is less appropriate and 'Team leadership' more suited. The key difference between the 'Solo leader' and 'Team leadership' revolves around the behaviour and participation of the two.

Solo and Team Leader:

- Solo Leader:
  - Plays unlimited role – the Solo Leader interferes in everything
  - Strives for conformity – the Solo Leader tries to mould people to particular standards
  - Collects acolytes – The Solo Leader collects admirers and sycophants
  - Directs Subordinates – subordinates take their leads and cues from the Solo Leader
  - Projects objectives – the Solo Leader makes it plain what everyone is expected to do 1. Chooses to limit role to preferred team roles – delegates roles to others

- Team Leader:
  - Chooses to limit role to preferred team roles – delegates roles to others
  - Builds on diversity – the Team Leader values differences between people
  - Seeks talent – The Team Leader is not threatened by people with special abilities
  - Develops colleagues – the Team Leader encourages the growth of personal strengths
  - Creates mission – the Team Leader projects the vision which others can act on as they see fit

Using Team Role theory the word 'shape' indicates to us 'shaper', whilst the word 'vision' implies 'plant'. Looking at leadership using Handy's definition is interesting for vision is certainly important to leadership, but does it have to be unique to an individual? Where it is unique to an individual with a drive to enact it such as a 'Shaper', strong Solo leadership is likely to prevail. Vision alternatively may be 'borrowed' by a 'Shaper' who treats it as a product of the self and similarly will adopt a Solo leadership style.

Many organisations have rewarded Solo leadership behaviour by promoting individuals to management and leadership positions, for such individuals have met past organisational needs In today's organisation the alternative approach, the Team Leader, is more appropriate. Whilst Team leadership may not be as natural as Solo leadership, Belbin suggests it can be learned through understanding the nature of leadership and the qualities required. In the rapidly changing and uncertain work environment of today no one person has all the answers to leadership. A Team leadership style based upon the development of the strengths and the allowable weaknesses of all of the roles will permit a more holistic, or participative, style of leadership where teamwork, problem solving, decision making and innovation can flourish with heightened teamwork and work performance.

Transactional and Transformational Leadership

James MacGregor Burns writing in his book 'Leadership' was the first to put forward the concept of "transforming leadership". To Burns transforming leadership "*is a relationship of mutual stimulation and elevation that converts followers into leaders and may convert leaders into moral agents*". Burns went on to also further define it by suggesting that:

- "[Transforming leadership] occurs when one or more persons engage with others in such a way that leaders and followers raise one another to higher levels of motivation and morality..."

Burns draws upon the humanistic psychology movement in his writing upon 'transforming leadership' by proposing that the transforming leader shapes, alters, and elevates the motives, values and goals of followers achieving significant change in the process. He proposed that there is a special power entailed in transforming leadership with leaders *"armed with principles [that] may ultimately transform both leaders and followers into persons who jointly adhere to modal values and end-values"*. Burns sees the power of transforming leadership as more noble and different from charismatic leadership, which he terms 'heroic' leadership, and executive or business leadership.

Despite this it is surprising that most of the application of Burns' work has been in these two types of leadership. Bernard Bass developed Burns' concept of transforming leadership in 'Leadership and Performance Beyond Expectations' into 'transformational leadership' where the leader transforms followers – the direction of influence to Bass is thus one-way, unlike Burns' who sees it as potentially a two-way process. Bass, however, deals with the transformational style of executive leadership that incorporates social change, a facet missing from Burns' work. For Bass 'transformational leaders' may:

- Expand a follower's portfolio of needs
- Transform a follower's self-interest
- Increase the confidence of followers
- Elevate followers' expectations
- Heighten the value of the leader's intended outcomes for the follower
- Encourage behavioural change
- Motivate others to higher levels of personal achievement.

Tichy and Devanna in their book 'Transformational Leadership' built further on the work of Burns and Bass in organisational and work contexts. They described the hybrid nature of transformational as "*... not due to charisma. It is a behavioural process capable of being learned*".

Bass writing with a research colleague Avolio suggested that *"Transformational leadership is closer to the prototype of leadership that people have in mind when they describe their ideal leader, and it is more likely to provide a role model with which subordinates want to identify"*. Transactional leadership has been the traditional model of leadership with its roots from an organisational or business perspective in the 'bottom line'. Stephen Covey writing in 'Principle-Centred Leadership' suggests that transformational leadership "... focuses on the 'top line'" and offers contrast between the two.

Comparison of Transactional and Transformational Leadership:

- Transactional Leadership:
  - Builds on man's need to get a job done and make a living
  - Is preoccupied with power and position, politics and perks
  - Is mired in daily affairs
  - Is short-term and hard data orientated
  - Focuses on tactical issues
  - Relies on human relations to lubricate human interactions

 - Follows and fulfils role expectations by striving to work effectively within current systems
 - Supports structures and systems that reinforce the bottom line, maximise efficiency, and guarantee short-term profits
- Transformational Leadership ddd. Builds on a man's need for meaning
 - Is preoccupied with purposes and values, morals, and ethics
 - Transcends daily affairs
 - Is orientated towards long-term goals without compromising human values and principles
 - Focuses more on missions and strategies
 - Releases human potential – identifying and developing new talent
 - Designs and redesigns jobs to make them meaningful and challenging
 - Aligns internal structures and systems to reinforce overarching values and goals

Both kinds of leadership are necessary. Transactional leadership has remained the organisational model for many people and organisations who have not moved into or encouraged the transformational role needed to meet the challenges of our changing times.

- "The goal of transformational leadership is to 'transform' people and organisations in a literal sense – to change them in mind and heart; enlarge vision, insight, and understanding; clarify purposes; make behaviour congruent with beliefs, principles, or values; and bring about changes that are permanent, self-perpetuating, and momentum building"

According to Bass and Avolio, transformational leaders display behaviours associated with five transformational styles. Transformational leadership is a process in which the leaders take actions to try to increase their associates' awareness of what is right and important, to raise their associates' motivational maturity and to move their associates to go beyond the associates' own self-interests for the good of the group, the organisation, or society. Such leaders provide their associates with a sense of purpose that goes beyond a simple exchange of rewards for effort provided.

The transformational leaders are proactive in many different and unique ways. These leaders attempt to optimize development, not just performance. Development encompasses the maturation of ability, motivation, attitudes, and values. Such leaders want to elevate the maturity level of the needs of their associates. They convince their associates to strive for a higher level of achievement as well as higher levels of moral and ethical standards.

Through the development of their associates, they optimize the development of their organisation as well. High performing associates build high performing organisations. Hooper and Potter extend the notion of transformational leadership to identify seven key competences of "transcendent leaders": those able to engage the emotional support of their followers and thus effectively transcend change.

- Setting direction
- Setting an example
- Communication
- Alignment
- Bringing out the best in people
- The leader as a change agent
- Providing decision in a crisis and on the ambiguous

DISPERSED LEADERSHIP

The importance of social relations in the leadership contract, the need for a leader to be accepted by their followers and a realisation that no one individual is the ideal leader in all circumstances have given rise to a new school of leadership thought. Referred to as 'informal', 'emergent' or 'dispersed' leadership, this approach argues a less formalised model of leadership where the leaders' role is dissociated from the organisational hierarchy. It is proposed that individuals at all levels in the organisation and in all roles can exert leadership influence over their colleagues and thus influence the overall leadership of the organisation. Heifetz distinguishes between the exercise of "leadership" and the exercise of "authority" – thus dissociating leadership from formal organisational power roles whilst Raelin talks of developing "leaderful" organisations through concurrent, collective and compassionate leadership.

The key to this is a distinction between the notions of "leader" and "leadership". "Leadership" is regarded as a process of sense-making and direction-giving within a group and the "leader" can only be identified on the basis of his/her relationship with others in the social group who are behaving as followers. In this manner, it is quite possible to conceive of the leader as emergent rather than predefined and that their role can only be understood through examining the relationships within the group.

The origins of such an approach have their foundations more in the fields of sociology and politics than the more traditional management literature and draw on concepts such as organisational culture and climate to highlight the contextual nature of leadership. It is a more collective concept, and would argue for a move from an analysis and development of individual leader qualities to an identification of what constitutes an effective leadership process within an organisation. A move in focus from the individuals to the relationships themselves.

THE CONTINGENCY APPROACH TO LEADERSHIP

The trait approach was based on the idea that leadership can be predicted by considering the impact of one variable, the personality of the leader. The style approach was also based on the idea that leadership can be explained through the effect of one variable, the manner by which the leader leads. The situational approach was likewise based on the idea that the style that a leader should adopt is based on one variable, the situation in which the leader is in. The contingency approach to leadership is based on the idea that scientists can account for leadership by examining the ways in which two or more variables work together to determine leadership. As we have discussed, the various earlier approaches were unsuccessful in describing how leadership works. In contrast, there is some reason to believe that considering the impact of multiple variables simultaneously may lead to some success.

The most well known example of a contingency perspective towards leadership is Fiedler's "contingency theory" (1964, 1978). Fiedler's work involved not only the relationship between trait and situation, but also style variables. He thus incorporated into his theory all of the various approaches that we have discussed.

In the following section, we will describe Fiedler's theory in detail. We shall begin with his proposed leadership trait and its effect on leadership style. We will then turn to his typology of situations. We shall finish our discussion of Fiedler's work by examining his view concerning the manner in which trait and situation interact.

LEADER TRAIT - LPC

Fiedler devised a test that he used to help him determine what he could consider a leadership trait. Imagine that you are taking this test. You are given a questionnaire with the following opening instructions:

Think of all the people you have ever known or with whom you have worked. Describe the one person with whom it has been the most difficult to work. In other words, think of the person who has been your least preferred coworker. In order to describe the person, rate him or her on a scale of 8 (positive side) to 1 (negative side) on the following pairs of items:

Pleasant/Unpleasant	Friendly/Unfriendly
accepting/rejecting	relaxed/tense
close/distant	warm/cold
supportive/hostile	interesting/boring
harmonious/quarrelsome	cheerful/gloomy
open/guarded	loyal/backbiting
trustworthy/untrustworthy	considerate/inconsiderate
nice/nasty	agreeable/disagreeable
sincere/insincere	kind/unkind

According to Fiedler, your answers to this questionnaire indicate the degree to which you possess a certain trait. For want of a better name, Fiedler called this permanent characteristic the "Least Preferred Coworker" trait. Scientists call it "LPC" for short. What is this characteristic? Fiedler would not necessarily agree with our interpretation of LPC, but the following discussion reveals how we believe LPC functions.

"High" LPC score. Suppose your answers on the questionnaire averaged 6 or higher on each item. This would give you a total score of at least 108 out of a possible total score of 144. With this high score, Fiedler would say that you are a "high" LPC person. What does this mean? As you recall, Fiedler's questionnaire asked you to describe the person you would least like to have as a coworker. A high score on this questionnaire means that you have judged this "least preferred coworker" to be, nevertheless, a pleasant, friendly individual. The evaluation may seem a bit of an inconsistency on your part.

However, what you have done is come to two separate conclusions about the person. On the one hand, you do not want to work with him or her. You have made a negative task-oriented judgement of the person. On the other hand, you think the person is relaxed, friendly, and so on. You have thereby made a positive social judgement of this person. Apparently, you are able to differentiate between how this least preferred coworker is as a worker and how he or she is as a person. In essence, you are able to separate the task and social aspects of the people around you. This ability makes you a high LPC person.

"Low" LPC score. In contrast, suppose your answers on each item on the questionnaire averaged 3 or lower. This would give you a low score, of only 54 at most, with 18 points being the lowest possible outcome. In this case you have judged your least preferred coworker to be an unfriendly, unpleasant person. This means that you give your coworker a negative rating for both task-oriented and social skills. The implication is that you cannot differentiate between the person's abilities as a worker and his or her skills as a person. You appear to be unable to separate the task and social aspects of people. This makes you a "low" LPC person.

LPC and leadership. How does the LPC trait affect a person in a leadership position? It appears that LPC has an influence on the leadership style that the person prefers to use. High LPC leaders like to follow a style that is maintenance oriented. When they feel pressured, they try to relieve the pressure by improving social relationships.

Low LPC leaders, on the other hand, prefer a task-oriented style. They receive their greatest satisfaction from the successful performance of a work assignment. When they feel pressure, they respond by working harder on the task than they had previously. In comparison with high LPC leaders, Fiedler has found that low LPC people tend to be more task-oriented during group discussion. They ask for and give more suggestions, demand greater member participation, and make negatively toned statements more often. The low LPC leaders also tend to be more active. They talk and interrupt more frequently and control the conversation to a greater degree than high LPC people do. Finally, there is a third possible type of LPC trait. This is medium LPC. Medium

LPC people have scores from each questionnaire item that average between 3 and 6, with total points ranging from 54 to 108. Fiedler finds that these people are socially independent. They are unconcerned with other people's evaluations of them and uninterested in leadership. Beyond identifying that they can exist, Fiedler ignores medium LPC people in his leadership theory.

GROUP SITUATION

One of the strong points of Fiedler's theory is the way in which he views the group situation. He does not present an unorganized list of possible circumstances. Instead, Fiedler has turned his attention to the features that make up a circumstance. This viewpoint has led to an orderly typology of group situations.

In general, Fiedler classifies situations according to their favourableness to a group leader. Different features within the circumstance can increase or decrease how favourable the circumstance is for a leader. Favourableness is the extent to which a leader can make decisions and take actions in his or her group. Further, it is the degree to which a leader can be confident these decisions and actions will lead to the outcomes that he or she intended.

Specifically, Fiedler defines situations in terms of the following three features:

- Leader-member relations. This is the most important feature. Fiedler defines it as the degree to which a leader has the support and loyalty of the other group members. He categorizes this feature as existing only at either end of the continuum. The continuum runs from "good" to "bad." If relations are good, the leader is confident that group members will follow his or her directions. According to our definition above of "favourableness," good relations are favourable to the leader. If relations are bad, a leader lacks confidence. This is unfavourable for him or her.
- Task structure. This feature is half as important as leader-member relations. Fiedler defines it as the extent to which the group can clearly specify the requirements for completing the task. The task structure also exists along a continuum. "Clear" is at one end of the continuum, and "unclear" is at the other end. A task structure is clear if the group members know the requirements for completing the task, if there is only one method for performing the task, if there is only one best solution, and if the group can verify whether a proposed solution is the best one. This is a favourable structure for leaders. In contrast, the task structure is unclear if the group members do not know the requirements for completing the task, if there is more than one method for performing the task, if there may be many "best" solutions, and if the group cannot verify which proposal is the best. Such a situation is unfavourable for a leader.

- Position power. This feature is half as significant for a group situation as task structure is, and thus one-fourth as important as leader-member relations. Fiedler defines position power as the extent to which a leader has legitimacy in a group. A leader's legitimacy is measured by the degree to which the leader has a position that allows him or her to reward and punish the other group members. The continuum for this feature runs from "strong" to "weak." A strong level of position power is favourable for a leader, whereas a weak level is unfavourable. A leader has strong position power if he or she has legitimacy as part of an organisational chain of command, as in the military. Position power is weak if a leader does not have such legitimacy.

THE PERCEPTUAL APPROACH TO LEADERSHIP

One of the most important legacies of the emergent approach is the idea that a leader has successfully emerged from a group when the members of the group believe that person to be the group's leader. Thus, the emergent approach emphasizes the notion that group members' perceptions about leadership are critical to the process of leader emergence.

The perceptual approach to leadership grows out of that notion. It is an attempt to understand how the average group member judges the leadership abilities of other members. Hence, it focuses on an important aspect of the leader emergence process

The perspectives we have discussed differ mainly in only one point. This is in regard to which factors they claim are important. Respectively, we have seen approaches towards leadership that maintain that a leader's success is due to his or her traits, his or her style, or the situation of the group. Further, we have discussed viewpoints that claim that the most important factors affecting leadership are the behaviours of all group members or the interaction between a leader's traits and the situation of the group. Despite these differences, scientists who advocate these approaches are united in their belief that they can objectively define "leadership" as a variable. Advocates of the perceptual approach do not share this belief. They believe that leadership exists primarily within the mind of each group member. Thus they believe that the way to study leadership is to examine what group members think leadership is.

IMPRESSION FORMATION PROCESS

The perceptual approach views leadership as an "impression formation process." We discussed the process by which personality impressions. Let's review it now. For example, Sue wants to form an impression of Charlie; so she watches how he behaves. Sue particularly notices attention-grabbing, or salient behaviour, on Charlie's part. Sue then decides whether his character is responsible for his behaviour or if he is just reacting to the situation. If she decides that Charlie is responsible for the way he acts, she forms an impression of him. This impression starts with a trait that describes the behaviour she has observed. The impression then builds, by adding other traits that Sue believes are associated with Charlie's first trait.

"Halo" and "Horns" Effects

If Sue observes something she believes is a "good" trait, she will tend to believe that Charlie has more "good" traits. Scientists call this tendency the "halo effect." If, on the other hand, Sue thinks Charlie has a "bad" initial trait, she will build up her impression by assigning more "bad" traits to him. This is the "horns effect." Finally, Sue will judge whether she likes Charlie based on her impression.

Biases enter into our impressions because of the halo and horns effects. As we have discussed, once we assign a trait to a person, we tend to further assign related traits. We can do this because we have a pre-existing idea of which traits are associated. Such a process of judgement often can be wrong. It is not always true that clumsy people are stupid, for example. We described how the halo effect often causes people to make "good" judgements about persons who are physically attractive. People tend to say that attractive people are intelligent, mentally stable, and so on, without seeing any relevant evidence that this is true. Clearly, attractive people are not always "good" in all ways.

IMPRESSION FORMATION PROCESS AND LEADERSHIP

The way in which we form impressions and make judgements about the leadership ability of our fellow group members works in the same way as any impression formation process. First, we watch the other members of our group to see which leadership behaviours they generally exhibit. We are particularly attentive to the most salient of those behaviours. Next, we decide whether each person's character is responsible for any leadership behaviours or whether the situation is responsible. If we decide that a person is responsible for his or her actions, we form an impression of the person as a leader. Our impression will include not only the behaviours we have actually observed but also the traits that we believe are associated with leadership.

For example, we see that Joan speaks her mind readily. We think that is what a leader should do. We then may come to believe that Joan also has integrity, spirit, organisational skills, and other traits that we think leaders should have, even if we do not see her exhibiting them. We may then decide that Joan is truly the leader of the group.

Behavioural Salience

We have noted that impression formation begins when an observer notices a particularly salient behaviour. Behavioural salience is an important part of the process by which group members come to judge one another's leadership. In fact, some of the variables involved in leader emergence work the way they do because they make a person's behaviour particularly salient.

Amount of communication. When someone is talking, we are likely to pay attention to them. Thus, the more a person talks during group discussion, the more attention they receive from the other members. Given this, it should not be surprising that talkative members are more likely to emerge as leaders than non-talkative members.

Further, anything that increases a talkative member's salience would increase the likelihood of that member emerging as group leader. For example, consistently with the material on deviance and minority, a small subgroup within the larger group is likely to gain the attention of the entire group if they are deviating from the group consensus. Thus, the behaviour of a talkative member of that subgroup would be particularly salient to the rest of the group, and especially likely to emerge as a leader. In their review of literature about the relationship between amount of talk and leader emergence, Mullen *et al.* (1989) found research evidence for this effect.

Seating position. One of the reasons that the ends or head of a table are the "leadership seats" is that a person who sits at one of those positions becomes perceptually salient to the other members of the group. Perceptual salience can increase the odds that a member will become group leader for two reasons. First, they are more likely to be in the normal line of sight of other group members. The other group members are then more likely to direct their attention to them. Second, placing group members where they will receive the comments of other members is likely to lead them to talk frequently. As discussed, frequent talking will likely result in other group members judging them to be leaders.

Implicit Leadership Theories

As we have described, if an observer decides that a person is responsible for their behaviour, the observer begins to form an impression of the person. This impression begins with a trait that describes the observed behaviour, and then grows through the addition of other traits that the observer believes are associated with the first trait.

But where do these beliefs about the association among traits come from? They come from what researchers call implicit personality theories. An implicit personality theory is a person's beliefs about what traits and behaviours go together. For example, people's implicit personality theories usually associate "good" traits, such as intelligence and attractiveness, together. This is the reason why "halo effects" occur in impression formation. Similarly, implicit personality theories normally link "bad" traits, such as clumsiness and stupidity, with one another. This is the source of "horns effects" in impressions.

Research has shown that people have beliefs about the attributes that the "ideal leader" should possess. We can call these beliefs implicit leadership theories. Our own research (Pavitt and Sackaroff, 1990) has shown that implicit leadership theories tend to include traits such as "forceful" and "enthusiastic." These theories also include behaviours such as "states the group's procedure" and "encourages group member participation." Thus, these are included in the list of attributes that most people feel that the "ideal leader" should exhibit.

Group members use these implicit leadership theories when they form impressions of one another's leadership. For example, a group consists of Leon, Marvin, and Bram. Leon believes that an ideal leader who "encourages group member participation" is also "enthusiastic." He saw those two attributes as "going together" in an ideal leader.

This judgement carries over into how Leon judges his fellow group members. For instance, if he were to think that Marvin exhibited a high level of "encouragement" behaviours, he would also judge Marvin as "enthusiastic." If Leon made a negative judgement about someone, he would connect similar negative attributes. If Leon judged that Bram exhibited a low level of encouragement behaviours, he would also think that Bram had low levels of the trait of "enthusiasm."

Leon is basing one judgement on another. He first observes Marvin and Bram and judges how much they encourage group members. As we have noted, Leon then believes that "encouragement" and "enthusiasm" go together in an "ideal leader." Therefore, he uses this belief and his previous judgement to decide how to assign the trait of "enthusiasm" to Marvin and Bram.

Further, group members use their implicit leadership theories as a basis for evaluating one another's leadership skills. If we form an impression of a group member that is similar to our preconceptions of the "ideal leader," then we would judge that group member to be a good leader. Analogously, if our impression is very different from our implicit leadership theory, then we would evaluate that member to be a poor leader.

We can use our example of Leon, Marvin, and Bram again to show this. Leon thought that Marvin had high levels of "encouragement" and "enthusiasm" attributes. Thus, Marvin's attributes were similar to those in Leon's vision of an "ideal leader." Hence, Leon evaluated Marvin as a good leader. In contrast, Leon thought that Bram had low levels of the attributes of "encouragement" and "enthusiasm." Thus, Bram was unlike Leon's vision of an "ideal leader." Accordingly, Leon, judged Bram to be a poor leader.

7

Alternative Framework of Leadership

REVIEW OF COMPETENCIES

From the review of leadership theory, current models and competency frameworks in use throughout the public and private sectors it would appear that a somewhat limited version of "transformational" leadership is being promoted. Most frameworks go beyond simple definitions of behaviours, to also consider some of the cognitive, affective and inter-personal qualities of leaders, however, although the role of followers may be recognised it is usually in a rather simplistic, unidirectional manner. Leadership, therefore, is conceived as a set of values, qualities and behaviours exhibited by the leader that encourage the participation, development, and commitment of followers. It is remarkable how few of the frameworks refer to the leader's ability to "listen" and none refer to the word to "follow".

The "leader" is thus promoted as the sole source of "leadership". He/she is seen to act as an energiser, catalyst and visionary equipped with a set of tools that can be applied across a diverse range of situations and contexts. Whilst contingency and situational leadership factors may be considered, they are not generally viewed as barriers to an individuals' ability to lead under different circumstances. Fewer than half of the frameworks cited refers directly to the leaders' ability to respond and adapt their style to different circumstances.

In addition to the "soft" skills, the leader is also expected to display excellent information processing, project management, customer service and delivery skills, along with proven business and political acumen. They build partnerships, walk the talk, show incredible drive and enthusiasm, and get things done. Furthermore, the leader demonstrates innovation, creativity and thinks "outside the box".

They are entrepreneurs who identify opportunities - they like to be challenged and they're prepared to take risks. Of interest, too, is the emphasis on the importance of values such as honesty, integrity, empathy, trust, ethics and valuing diversity. The leader is expected to show a true concern for people that is drawn from a deep level of self-awareness and personal reflection.

This almost evangelistic notion of the leader as a multi-talented individual with diverse skills, personal qualities and a large social conscience, however, posses a number of difficulties. Firstly it represents almost a return to the trait theory of leadership, just with a wider range of attributes. Secondly when you attempt to combine attributes from across a range of frameworks the result is an unwieldy, almost over-powering list of qualities such as that identified in the CEML research. And thirdly there is little evidence in practice that the "transformational" leader is any more effective than his/her alternatives.

Personal qualities of the leader are undoubtedly important but are unlikely to be sufficient in themselves for the emergence and exercise of leadership. Furthermore, the manner in which these qualities translate into behaviour and group interaction is likely to be culturally specific and thus depend on a whole host of factors, such as the nature of the leader, followers, task, organisational structure, national and corporate cultures, etc.

LEADERSHIP MODELS AND COMPETENCY FRAMEWORKS

This part of the report will look at some different leadership models and frameworks used in practice across the public and private sector organisations. The chosen models were selected as the organisations were known to researchers at the Centre for Leadership Studies and/or details of the framework were publicly available. They are not intended to represent a comprehensive, or even representative, sample of available frameworks but rather a preliminary examination of readily available materials. The inclusion of a particular framework does not necessarily indicate that it is in any way assumed "better" or more "typical" than those that were not included and, indeed, there may well be many excellent models which have not been discussed.

To many participating organisations the material reviewed represents an element of their "competitive advantage" and is thus confidential. We have therefore chosen in this report, not to include the full framework but simply to refer to the key elements. Where further information is available on the Internet we have included the web address. For ease of presentation, they have been divided into private-sector, public-sector and generic frameworks.

PRIVATE SECTOR FRAMEWORKS

AstraZeneca Leadership Capabilities

The AstraZeneca Leadership Capabilities were defined shortly after merger in 1999 and have been used in performance management, development planning and management planning across the global company. They are a central part of leadership development programmes and a 360 degree feedback tool has been developed to support their application.

The leadership behaviours provide a link between business priorities and the AZ values of: respect for the individual and for diversity; openness, honest, trust and support for each other; integrity and high ethical standards; and leadership by example at all levels. There are seven key capabilities, each with associated indicators/behaviours:

- Provides clarity about strategic direction
- Ensures commitment
- Focuses on delivery
- Builds relationships
- Develops people
- Demonstrates personal conviction
- Builds self-awareness

BAE Performance Centred Leadership

Performance Centred Leadership competencies provide a set of related behaviours used to improve business performance. They have been developed from 360 degree feedback information, benchmarked against the competencies of high performing organisations, changed to reflect input from the Senior leader focus groups and statistically evaluated by London University. The competencies and related behaviours are used to evaluate performance in Peer Recognition and Employee opinion survey, identifying development opportunities through 360 degree feedback and are used as part of the appointment process. There are five core competences, each with a set of related behaviours:

- Achieving High Performance
- Focusing on the Customer
- Developing Others
- Continuously Improving
- Working Together

The framework forms a basis for leadership development in BAE which is fully integrated with all other strategic processes in the organisation through the Performance Centred Leadership Development Framework.

Federal Express Leadership Qualities

FedEx has a system for rating aspiring leaders according to 9 attributes:

- Charisma
- Individual consideration
- Intellectual stimulation
- Courage
- Dependability
- Flexibility
- Integrity
- Judgement
- Respect for others

Lufthansa Leadership Compass

The Lufthansa Leadership Compass sets out a framework for effective leadership that is used by the Lufthansa School of Business in its leadership development education. It includes the following six key categories, which set out a range of skills and behaviours including: vision, decisiveness, concern for people, self-reflection and professional know-how:

- Entrepreneurial leadership
- Breakthrough problem solving
- Winning others
- Leading people
- Attitude and drive
- International business competencies

Development Centres based on this framework are used to help "high potential" employees define their current position and determine the next steps for their professional career. This involves a self-assessment exercise, development centre and a post DC process whereby the participant develops an individual development plan with the support and coaching of their superior. It is intended that this process should occur about 1 year before moving into a C grade post.

Philips Leadership Competencies

Six Leadership Competencies define the behaviour that is required to achieve business success in Phillips. They provide a balanced approach, stating the importance of task aspects while recognising that results are obtained through people. These competencies are as follows:

- Shows determination to achieve excellent results
- Focuses on the market
- Finds better ways
- Demands top performance
- Inspires commitment
- Develops self and others

Shell Leadership Framework

The Leadership Framework used by Shell includes nine key elements as indicated below:

- Builds Shared Vision
- Champions Customer Focus
- Maximises Business Opportunities
- Demonstrates Professional Mastery
- Displays Personal Effectiveness
- Demonstrates Courage

- Motivates, Coaches and Develops
- Values Differences
- Delivers Results

Vodafone Global Leadership Competencies

The Vodafone leadership competencies underlying their Global Leadership Programme are divided into five categories:

- Values communication
- International team development
- Strategic vision
- Building organisational capability
- Commercial drive

PUBLIC SECTOR FRAMEWORKS

Senior Civil Service Competency Framework

This framework sets out key attributes that have been identified by Civil Service Corporate Management as required for the *Senior Civil Service* (SCS). There are six main sets of competences, each with a series of related behaviours. The competencies are as follows:

- Giving purpose and direction
- Making a personal impact
- Thinking strategically
- Getting the best from people
- Learning and improving
- Focusing on delivery

DfES - Management and Leadership Attributes

This framework sets out what is expected of managers and leaders in the Department for Education and Skills as the organisation moves forward to deliver the Department's Strategic Framework. It is based on the SCS Competency Framework and was developed following a period of internal consultation in the DfES. It distinguishes between "effective" and "ineffective" behaviours in relation to three clusters of attributes each of which comprises a set of behaviours, skills and knowledge.

- Interpersonal Attributes: Making a personal impact, Giving purpose and direction
- Delivery Attributes: Focussing on delivery, Thinking strategically
- Improvement Attributes: Getting the best from people, Learning and improving

The framework takes a situational/contingency view of leadership in that it states that:

- Competent DfES managers and leaders at all levels will demonstrate varying combinations of these attributes in different circumstances and at different times. The effective behaviours and skills within each attribute are examples of what competent managers and leaders do when they are modelling good management and leadership – they may not do all of them all of the time!"

Northern Ireland Senior Civil Service Core Criteria

This is the Northern Ireland equivalent of the SCS Competency Framework, covering 8 key competencies including leadership.

- Leadership: Envisioning, Team building, Standards and integrity
- Conceptual and strategic thinking and planning: Conceptual thinking, Strategic thinking, Planning
- Focus on outcomes: Customer orientation, Outcomes focus, Meeting and improving performance standards
- Managing and developing staff: Managing staff effectively, Promoting and facilitating development
- Managing relationships and partners
- Communication: Oral/written, Influencing, Presentation
- Managing resources innovatively: Cost awareness, Improvement orientation
- Personal effectiveness: Change orientation, Develop orientation, Self confidence and resilience, Commitment, Intellect in action

Scottish Executive Framework

This framework, devised for the Scottish parliament, identifies seven sets of criteria and, for each, what everyone should do and what managers and leaders should also do. Indicators are also given as to when development needs may be identified. The specific leadership dimensions of the framework are as follows:

- Achieving
- Self management
- Analysis and investigation
- Outward focus
- Communication
- Managing others
- Working with others

Ministry of Defence

The MoD uses a number of competency frameworks related to leadership for annual appraisal, including a revised SCS Competency Framework and *Officers Joint Appraisal Report* (OJAR).

MoD Senior Civil Service Competency Framework

This is based on the SCS Competency Framework and redefines it as indicated below.

- Leading and working together: Working together, Providing the lead, Enabling others to give of their best
- Being personally effective: Striving to achieve results, Promoting change and continuous improvement, Communicating and influencing, Solving problems and taking decisions, Taking a wider perspective
- Delivering results: Focussing on customers and service delivery, Developing and delivering effective policies and programmes, Managing work and resources to achieve results, Exploiting information and knowledge

Officers Joint Appraisal Report

The OJAR, introduced in March 2001, covers 10 performance attributes explored during annual appraisals for officers across the forces. These are as follows:

- Leadership
- Professional effectiveness
- Effective intelligence
- Judgement
- Management
- Initiative
- Reliability
- Powers of communication
- Subordinate development
- Courage and values.

EO for Local Government – Compendium of Competencies

The *Employers' Organisation* for local government's (EO) role is to help councils achieve the high standards of people management needed to ensure the continuous improvement of services. Their web site includes a compendium of leadership competencies developed by and/or used by local authorities across the UK. These have been classified into 20 different categories as indicated below.

- Change: includes Challenge, Leadership for Change, Managing Change/Strategic Thinking.
- Communication: includes Communicating, Communication and Customer Care, Listening and Organising
- Corporate Focus: includes Collective Responsibility, Corporate Focus, Developing a Learning Organisation, Evaluating and Improving Organisational Performance, Organisational Awareness, Organisational Effectiveness

- Customer Focus: includes Commitment to Quality Customer Service, Customer Focused Service Delivery, Sharpening Customer and Service Focus
- Decision Making: includes Analysing and Solving Problems, Decision Making, Identifying and Solving Problems, Judgement.
- Equality and Diversity: includes Achieving Equal Opportunities, Demonstrating Leadership in Implementing Equalities, Managing Equitably, Valuing Diversity
- Focus on Results: includes Achievement Focused, Focusing on Results, Managing for Results
- Impact and Influence: includes Acting Assertively, Impact and Influence, Interpersonal Skills, Networking and Influencing, Partnership Working, Persuasiveness
- Information Management: includes Gathering and Using Information, Getting Unbiased Information, Giving Clear Information, Information and Communication Management, Searching for Information
- Integrity: includes Behaving Ethically, Integrity
- Leading People: includes Appraising People and Performance, Developing Others, Disciplining and Counselling, Enabling, Leadership, Managing People, Managing, Developing and Understanding Others, Personal and Staff Development, Training, Coaching and Delegating, Valuing People
- Partnerships: includes Community Leadership, Co-operating with Others, Leading Integrated Working, Networking and Influencing, Working in Partnership
- Personal Management and Drive: includes Determination, Managing Self, Motivation and Drive, Personal Effectiveness, Personal Management, Planning and Scheduling Work, Setting Goals and Standards, Time Management and Prioritising
- Political Awareness: includes Democratic Support, Political and Organisational Awareness, Working Competently within the Political Environment
- Project and Process Management: includes Managing Projects, Organisational and Project Management
- Resource Management: includes Managing Resources
- Safety
- Service Improvement: includes Continuous Improvement to Service Delivery, Delivering Excellence, Leading the Challenge on Continuous Service Improvement, Managing the Executive Programme and Performance, Service Co-ordination and Management, Sharpening Customer and Service Focus
- Strategic Focus: includes: Acting Strategically, Developing Strategy, Managing Change/Strategic Thinking, Strategic Behaviour, Vision

- Team Building: includes Building Teams, Working in and Developing Teams

NHS Leadership Qualities Framework

The NHS Leadership Qualities Framework, developed by the NHS Leadership Centre, identifies 15 key qualities across three broad clusters: Personal qualities, Setting direction and Delivering the service.

- Personal qualities: Self belief, Self awareness, Self management, Drive for improvement, Personal integrity
- Setting Direction: Seizing the future, Intellectual flexibility, Broad scanning, Political astuteness, Drive for results
- Delivering the service: Leading change through people, Holding to account, Empowering others, Effective and strategic influencing, Collaborative working

As with the DfES model, there is an emphasis on the situational nature of leadership and an attempt to indicate the circumstances under which different leadership qualities will take precedence.

National College for School Leadership – Hay McBer Model

In 1999 the NCSL commissioned Hay McBer to research leadership in schools. This research led to the development of a model of school leadership which formed the basis of further discussion. The NCSL now seems to be moving away from this approach towards an integrated leadership development framework. The 17 school leadership qualities in the Hay McBer Model are as follows:

- Analytical Thinking
- Challenge and Support
- Confidence
- Developing Potential
- Drive for Improvement
- Holding People Accountable
- Impact and Influence
- Information Seeking
- Initiative
- Integrity
- Personal Convictions
- Respect for Others
- Strategic Thinking
- Teamworking
- Transformational Leadership
- Understanding the Environment
- Understanding Others

Senior Executive Service

This framework sets out leadership competencies for the *Senior Executive Service* (SES) in the US. It identifies 26 competencies across five categories:

- Leading Change: Continual Learning, Creativity and Innovation, Resilience, Service Motivation, Strategic Thinking, Vision.
- Leading People: Conflict Management, Leveraging Diversity, Integrity/Honesty, Team Building
- Results Driven: Accountability, Customer Service, Decisiveness, Entrepreneurship, Problem Solving, Technical Credibility
- Business Acumen: Financial Management, Human Resources Management, Technology Management
- Building Coalitions/Communication: Influencing/Negotiating, Interpersonal Skills, Oral Communication, Partnering, Political Savvy, Written Communication

GENERIC FRAMEWORKS

CEML Framework of Management and Leadership Abilities

The Council for Excellence in Management and Leadership conducted an extensive piece of research using primary and secondary data sources to identify a key set of management and leadership abilities. The resultant framework identified 83 distinct management and leadership abilities which were grouped into 8 meta-groups and three generic categories. The categories and meta-groups are as follows:

- Thinking Abilities: Think Strategically
- People Abilities: Manage self, Manage and lead people, Lead direction and culture, Manage relationships
- Task Abilities: Manage information, Manage resources, Manage activities and quality

METO Management Standards

These are the previous management standards developed by METO, the Management Education Training Organisation. The seven key roles are as follows:

- Manage Activities
- Manage Resources
- Manage People
- Manage Information
- Manage Energy
- Manage Quality
- Manage projects

Investors in People Leadership and Management Model

The IIP Leadership and Management Model sets out a framework for the assessment of leadership and management capabilities in relation to the new "leadership and management" dimension of the Investors in People Award. There are four main principles each with associated indicators.

EFQM Business Excellence Model

The European Foundation for Quality Management Award is an internationally recognised quality award based around business processes. The leadership dimension covers the following four areas:

- 1a Leaders develop the mission, vision and values and are role models of a culture of Excellence;
- 1b Leaders are personally involved in ensuring the organisation's management system is developed, implemented and continuously improved;
- 1c Leaders are involved with customers, partners and representatives of society;
- 1d Leaders motivate, support and recognise the organisation's people.

Institute of Chartered Management – Chartered Management Skills

Chartered Manager candidates need to demonstrate learning, development and impact in the workplace against two of these six categories.

- Leading People
- Meeting Customer Needs
- Managing Change
- Managing Information and Knowledge
- Managing Activities and Resources
- Managing yourself

IMF Management Competencies

As a first step in fostering effective managerial practices, the International Monetary Fund has defined a set of effective managerial behaviours, encapsulated in management competencies. Management competencies comprise a set of critical knowledge, skills, and behaviours that lead to effective management practices.

These management competencies are tools you, as a manager, can use to perform your supervisory functions. Effective performance of each competency is described by a series of behavioural benchmarks. Below are the 15 different management competencies, grouped in 6 broad categories.

- Intellectual Leadership Factor: Sound Judgement/Analytical Skills, Strategic Vision

- Work Management Factor: Planning and Organising, Drive for Results, Adaptability
- Communication Factor: Oral Presentation Skills, Creating Open Communication, Written Communication Skills
- Interpersonal Factor: Building Relationships, Negotiating and Influencing, Country/Client Relations
- People Management Factor: Motivating Performance, Delegating, Fostering Teamwork, Appraising and Developing Staff

IMF Management competencies are used in a number of ways:

- They are the starting point for developing managerial performance expectations. Competencies can help senior managers articulate the skills needed to be an effective manager—as distinct from those needed to be an effective economist or technical contributor.
- Competencies are the basis for assessing potential managers in the Management Development Center.
- Competencies are the basis for identifying training and development areas.
- They form a common basis on which to assess managers within and across departments.

Hamlin's Generic Model of Managerial and Leadership Effectiveness

This model is based upon a meta analysis of leadership and management behaviours in four UK public-sector organisations. It distinguishes between positive and negative indications of management and leadership.

- Positive indicators:
  - Effective organisation and planning/proactive management
  - Participative and supportive leadership/Proactive team leadership
  - Empowerment and delegation
  - Genuine concern for people/Looks after the interests and development needs of staff
  - Open and personal management approach/Inclusive decision making
  - Communicates and consults widely/Keeps people informed
- Negative indicators:
  - Shows lack of consideration or concern for staff/ineffective autocratic or dictatorial style of management
  - Uncaring, self serving management/undermining, depriving and intimidating behaviour
  - Tolerance of poor performance and low standards/ignoring and avoidance
  - Abdicating roles and responsibilities
  - Resistant to new ideas and change/negative approach

The results have been compared to the Zenger Miller Grass-Roots Leadership Model and used to argue for a universalistic model of leadership/ management.

The Zenger Miller Grass-Roots Leadership Model

This model was developed from empirical research in which collected 1,871 "critical incidents" from 450 US and Canadian organisations. The model has been refined from the original Zenger Miller CLIMB strategies model.

- Create a compelling future: Create and describe a vision, Manager changes required to realize a vision
- Let the customer drive the organisation: Respond to identified customer needs
- Involve every mind: Support individual effort, Support team effort, Share information, Make decisions that solve problems, Manage work horizontally, Build personal credibility
- Manage work horizontally: Manage cross-functional processes, Display technical skills, Manage projects, Manage time and resources
- Build personal credibility: Take initiative beyond job requirements, Take responsibility for your own actions and the actions of your group, Handle emotions in yourself and others, Display professional ethics, Show compassion, Make credible presentations

EXPERIENCE OF USING COMPETENCY FRAMEWORKS

The very fact that organisations will go to great effort and expense to develop their own leadership framework is perhaps evidence in itself that there is no "one size fits all" even though there does seem to be a remarkably great degree of similarity between them. Perhaps, in this case, it is not so much the framework in itself that is important, but the process by which it is developed.

The identification of what is required of leaders and the manner in which this integrates with other activities is an important voyage of discovery for the organisation and one for which it is vital that key players take ownership.

To achieve this takes time, reflection and discussion - simply printing off or copying a pre-defined set of standards wouldn't achieve the same results. In the organisations with whom we've spoken the leadership competency framework is an integral element of the leadership development process – whereby it is used to define the content and mechanism of delivery and to help individuals measure and explore their own level of development. It frequently forms the basis of the 360-degree feedback process, by which they can monitor their progress and identify personal learning and development needs, and also underlies assessment and appraisals. Astrazeneca expressed the importance of keeping the framework to a manageable number of dimensions so that it remains easier to operationalise.

Experience of larger frameworks confirms that longer lists may result in a box-ticking mentality which does little, if anything, to enhance leadership and management capability. A further challenge also remains: what is the realistic life-span of a framework? Once formalised and implemented it is becomes easy to stop challenging and developing the framework - the search for leadership competencies within an organisation could thus become self-fulfilling and stagnate. Like any continuous improvement process, the development and identification of leadership talent needs to remain dynamic and current. It needs to move with the times and encourage creativity and diversification.

EVIDENCE-BASED LEADERSHIP DEVELOPMENT

Whilst it has been argued that the leadership and management frameworks may suffer from an over-emphasis on the individual leader, they may also suffer from a lack of research basis. For many of the frameworks little, if no information, was available on how they were developed and it seems likely that no detailed research was conducted. Alan Hooper reported that following his research with companies to develop the "transcendent leadership" competencies he found the majority of corporate leadership frameworks to be loosely based on notions of the company culture, guidance of the CEO and "what seems to be acceptable around here".

Even for those frameworks where research has been performed, there are some concerning methodological omissions. For example, the NHS Leadership Framework was developed following interviews with 150 Chief Executives yet is being used to direct leadership development at all levels within the organisation. Such a lack of empirical grounding is concerning for a number of reasons.

Firstly, there is a danger that the qualities identified have little bearing on the effectiveness of leadership in the organisation. Secondly, there is a danger of forming a clique, whereby people are selected into leadership positions because of their similarity to existing leaders, thus neglecting those individuals who don't fit this mould and forming leadership "blind spots".

And thirdly, a lack of concern over research at this stage is frequently translated into a lack of concern for the evaluation of leadership development activities. Research is increasingly stressing the necessity of building evaluation structures into leadership and management development. Huge spending is made on this type of activity yet to most organisations this remains a leap of faith. It may be a difficult task to evaluate beyond immediate post-course reactions but the ability to identify whether such activities are leading to behavioural, attitudinal and organisational changes is a major source of competitive advantage.

It not only enables the improvement of existing provision and identification of future provision but also an appreciation of the wider-scale impact of the intervention. Multi-stakeholder evaluation, for example, explores the aspirations and experiences of diverse stakeholder group and may well reveal that activities beneficial for one may have a negative effect on others.

James and Burgoyne argue that "evaluation, like breathing, is not optional" whether done formally or informally it will always influence subsequent decisions about investments and budgets. It would be best, therefore, that this is based on some proof rather than vague aspirations – few businesses would survive if they based business decisions on such weak logic.

EMERGENT AND COLLECTIVE LEADERSHIP DEVELOPMENT

The findings of our review are very similar to those of another recent review of leadership and leadership development literature for the Learning and Skills Research Centre. The authors developed a useful model for the consideration of both leadership and leadership development along two dimensions.

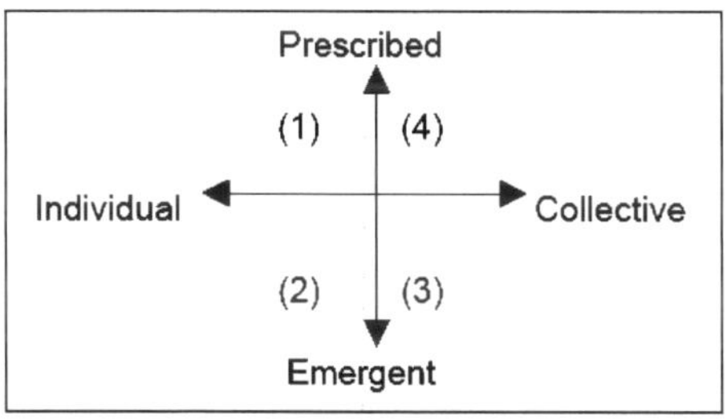

The model proposes that leadership development initiatives differ in the degree to which they focus on individual or collective processes and prescriptive or emergent models and approaches. It is proposed that the vast majority of leadership initiatives lie within cell of the grid, with about 15 per cent in cell and the remaining 5 per cent on the collective side. The authors also argue that there is an almost exclusive emphasis on the leadership inputs and outputs with little attention being paid to the processes in between and they challenge us to consider a more "relational" notion of leadership. Such an emergent and collective view of leadership is reflected. In the Lead2Lead and Leadership Game approaches, for example, far greater attention is paid to the processes than the specific inputs or outputs.

To this extent, the process is conceived as one which is likely to generate leadership insights, understanding and awareness but the exact inputs will be different in every case and the outputs will emerge from the process rather than being predefined. Indeed, there is also an extent to which emergent and collective methodologies are used within programmes closely associated with a competencies/qualities framework. For example, the study tours and exchanges on the NHS Chief Executives programme assume that relevant knowledge and understanding will somehow arise from these experiences.

Furthermore, in a review of the Experienced Chief Executives Development Programme, the programme designers report how they used Activity Theory as a basis for programme conception. The programme was "designed to help participants step back from day-today pressures, reflect on the activities in which they were engaged and their inherent dilemmas, and explore new options".

The National College for School Leadership is likewise looking for means to develop a more collective form of leadership within schools. It is moving away from the relatively individualistic approach of the Hay McBer framework to a more fluid Leadership Development Framework that specifies a strategy for developing school leaders at all levels.

AN ALTERNATIVE TO LEADERSHIP AND MANAGEMENT FRAMEWORKS?

In our research and discussion related to the current review, we have begun to hear voices of dissent. The Scottish Leadership Foundation, for example, is currently working with public-sector organisations in Scotland to move them away from competency and standards frameworks.

The National College for School Leadership seems to be reconsidering its position; and the Institute for Leadership and Management is launching a process to develop its own leadership standards in reaction to the current project under way by the Management Standards Centre.

It seems much has already been done to define what "qualities", "competencies", "standards" should be sought from our leaders but, as the current debate would imply, this has done little to improve the quality of our leaders and leadership other than, perhaps, for specific organisations. Take, for example, the work of CEML on identifying management and leadership abilities.

They produced a list of 83 attributes based on a meta analysis of previous research, however, this has not been adopted as the norm as the current exercise contests. What is to ensure that the new National Occupational Standards in Management and Leadership will be any more successful? Perhaps, therefore, it is time to conceive of alternative ways to view management and leadership standards:

- Should we be recommending ethically and socially acceptable forms of behaviour? – almost a "Leadership Charter" that leaders can sign up to?
- Should we be promoting "mindsets" that leaders need to master rather than the behaviours they exhibit?
- Should we be questioning leadership styles, approaches, behaviours and methods to reveal their weaknesses rather than searching for some Holy Grail of leadership?

- Should we focus instead on leadership development to explore what does and doesn't help improve organisational performance rather than providing a post-hoc description of leadership qualities?

In many ways a leadership competencies or standards framework is like a psychometric profile – useful for illuminating current practice in comparison to a norm but dangerous and potentially damaging if misused. To work as a psychometric assessor you must be qualified in the tools' application and interpretation – perhaps the same should be true of leadership and management frameworks to prevent their abuse.

LEADERSHIP BY A GROUP

In contrast to individual leadership, some organisations have adopted group leadership. In this situation, more than one person provides direction to the group as a whole. Some organisations have taken this approach in hopes of increasing creativity, reducing costs, or downsizing. Others may see the traditional leadership of a boss as costing too much in team performance. In some situations, the maintenance of the boss becomes too expensive - either by draining the resources of the group as a whole, or by impeding the creativity within the team, even unintentionally.

A common example of group leadership involves cross-functional teams. A team of people with diverse skills and from all parts of an organisation assembles to lead a project. A team structure can involve sharing power equally on all issues, but more commonly uses rotating leadership. The team member(s) best able to handle any given phase of the project become(s) the temporary leader(s).

For example, the Orpheus orchestra has performed for over thirty years without a conductor — that is, without a sole leader. As a team of over 25 members, it has drawn discriminating audiences, and has produced over 60 recordings for Deutsche Grammophon in successful competition with other world-class orchestras.

Rather than an autocratic or charismatic conductor deciding the overall conception of a work and then dictating how each individual is to perform the individual tasks, the Orpheus team generally selects a different "core group" for each piece of music. The core group provides leadership in working out the details of the piece, and presents their ideas to the whole team. Members of the whole team then participate in refining the final conception, rehearsal, and product, including checking from various places in the auditorium how the sound balances and verifying the quality of the final recording.

At times the entire Orpheus team may follow a single leader, but whom the team follows rotates from task to task, depending on the capabilities of its members.

The orchestra has developed seminars and training sessions for adapting the Orpheus Process to business.

CO-LEADERSHIP

As a compromise between individual leadership and an open group, leadership structures of two or three people or entities occur commonly. Ancient Rome preferred two consuls to a single king, and the Roman Empire grew to accommodate two Emperors - those of the East and of the West - simultaneously. The Middle Ages saw leadership divided between the secular and spiritual realms - between Emperor and Pope. Some groups - often left-wing or Green in orientation - employ a co-leader structure today.

Triumvirates have long served to balance leadership ambitions - notably in Rome in the first century BC, but also as recently as in the Soviet Union troikas of the 20th century. Compare the separation of powers (legislative, judicial and executive) formalised (for example) in the constitution of the United States of America.

DIVIDED LEADERSHIP

Whereas sometimes one can readily and definitively identify the locus of leadership, in other circumstances the situation remains obscured. Pre-modern Japan offers a classical example: the emperors provided symbolic and religious leadership, but the shoguns embodied virtually all political and administrative leadership.

Similar dichotomies appear in many places and in many periods. Any constitutional monarch has a potentially confusing relationship with the day-to-day leader (typically a prime minister) who remains (at least theoretically) subordinate - socially as well as politically. Regents may stand against monarchs (and their supporters) during the minority or absence of those monarchs. Heads of state may operate at cross-purposes with heads of government (see governmental co-habitation). Political leaders may or may not align closely with religious leaders. And in federal-type systems, regional leadership and its potentially different systems may cross swords with national leaders. Not to mention the potentially conflicting leadership manifestations of boards of directors and of Chief Executives.

Greiner's study of the language of U.S. Presidents examined the relationship between leader and followers and observed that changes have taken place in the presidential use of words that define the leader and the community as one. Modern US presidents have an observed tendency to make more use of inclusive words like we, us and our in their inaugural speeches. The use of inclusive words may suggest an effort by these democratically selected leaders to make the community work together to solve problems collectively.

Aristocratic thinkers have postulated that leadership depends on one's blue blood or genes: monarchy takes an extreme view of the same idea, and may prop up its assertions against the claims of mere aristocrats by invoking divine sanction: see the divine right of kings. Contrariwise, more democratically-inclined theorists have pointed to examples of meritocratic leaders, such as the Napoleonic marshals profiting from careers open to talent.

In the autocratic/paternalistic strain of thought, traditionalists recall the role of leadership of the Roman pater familias. Feminist thinking, on the other hand, may damn such models as patriarchal and posit against them emotionally-attuned, responsive, and consensual empathetic guidance and matriarchies.

Comparable to the Roman tradition, the views of Confucianism on "right living" relate very much to the ideal of the (male) scholar-leader and his benevolent rule, buttressed by a tradition of filial piety.

Within the context of Islam, views on the nature, scope and inheritance of leadership have played a major role in shaping sects and their history. See caliphate.

In the 19th century, the elaboration of anarchist thought called the whole concept of leadership into question. (Note that the Oxford English Dictionary traces the word "leadership" in English only as far back as the 19th century.) One response to this denial of élitism came with Leninism, which demanded an élite group of disciplined cadres to act as the vanguard of a socialist revolution, bringing into existence the dictatorship of the proletariat.

Other historical views of leadership have addressed the seeming contrasts between secular and religious leadership. The doctrines of Caesaro-papism have recurred and had their detractors over several centuries. Christian thinking on leadership has often emphasized stewardship of divinely-provided resources - human and material - and their deployment in accordance with a Divine plan. Compare servant leadership.

A SELECTION OF LEADERSHIP DEVELOPMENT INITIATIVES

In most cases, used as a basis for the development of leadership and management development provision within organisations as well as appraisal and performance review.

It is beyond the scope of this report to offer a detailed review of the associated programmes and the range of leadership and management development initiatives available, however, we would like to introduce a number of approaches that we feel are particularly interesting in the manner in which they seek to develop the behaviours, skills and attitudes of leaders.

NHS CHIEF EXECUTIVES PROGRAMMES

The NHS manage a wide range of programmes through their Leadership Centre, including a suite of programmes for Chief Executives.

These comprise a number of initiatives based upon the NHS Leadership Qualities Framework, including: National and International Learning Experiences:

- Development Assignments
- Transformational Thinking

- Study Tour to Canada
- Duality Leadership Programme
- Action Learning Sets

Modular Programmes:

- Experienced Chief Executives Development Programme
- Drive for Results

Of interest here, is the range of learning opportunities being offered, from action learning sets, study tours and exchanges to modular programmes. The participants are free to choose their preferred modes of learning yet the thinking behind the programme implies that each will contribute towards developing qualities from the Leadership Qualities Framework.

NCSL LEADERSHIP DEVELOPMENT FRAMEWORK

The National College for School Leadership is one of the leading organisations in relation to their awareness of the importance of distributed leadership. Recent years have seen an increasing move from the competency-based approach of the Hay McBer Model to the development of a Leadership Development Framework. The outcomes of a Think Tank report lead to 10 propositions about school leadership. School leadership must:

- Be purposeful, inclusive and values driven
- Embrace the distinctive and inclusive context of the school
- Promote an active view of learning
- Be instructionally focused
- Be a function that is distributed throughout the school community
- Build capacity by developing the school as a learning community
- Be futures oriented and strategically driven
- Be developed through experiential and innovative methodologies
- Be served by a support and policy context that is coherent and implementation driven
- Be supported by a National College that leads the discourse around leadership for learning

These propositions have been actualised through a series of programmes aimed at five different stages in a school leader's career:

- Emergent leadership, when a teacher is beginning to take on management and leadership responsibilities and perhaps forms an aspiration to become a headteacher
- Established leadership, comprising assistant and deputy heads who are experienced leaders but who do not intend to pursue headship
- Entry to headship, including a teacher's preparation for and induction into the senior post in a school
- Advanced leadership, the stage at which school leaders mature in their role, look to widen their experience, to refresh themselves and to update their skills

- Consultant leadership, when an able and experienced leader is ready to put something back into the profession by taking on training, mentoring, inspection or other responsibilities

The focus on, and research into, leadership at different organisational levels and career stages is refreshing when contrasted to the majority of competency/ quality frameworks which tend to be based on research with senior managers only. The model therefore, reflects a contingency approach, but without being prescriptive, and seeks to develop a "leadership culture" rather than just a finite number of "leaders".

ACEVO - LEADERSHIP JOURNEY

The "leadership journey" currently being delivered to members of the *Association of Chief Executives of Voluntary Organisations* (ACEVO) uses a somewhat emergent group learning process to develop and explore leadership capabilities, whereby a group of 12 or so Chief Executives from different voluntary-sector organisations embark on a one-year learning experience together.

The programme, run by a consultancy organisation is based around a series of two-day residential modules and associated action learning sets and individual and group challenges. Whilst the basic structure of the programme is outlined in advance, the emphasis is very much on getting the group to agree on future topics, activities and speakers and thus input and develop the programme as it proceeds.

A further central element of the programme is the "make a difference challenge" which is an active development challenge for participants to complete within their organisation and share with other members of the group. The programme is, therefore, very experiential and depends to a large extent on peer-group interaction, support and development.

LEAD2LEAD

The Lead2Lead programme, managed by Lancaster University, uses the process of leadership exchange and reflection to help improve leadership awareness. It involves a process of careful paring of participants, often from different organisations, sectors, and even countries. Once matched, participants are given training in observation and reflection techniques, followed by a three-day exchange to each others work place, and a facilitated debriefing session.

The process of observing and being observed can generate significant insights and awareness that could not be delivered through more formalised training. It gives first-hand experience, stories, and personal insights that can be very important to leadership. Furthermore, the "time-out" and reflection elements give the leader space to think and consider their leadership practises.

INTERNATIONAL MASTERS IN PRACTISING MANAGEMENT (IMPM)

The International Masters Programme in Practicing Management is designed to be the "Next Generation" Masters Programme, combining management development with management education. It is a degree programme that focuses directly on the development of managers in their own contexts - their jobs and their organisations. The IMPM is therefore deeper than conventional programmes of management development and more applied than traditional degree programmes. It was launched in March of 1996 to acclaim from participants and their companies alike, as well as from the international business press.

The IMPM seeks to break the mold of the functional "silos" so common in management education - marketing, finance, organisation behaviour, and so on. Instead, the Programme is structured around managerial "mindsets", one for each module. It opens in Lancaster with Managing in general and the *reflective* mindset in particular. Then it moves to McGill, where attention turns to Managing Organisations and the *analytic* mindset. Bangalore follows with Managing Context, the *worldly* mindset. In Japan, it takes up Managing Relationships, the *collaborative* mindset. The Programme closes at INSEAD with Managing Change, the *action* mindset. More detail is given about each of these mindsets by Mintzberg and Gosling:

- The reflective mindset refers to "managing self" – developing the ability to reflect and make meaning – a form of emotional intelligence.
- The analytic mindset refers to "managing organisations" – developing the ability to analyse and synthesise not only the hard data, but also the soft – "to appreciate scores and crowds while never losing sight of the ball".
- The worldly mindset refers to "managing contexts" – to appreciate cultural and local differences and similarities and respond accordingly.
- The collaborative mindset refers to "managing relationships" – developing partnerships and networks; working with people – managing "relationships" not "people".
- The action mindset refers to "managing movement"– managing change without losing track of continuity.

It is argued that the good manager/leader must master and integrate each of these mindsets and so offers a more cognitive and reflective approach to management development than more traditional behaviour and skills-based programmes.

THE LEADERSHIP GAME

The Leadership Game is a dynamic action-learning event for senior to middle managers designed to maximise learning through experiential techniques supported by expert analysis, feedback and coaching. It is a two-day programme that creates a temporary learning zone to explore issues such as:

- Leadership and decision-making under pressure
- Leaders within hierarchies, virtual teams and self-managed teams
- Team effectiveness under different leadership styles/structures
- How teams work together across functional boundaries
- Understanding the big picture: strategic vision and organisational dynamics.

Day 1 – "The leadership Game" uses a mixture of plenary, work team and cross-team groups and a real-life work related challenge. The process is observed by expert consultants who give team and individual analysis and feedback as required. Day 2 – "Learning Assessment and Implementation" unleashes the learning from Day 1 to address the personal and organisational challenges that arise from the Leadership Game. The programme is run in conjunction with the Tavistock Consultancy Service and represents a current manifestation of the "Human Relations" school started by Kurt Lewin and applied through the National Training Labs of the 1950s. This approach encourages a contextualisation of emotional intelligence and a coming to terms with authority. It offers an alternative to the trait theories of leadership and provides a forum for exploring the emotional aspects of leadership in context and through activities.

8

Transformational Leadership

Transformational leadership is a style of leadership where the leader works with employees to identify the needed change, creating a vision to guide the change through inspiration, and executing the change in tandem with committed members of the group. It also serves to enhance the motivation, morale, and job performance of followers through a variety of mechanisms; these include connecting the follower's sense of identity and self to the project and the collective identity of the organisation; being a role modelfor followers in order to inspire them and raise their interest in the project; challenging followers to take greater ownership for their work, and understanding the strengths and weaknesses of followers, allowing the leader to align followers with tasks that enhance their performance.

ORIGINS

The concept of transformational leadership was initially introduced by leadership expert and presidential biographer James MacGregor Burns. According to Burns, transformational leadership can be seen when "leaders and followers make each other advance to a higher level of morality and motivation." Through the strength of their vision and personality, transformational leaders are able to inspire followers to change expectations, perceptions, and motivations to work towards common goals. Unlike in the transactional approach, it is not based on a "give and take" relationship, but on the leader's personality, traits and ability to make a change through example, articulation of an energizing vision and challenging goals. Transforming leaders are idealized in the sense that they are a moral exemplar of working towards the benefit of the team, organisation and/or community. Burns theorized that transforming and transactional leadership were mutually exclusive styles. Later, researcher Bernard M. Bass expanded upon Burns' original ideas to develop what is today referred to as Bass' Transformational Leadership Theory. According to Bass, transformational leadership can be defined based on the impact that it has on followers. Transformational leaders, Bass suggested, garner trust, respect, and admiration from their followers. Bernard M. Bass (1985), extended the work of Burns (1978) by explaining the psychological mechanisms that underlie transforming and transactional leadership. Bass introduced the term "transformational" in place of "transforming." Bass added to the initial concepts of Burns (1978) to help explain how transformational leadership could be measured, as well as how it impacts follower motivation and performance. The extent to which a leader is transformational, is measured first, in terms of his influence on the followers.

The followers of such a leader feel trust, admiration, loyalty and respect for the leader and because of the qualities of the transformational leader are willing to work harder than originally expected. These outcomes occur because the transformational leader offers followers something more than just working for self-gain; they provide followers with an inspiring mission and vision and give them an identity. The leader transforms and motivates followers through his or her idealized influence, intellectual stimulation and individual consideration. In addition, this leader encourages followers to come up with new and unique ways to challenge the status quo and to alter the environment to support being successful. Finally, in contrast to Burns, Bass suggested that leadership can simultaneously display both transformational and transactional leadership.

DEFINITIONS

According to Bass, transformational leadership encompasses several different aspects, including:

- Emphasizing intrinsic motivation and positive development of followers
- Raising awareness of moral standards
- Highlighting important priorities
- Fostering higher moral maturity in followers
- Creating an ethical climate (share values, high ethical standards)
- Encouraging followers to look beyond self-interests to the common good
- Promoting cooperation and harmony
- Using authentic, consistent means
- Using persuasive appeals based on reason
- Providing individual coaching and mentoring for followers
- Appealing to the ideals of followers
- Allowing freedom of choice for followers

Transformational leaders are described to hold positive expectations for followers, believing that they can do their best. As a result, they inspire, empower, and stimulate followers to exceed normal levels of performance. Transformational leaders also focus on and care about followers and their personal needs and development. Transformational leaders fit well in leading and working with complex work groups and organisations, where beyond seeking an inspirational leader to help guide them through an uncertain environment, followers are also challenged and feel empowered; this nurtures them into becoming loyal, high performers.

There are 4 components to transformational leadership, sometimes referred to as the 4 I's:

- Idealized Influence (II) - the leader serves as an ideal role model for followers; the leader "walks the talk," and is admired for this.
- Inspirational Motivation (IM) - Transformational leaders have the ability to inspire and motivate followers. Combined these first two I's are what constitute the transformational leader's charisma.
- Individualized Consideration (IC) - Transformational leaders demonstrate genuine concern for the needs and feelings of followers. This personal attention to each follower is a key element in bringing out their very best efforts.
- Intellectual Stimulation (IS) - the leader challenges followers to be innovative and creative. A common misunderstanding is that transformational leaders are "soft," but the truth is that they constantly challenge followers to higher levels of performance.

Transformational leadership is said to have occurred when engagement in a group results in leaders and followers raising one another to increased levels of motivation and morality.

CHARACTERISTICS

Five major personality traits have been identified as factors contributing to the likelihood of an individual displaying the characteristics of a transformational leader. Different emphasis on different elements of these traits point to inclination in personality to inspirational leadership, transactional leadership, and transformational leadership. These five traits are as follows.

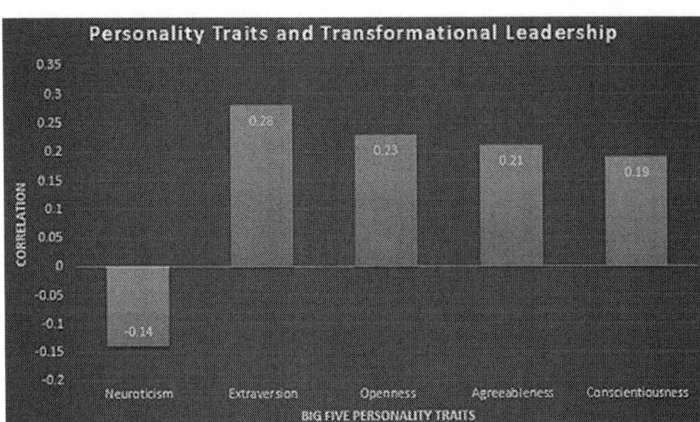

Results of Meta Analysis finding correlation between personality traits and transformational leadership from data gathered by Joyce Bono and Timothy Judge.

EXTRAVERSION

The two main characteristics of extraverts are affiliation and agency, which relate to the social and leadership aspects of their personality, respectively. Extraversion is generally seen as an inspirational trait usually exhibited in transformational leadership.

NEUROTICISM

Neuroticism generally gives an individual an anxiety related to productivity which, in a group setting can be debilitating to a degree where they are unlikely to position themselves in a role of transformational leadership due to lower self-esteem and a tendency to shirk from leadership responsibilities.

OPENNESS TO EXPERIENCE

Creative expression and emotional responsiveness have been linked to a general tendency of openness to experience. This trait is also seen as a component of transformational leadership as it relates to the ability to give big-picture visionary leadership for an organisation.

AGREEABLENESS

Although not a trait which specifically points to transformational leadership, leaders in general possess an agreeable nature stemming from a natural concern for others and high levels of individual consideration. Charisma and idealized influence is a classic ability of individuals who possess agreeability.

CONSCIENTIOUSNESS

Strong sense of direction and the ability to put large amounts of productive work into tasks is the by-product of conscientious leaders. This trait is more linked to a transactional form of leadership given the management-based abilities of such individuals and the detail oriented nature of their personality.

TRANSFORMATIONAL LEADERSHIP THEORY

According to Cox (2001), there are two basic categories of leadership: *transactional* and *transformational*. The distinction between transactional and transformational leadership was first made by Downton but the idea gained little currency until James McGregor Burns' (1978) work on political leaders was published. Burns distinguished between ordinary (*transactional*) leaders, who exchanged tangible rewards for the work and loyalty of followers, and extraordinary (*transformational*) leaders who engaged with followers, focused on higher order intrinsic needs, and raised consciousness about the significance of specific outcomes and new ways in which those outcomes might be achieved. The idea of transformational leadership was developed further by Bernard Bass, now Distinguished Professor Emeritus of Organisational Behaviour, at the State University of New York (Binghampton), who disputed Burns' conception of transactional and transformational leadership as opposites on a continuum. He suggested instead that they are separate concepts and that good leaders demonstrate characteristics of both.

Interest in transformational leadership over the past three decades is the result of two tendencies. First, significant global economic changes from the early 1970s – which followed on from about 25 years of post-World War 2 stability – meant that many large western companies such as General Motors and AT&T had to consider radical changes in their ways of doing business. Factors such as rapid technological change, heightened levels of competition, a rising flow of products from newly industrialized countries, volatility in OPEC (Organisation of Petroleum Exporting Countries) pricing strategies, and changing demographic structures created a turbulent, unstable and competitive environment in which significant organisational change was imperative. Changes often included downsizing and the adoption of new forms of organisational arrangement. These amendments took their toll on worker satisfaction and empowerment and broke "the old social contract of long-term employment in return for employee loyalty". Because companies needed to resolve the apparently contradictory challenge of finding new ways of affecting change while simultaneously building employee morale, new approaches to leadership were needed. Second, the theoretical base of work on leadership that prevailed in the 1970s was founded in explorations of traits, behaviours, and situations (contingency theories) and failed to account of some 'untypical' qualities of leaders.

Transformational leadership is that which:

... facilitates a redefinition of a people's mission and vision, a renewal of their commitment and the restructuring of their systems for goal accomplishment. It is a relationship of mutual stimulation and elevation that converts followers into leaders and may convert leaders into moral agents. Hence, transformational leadership must be grounded in moral foundations.

Transformational leadership fosters capacity development and brings higher levels of personal commitment amongst 'followers' to organisational objectives. According to Bass transformational leadership "occurs when leaders broaden and elevate the interests of their employees, when they generate awareness and acceptance of the purposes and mission of the group, and when they stir employees to look beyond their own self-interest for the good of the group." Together, heightened capacity and commitment are held to lead to additional effort and greater productivity.

Transformational leaders elevate people from low levels of need, focussed on survival (following Maslow's hierarchy), to higher levels. They may also motivate followers to transcend their own interests for some other collective purpose but typically help followers satisfy as many of their individual human needs as possible, appealing notably to higher order needs (*e.g.* to love, to learn, and to leave a legacy). Transformational leaders are said to engender trust, admiration, loyalty and respect amongst their followers. This form of leadership requires that leaders engage with followers as 'whole' people, rather than simply as an 'employee' for example. In effect, transformational leaders emphasize the actualization of followers. Transformational leadership is also based on self-reflective changing of values and beliefs by the leader and their followers. From this emerges a key characteristic of transformational leadership. It is said to involve leaders and followers raising one another's achievements, morality and motivations to levels that might otherwise have been impossible.

Though an understanding of transformational leadership predicated on its outcomes appears to have been achieved, Leithwood and Jantzi (2000) observe that despite (or perhaps as a result of) over four decades of work in the field, the literature in educational leadership offers no single conception of the processes that constitute transformational leadership. For instance, Gronn (1996) remarks on the close relationship between charismatic and transformational leadership while pointing out the absence of notions of charisma in some work transformational leadership. And most authors in the field propose that four factors make up transformational leadership whereas Leithwood suggests six. These are set out in Table below.

Table : Dimensions of Transformational Leadership.

The Four Common I's	Leithwood's Six
1. Idealized influence. *Charismatic vision and behaviour that inspires others to follow.*	1. Building vision and goals.
2. Inspirational motivation. *Capacity to motivate others to commit to the vision.*	2. Providing intellectual stimulation.
3. Intellectual stimulation. *Encouraging innovation and creativity.*	3. Offering individualized support.
4. Individualized consideration. *Coaching to the specific needs of followers.*	4. Symbolizing professional practices and values.
	5. Demonstrating high performance expectations.
	6. Developing structures to foster participation in decisions.

Nevertheless, it is clear that general understandings of transformational leadership are dominated by acceptance of the four dimensions set out in the left-hand column of Table 1. These factors have been confirmed by empirical work in the area. In 1985 Bernard Bass devised the Multifactor Leadership Questionnaire (MLQ), an instrument intended to measure transformational and transactional leader behaviours. Over the past two decades, and following application in scores of research studies involving military, educational, and commercial organisations, the MLQ has emerged as the primary means of quantitatively assessing transformational leadership. An outcome of this work is the isolation of four factors now accepted as being exhibited by effective transformational leaders.

Idealized influence (attributes and behaviours)
+
Individualized consideration
+
Inspirational motivation
+
Intellectual stimulation
=
Performance Beyond Expectations

Fig. The Additive Effect of Transformational Leadership.

Idealized influence is about building confidence and trust and providing a role model that followers seek to emulate. Leaders are "admired, respected, and trusted". Confidence in the leader provides a foundation for accepting (radical) organisational change. That is, followers who are sure of the virtues of their leader will be less likely to resist proposals for change from her/him. Clearly, idealized influence is linked to charisma. Charismatic leadership is a characteristic of transformational leadership and depends on leaders as well as followers for its expression. The link between charismatic and transformational leadership is clearest during times of crisis within an organisation such as when Lee Iacocca took over and resurrected the ailing Chrysler Corporation in the 1970s and 1980s.

Inspirational motivation is related to idealized influence but whereas charisma is held to motivate individuals, inspirational leadership is about motivating the entire organisation to, for example, follow a new idea. Transformational leaders make clear an appealing view of the future, offer followers the opportunity to see meaning in their work, and challenge them with high standards.

They encourage followers to become part of the overall organisational culture and environment. This might be achieved through motivational speeches and conversations and other public displays of optimism and enthusiasm, highlighting positive outcomes, and stimulating teamwork (Simic, 1998, p. 52). Martin Luther King's "I have a dream" speech and US President John F. Kennedy's vision of putting a man on the moon by 1970 stand out as exceptional examples of this characteristic (Yukl, 1989, p. 221). Through these sorts of means, transformational leaders encourage their followers to imagine and contribute to the development of attractive, alternative futures.

Intellectual stimulation involves arousing and changing followers' awareness of problems and their capacity to solve those problems. Transformational leaders question assumptions and beliefs and encourage followers to be innovative and creative, approaching old problems in new ways. They empower followers by persuading them to propose new and controversial ideas without fear of punishment or ridicule. They impose their own ideas judiciously and certainly not at any cost (Simic, 2003, p. 52).

Individualized consideration involves responding to the specific, unique needs of followers to ensure they are included in the transformation process of the organisation (Simic, 1998, p. 52). People are treated individually and differently on the basis of their talents and knowledge and with the intention of allowing them to reach higher levels of achievement than might otherwise have been achieved. This might take expression, for example, through expressing words of thanks or praise, fair workload distributions, and individualized career counseling, mentoring and professional development activities. Clearly then, besides having an overarching view of the organisation and its trajectory, the transformational leader must also comprehend those things that motivate followers individually (Simic, 2003, p. 52).

Together, the four main dimensions of transformational leadership are interdependent; they must co-exist; and they are held to have an additive effect that *yields performance beyond expectations*.

Table: Characteristics of Transformational Leaders.

- Clear sense of purpose, expressed simply (*e.g.* metaphors, anecdotes)
- Value driven (*e.g.* have core values and congruent behaviour)
- Strong role model
- High expectations
- Persistent
- Self-knowing
- Perpetual desire for learning
- love work
- Life-long learners
- Identify themselves as change agents
- Enthusiastic
- Able to attract and inspire others
- Strategic
- Effective communicator
- Emotionally mature
- Courageous
- Risk-taking

- Risk-sharing
- Visionary
- Unwilling to believe in failure
- Sense of public need.
- Considerate of the personal needs of employees
- Listens to all viewpoints to develop spirit of cooperation
- Mentoring
- Able to deal with complexity, uncertainty and ambiguity

The characteristics that, according to the extant literature, accompany the four foundational attributes of a transformational leader. Collectively, they do suggest a human being of remarkable capabilities! Nevertheless, on foundations provided by the four dimensions of transformational leadership and the various associated characteristics, transformational leaders are people who can create significant change in both followers and the organisation with which they are associated. They lead changes in mission, strategy, structure and culture, in part through a focus on intangible qualities like vision, shared values and ideas, and relationship building. They are able to give significance to diverse activities, illustrating, for example, the ways in which different people and groups might be working towards larger organisational objectives. Transformational leaders also find common ground that allows them to enlist followers in processes of change.

Following Carlson and Perrewe (1995), ERIC (1992), Lussier and Achua (2004), and Yukl (1989) there are four stages of organisational change under transformational leadership. First, it is necessary to *make a compelling case* for change. The transformational leader helps to bring about change by making a convincing case for it. This characteristically involves heightening followers' sensitivity to environmental changes and challenges and questioning the status quo.

For instance, the case for change within a school or some other educational environment might be made by inviting government department spokespeople to the school to present an overview of policy and related contexts or by highlighting levels of performance relative to other, similar organisations.

Second, it is important to *inspire a shared vision*, seeking broad input, and encouraging everyone to think of a new and better future. This needs to be cast in ideological rather than just economic terms. This might be achieved by involving all staff in the shaping and reshaping of the school/department's strategic plan on a regular basis. Staff might be surveyed to establish their wants and needs.

For example, in an educational context, a school principal or department head could also visit classrooms regularly (and encourage others to do the same) to better gauge collective requirements. Inspiring a shared vision will also be achieved through coaching and conscious role modeling strategies.

Third, *change needs to be led*. A sense of urgency must be instilled. Collaboration has to be encouraged and the self-confidence of followers' must be increased. In effect, it is vital to create an environment conducive to the creation and sharing of knowledge. Public recognition of achievements and successful (shared) initiatives might help serve these ends. Private notes of congratulation to successful followers can also help foster self-confidence. It is also necessary at this stage, to deal with the emotional resistance that typically accompanies change and this may be achieved through careful recognition of the individuals needs of staff or followers.

Finally, *change needs to be embedded*. This is achieved by, for example, monitoring progress, changing appraisal and reward systems, and hiring staff with a commitment to collaboration. Together these should also empower followers to help achieve the organisation's objectives. What leaders pay attention to, what they measure and how they measure it, and what they control are critical factors in transforming an organisation's culture and embedding new ways of thinking and acting.

In summary:

"the transformational leader articulates the vision in a clear and appealing manner, explains how to attain the visions, acts confidently and optimistically, expresses confidence in the followers, emphasizes values with symbolic actions, leads by example, and empowers followers to achieve the vision.

That transformational leadership is successful has been demonstrated by studies in a diverse range of professional and cultural settings, including military, schools and corporations. However, in their recent study of 'traditionality' in Taiwan and the United States, Spreitzer, Perttula and Xin (2005) make it clear that while transformational leadership is effective regardless of culture, the level of effectiveness depends to some extent on cultural values. People with traditional cultural values see weaker links between transformational leadership and leader effectiveness than those with less traditional values. Transformational leadership has also been demonstrated to result in a "high level of follower motivation and commitment and well-above-average organisational performance, especially under conditions of crisis or uncertainty". As Carlson and Perrewe observe, major changes in the organisation's mission, strategies and level of follower commitment are likely to emerge as a result of transformational leadership. On the basis of their analysis of several legal cases, Odom and Green (2003) argue that principles of transformational leadership (*i.e.*, intellectual stimulation, idealized influence) applied to ethical dilemmas faced by managers offers the prospect of less litigation and better ethical outcomes than the more common transactional approach to ethics. Within educational environments teachers are more likely to collaborate and are held to be more likely to have positive attitudes to school improvement and to new forms of instructional behaviour as a result of transformational leadership.

SUCCESSFUL TRANSFORMATIONAL LEADERS

Although the idea of transformational leadership is relatively recent, people who have demonstrated the characteristics of this form of leadership have existed for many years. For instance, Yates (2002) argues that Genghis Khan was a transformational leader who, during the late 12th and early 13th centuries, united fiercely independent Mongol tribes to ultimately create one of the largest land empires ever seen. Another transformational leader is Lou Gerstner – retired Chairman and CEO of IBM. He turned IBM around from $8.1 billion loss in 1993 after identifying part of the company's problem as 'success syndrome'. That is, having been one of the greatest commercial institutions on Earth from the 1960s-1980s, IBM had become insular and rigid. Gerstner completely transformed the culture of the organisation through, for example, modeling desired behaviour and abolishing IBM's notorious dress code to reflect better the attire of their customers. Lee Iacocca is a transformational leader who is credited with saving the Chrysler Corporation. He took over Chrysler when it was on the brink of bankruptcy and set about transforming the ideals of his closest subordinates. In turn, that began to reshape the corporation's culture. Because a transformational leader encourages others to becomes transformational leaders, soon the entire organisation was filled with effective leaders.

One high profile transformational leader from educational environments is Dr Ruth Simmons, the first African-American to be appointed President of an 'Ivy League' university (Brown) in the USA. Earlier, as President of Smith College Simmons had started an engineering programme - the first ever at a women's university in the USA. Simmons was a transformational leader who herself attributed her own successes to her kindergarten teacher, Ms Ida Mae Henderson, who had advised her she could do anything in her heart she set out to achieve. Within military and government contexts, General Colin Powell overcame entrenched racism (particularly in the US military) and low institutional expectations of African Americans to become chairman of the US Joint Chiefs of Staff in 1989. He went further, becoming in 1991 the first African American to become US Secretary of State, a position some said he filled with vision and the qualities of a transformational leader.

Other transformational leaders include Christine Nixon, the current Police Chief Commissioner in the Australian state of Victoria, who is popularly understood to have transformed the culture of that police force for the good, and Sir Richard Branson, responsible for international Virgin enterprises.

These are positive examples of transformational leaders but as critics point out, transformational leadership is not without its dark side and other flaws.

CRITICISMS OF TRANSFORMATIONAL LEADERSHIP

The morality of transformational leadership has been questioned, especially by libertarians and organisational development consultants. A key criticism is that within it transformational leadership has potential for the abuse of power (Hall, Johnson, Wysocki and Kepner, 2002). Transformational leaders motivate followers by appealing to strong emotions regardless of the ultimate effects on followers and do not necessarily attend to positive moral values. As Stone, Russell and Patterson observe, transformational leaders can exert a very powerful influence over followers, who offer them trust and respect. Some leaders may have narcissistic tendencies, thriving on power and manipulation. Moreover, some followers may have dependent characters and form strong and unfortunate bonds with their leaders. Further, as Bass (1997) notes, transformational leadership lacks the checks and balances of countervailing interests, influences and power that might help to avoid dictatorship and oppression of a minority by a majority. In the absence of moral rectitude it is self-evident then that transformational leadership might be applied for less-than-desirable social ends. Yukl describes this as the "dark side of charisma" and goes on to note (p. 227) that for every example of a positive transformational leader demonstrating charismatic qualities (*e.g.*, Mohandas [Mahatma] Ghandi), there is an equally negative example (*e.g.*, Charles Manson). The Rev Jim Jones, who led the massive Jonestown suicide, is an example of a transformational leader from the 'dark side'. These criticisms about the morality of transformational leadership have been addressed by the argument that to be truly transformational, leadership must have moral foundations. Thus: "To bring about change, *authentic* transformational leadership fosters the modal values of honesty, loyalty, and fairness, as well as the end values of justice, equality, and human rights."

There is an argument that transformational leadership is facilitative of change because it contributes to organisational improvement, effectiveness and institutional culture. As such, it is appropriate in environments of turbulence and change such as those that prevail in many organisations in the mid-2000s. However, this view is contested by Barnett, McCormick and Conners (2001) whose study of twelve secondary schools in New South Wales, Australia revealed that teachers may in fact be distracted from concentrating on learning-and-teaching by, for example, taking time away from students to be involved in the corporate school initiatives an inspirational, transformational principal expects of them.

Leithwood and Jantzi (2000) conclude that transactional leaders more commonly apply teleological ethics whereas transformational leaders deploy deontological ethics. In short, these two approaches to leadership stand on different moral foundations. As some recent work in ethics suggests (Israel and Hay, 2006), ethical decision-making is best founded on both approaches.

Bass (1997) usefully summarizes some of the other criticisms of transformational leadership. It lends itself to amoral self promotion by leaders since, it makes use of impression management. He suggests it is anthithetical to organisation learning and development involving shared leadership, equality, consensus and participative decision-making. It encourages followers to go beyond their own self-interests for the good of the organisation and may emotionally engage followers in pursuit of evil ends. This point is supported by Carlson and Perrewe (1995) who remind us that an organisation's culture socializes individuals into that culture. While acceptable behaviour might be supported in this way, so too might socially unacceptable behaviour. Finally, Bass notes that transformational leadership can see followers manipulated in ways that may see them lose more than they gain.

THE FUTURE OF TRANSFORMATIONAL LEADERSHIP

And so what is the future of transformational leadership? There seems to be an emerging orthodoxy in the literature favoring a blend of transactional and transformational leadership. However, Sanders, Hopkins and Geroy (2003) propose an extension to both through what they call 'transcendental leadership'. Their model suggests three structural levels of leadership accomplishment, these being transactional, transformational, and transcendental, and they suggest that a leader's development along three dimensions of spirituality – consciousness (mind), moral character (heart) and faith (soul) – is associated with these levels of leadership accomplishment. They argue for the need to society and organisations to recognize the need for and embrace spirituality. Traditional leadership theories are said to concentrate on external manifestations of leadership but the model proposed by Sanders, Hopkins and Geroy (2003) indicates that leadership is best understood by adding consideration of the leader's internal components. While their very new theory is yet to be tested empirically, their intent is to help bring spirituality out of the 'closet' (p. 29) and to weave it coherently into new understandings of leadership.

MEASUREMENT

One of the ways in which transactional leadership is measured is through use of the Multifactor Leadership Questionnaire (MLQ), a survey which identifies different leadership characteristics based on examples and provides a basis for leadership training. Early development was limited because the knowledge in this area was primitive, and as such, finding good examples for the items in the questionnaire was difficult. Subsequent development on the MLQ led to the current version of the survey, the MLQ5X.

The current version of the MLQ5X includes 36 items that are broken down into 9 scales with 4 items measuring each scale. Subsequent validation work by John Antonakis and his colleagues provided strong evidence supporting the validity and reliability of the MLQ5X. Indeed, Antonakis went on to confirm the viability of the proposed nine-factor model MLQ model, using two very large samples. Although other researchers have still been critical of the MLQ model, since, 2003 no one has been able to provide dis-confirming evidence of the theorized nine-factor model with such large sample sizes at those published by Antonakis.

In regards to transformational leadership, the first 5 components - Idealized Attributes, Idealized Behaviors, Inspirational Motivation, Intellectual Stimulation, and Individualized Consideration - are considered to be transformational leadership behaviors.

MEASUREMENT OF LEADERSHIP.

From 1930's to 1950, leadership was widely regarded as a 'gift' that required certain traits. However, there is little empirical support for personality trait theories, and early leadership measures based on traits suffered poor psychometric properties.

To test the usefulness of various leadership theories, researchers have measured leadership by examining:

- Traits of leaders and/or their followers (subordinates)
- Leader behaviour
- Follower behaviour
- Situations
- Interactions between leader and follower
- Charisma

The results are used to 'predict' performance/results. Instruments and theories are useful to organisations to the extent that are repeatable (reliable) and accurate (valid). Empirical support exists for only a small number of traits, and particular traits seem to suit certain situations.

No single model or theory has yet succeeded in encapsulating leadership, and can not do so until its definition has been agreed upon. In the absence of an accepted and tested universal theory of leadership, there can be no generic 'leadership' instrument.

Nearly all leadership studies to date have been about supervisory leadership, and therefore nearly all currently available leadership instruments are limited in application to supervisors and managers. Although there are many, we will consider only the most successful or evolutionarily important:

- Trait theories
- Social Exchange theories such as LMX (Leader-Member exchange)
- Transformational Leadership
- Value Based Leadership.

The optimal instrument for any organisation seeking to measure internal leadership, will depend upon exactly what information is required and what hierarchical level is to be measured. At the very beginning of a leadership career, an instrument is required to measure potential or emergent leaders. Other instruments would attempt to cover the range from supervisory through to national leadership levels.

LEADERSHIP SKILLS INVENTORY

This instrument identifies potential leaders and quantifies their leadership skills. It uses both 'self' and 'other' instruments (subordinate and supervisor). It measures congruency of desirable attributes. If subordinates and manager agree about the ownership of certain skills by the subordinate, then they probably exist. However, for this to work the Manager must have leadership skills. Once congruent validity is demonstrated in an organisation, only the subordinate is required to complete this instrument in future. It becomes a useful tool for locating potential leaders from within the organisation.

The Leadership Skills Inventory is a 125 item Likert-style instrument covering nine categories of leadership. Those categories are: fundamentals of leadership; written communication; speech communication skills; 'values' clarification; decision-making skills; group dynamic skills; problem solving skills; personal development skills, and planning skills. This instrument exposes the leadership strengths and weaknesses of a person, enabling clear training plans to be tailor-made for that individual.

A supporting study of the instrument provides empirical support of concurrent, content, and construct validity. Concurrent validity was supported by correlation ($r=.34$, $p<.01$) between LSI score and observed leadership behaviour. Content validity was gained through expert jury agreement on content applicability of each question. Finally, a single factor was evenly and heavily loaded by each component (.636 to.876), supporting the construct validity, but not supporting the nine categories as separate components. The categories had much in common, with correlations between them ranging from $r=.295$ to.761, $p<.01$. The authors recommend that this instrument be used to guide developmental studies rather than as a basis for selecting from amongst potential leaders.

Comment: This is to test members of a group to predict emergent leadership or to assign group leadership, or to monitor the effectiveness of leadership training.

LEADER MEMBER EXCHANGE (LMX-7)

LMX theory is describes the dyadic relationship between an individual member and his or her supervisor, and describes reciprocal fulfillment of expectations (Graen et al., 1982). An important ingredient of the dyadic theory is the differentiated relationships yielding different qualities of exchange, in turn creating 'in' groups and 'out' groups of subordinates (Dansereau et al., 1975). LMX theory maintains that a work group should not be considered a single entity. Instead, it considers the relationships between leader and each group member as being a socially influencing behaviour of 'leadership'. LMX has been shown to positively relate to performance and satisfaction (Graen et al., 1986), locus of control and time-based pressure, delegation, job attitudes and performance evaluations, and commitment and citizenship behaviour. LMX relates negatively to turnover (Graen et al., 1982)(good for the organisation) and performance (bad for the organisation). Literature showed more studies with positive LMX-performance relationships than negative, but there was considerable variation. An explanation is offered by way of conversation quality of the relationship.

The LMX-7 instrument contains 7 items that examine the quality of exchange between leader and subordinate, and is completed by the subordinates of the supervisor/manager/leader. There is, however, considerable literature using the 7-item LMX measure from, with most users reporting high alphas such as.91,.86 and.9 (Wayne et al., 1997).

The LMX7 instrument can be used to examine the quality of social relationships perceived by subordinates to exist between themselves and their immediate leader. The testing of the instrument has been confined to organisational settings and is aimed at middle to lower management.

Comment: The LMX seems more useful in hierarchical organisation with managers and supervisors, rather than organisations with a flat structure. LMX does not apply at executive level because high levels do not have the same co-worker/superior social support relationships. LMX also may not suit excessively high stress environments if there is a tendency for 'directing' behaviours to replace 'social influence' behaviours by supervisors under stress. report that decisions made under stressful circumstances are, unlike LMX behaviour, likely to exhibit symptoms rigidity of response.

MULTIFACTOR LEADERSHIP QUESTIONNAIRE (MLQ)

Charismatic leadership theory regards charismatic leaders as exceptionally self-confident, strongly motivated to influence, and with strong convictions of the morality of their beliefs. This theory applies to all levels of leadership within or external to organisations. It has been supported in a wide range of situations. Over the same general period that charismatic theory has been developed, others such as transformational leadership, attributional theory of leadership and the value based leadership theory also emerged. The interest in these theories result from their generalisability across levels, genders, and cultures (summarised in House and Aditya, 1997), and the high level of follower commitment and performance, especially when the organisation is under stress

However, these theories have been critisised for limitations regarding measures of effects on followers, the single lumping of charismatic behaviours as a single undifferentiated syndrome, and inattention to important group characteristics. There is scant attention to the social implications of leadership.

The instrument used most frequently for this form of leadership is the MLQ. While there are several revisions of the MLQ, they all comprise subscales and use a 5 point Likert type scale. MLQ looks at traits and at the effects of leaders on followers, all measured through the eyes of the followers. The MLQ attempts to measure transactional, transformational, and laissez-faire leadership in a leader's performance, where transactional and transformational leadership styles each comprise several sub-scale dimensions and accompanying behaviours. The three-factor model of this leadership theory remains a valid concept for training purposes, but the high correlation suggests caution when interpreting sub-scales.

More recently, the MLQ is being used to not just measure the transformational leadership, but the ratio of the three styles as perceived by the followers.

Comment: The MLQ is broadly applicable to a wide range of organisational, political, or other leadership situations, and at any level where there is responsibility to influence the actions of others. It can apply to managers, supervisors, or CEO's, and can indicate the extent of transactional, transformational, or laissez-faire leadership experienced by followers. It is probably wasted in a strict rule-driven bureaucratic environment where there is little opportunity for doing things differently or for personal growth.

LPI LEADERSHIP PRACTICES INVENTORY

This instrument grew not from a model, but from a desire to measure actual successful organisational leadership behaviours, and to shift away from psychological characteristics. It moved from 'what they are like' to 'what do they do'. Surveys and interviews of over 1,100 leaders about their best personal leadership experiences yielded data about the ideal behaviours of leaders. A process of testing on another 2,100 managers and narrowing down the data, resulted in two 5 point Likert-style instrument of 30 questions covering 5 leadership practices. The 5 practices are: challenging the process, inspiring a shared vision, enabling others to act, modeling the way, and encouraging the heart. One of the instruments (LPI Observer) is for subordinates to report on their manager. The other (LPI Self), is for the manager to self-report. Reliability and validity tests involved another 2,876 managers and their subordinates, representing both genders, and 4 foreign countries. Internal consistency of the 5 sub-scales ranged from.70 to.91, with test-retest reliability.93 and above.

Further psychometric investigation using data from 5,298 managers and 30,913 subordinates confirmed 5 factors corresponding to the hypothesised dimensions. The authors also reported small gender differences with females reportedly engaging more in modeling and encouraging. Female subordinates reported their managers as more challenging and higher modeling, regardless of manager gender, and LPI Self scores tend to be higher than LPI Observer.

LPI scores have been shown to relate to organisational effectiveness, work group vitality, job satisfaction and organisational commitment. LPI has differentiated between transactional and transformational styles, where challenging the process and inspiring a shared vision related to transformational leadership, while enabling others related to transactional leadership. Encouraging the heart and modeling the way related to both styles.

Comment: The LPI can quantify the five sub-scale qualities of leadership practice and also distinguish between transformational and transactional leadership style. Such a comprehensive range of information from a modest 30-item instrument may be useful to assess adjustments during periods of organisational change, regardless of cultures or genders involved. This instrument is restricted to intra-organisational leadership.

EFFECTIVENESS AS COMPARED TO OTHER LEADERSHIP STYLES

Studies have shown that transformational leadership styles are associated with positive outcomes in relation to other leadership styles. According to studies performed by Lowe, Kroeck, and Sivasubramaniam, charisma (or Idealized Influence) was found to be a variable that was most strongly related to leader effectiveness among MLQ scales. Other studies show that transformational leadership is positively associated with employee outcomes including commitment, role clarity, and well-being.

TRANSACTIONAL LEADERSHIP

In contrast to transformational leadership, transactional leadership styles focus on the use of rewards and punishments in order to achieve compliance from followers. Transformational leaders look towards changing the future to inspire followers and accomplish goals, whereas transactional leaders seek to maintain the *status quo*, not aiming for progress.

The MLQ does test for some transactional leadership elements - Contingent Reward and Management-by-Exception - and these results for these elements are often compared to those of the transformational elements that the MLQ tests for. Studies have shown transformational leadership practices lead to higher satisfaction with leader among followers and greater leader effectiveness, while transactional practices lead to higher follower job satisfaction and leader job performance

LAISSEZ-FAIRE LEADERSHIP

In a laissez-faire leadership style, a person may be given a leadership position without providing leadership, which leaves followers to fend for themselves. This leads to subordinates having a free hand in deciding policies and methods.

Studies have shown that while transformational leadership styles are associated with positive outcomes, laissez-faire leadership is associated with negative outcomes, especially in terms of follower satisfaction with leader and leader effectiveness. Also, other studies comparing the leadership styles of men and women have shown that female leaders tend to be more transformational with their leadership styles, whereas laissez-faire leadership is more prevalent in male leaders

CULTURAL FACTORS AFFECT LEADERSHIP

In 1993 House launched The Global Leadership and Organisational Behaviour Effectiveness Research Programme (GLOBE) to test leadership hypotheses in various cultures. Over the past six years GLOBE has evolved into a multi-phase, multi-method research project in which some 170 investigators from over 60 cultures representing all major regions of the world collaborate to examine the interrelationships among societal culture, organisational culture and practices and organisational leadership. GLOBE has focused on universals and culture-based differences in perceived effectiveness of leadership attributes by asking middle managers whether certain leader characteristics and behaviors would help or hinder a person in becoming an outstanding leader.

GLOBE recently completed the second of four phases envisioned by House and his colleagues. Phase II found that there are universally endorsed leader attributes. In addition, the study also found that there are attributes that are universally seen as impediments to outstanding leadership. The most important finding, however, is that there are culturally-contingent attributes that can help or hinder leadership. What is seen as a strength in one culture may be a considerable impediment in another culture. These findings appear in a paper titled: "EMICs and ETICS of Culturally-Endorsed Implicit Leadership Theories: Are Attributes of Charismatic/ Transformational Leadership Universally Endorsed?"which is being published in 1999 in Leadership Quarterly.

Business is global, but each business organisation has a culture shaped by the business it is in and the people who run the business. Executives are themselves products of the unique cultures in which they have learned and conducted business. To see how cultures might come into play, we can easily imagine a situation in which a British executive who was trained at an American business school is asked to run the Argentine manufacturing facility of a Japanese firm. What leadership attributes should this executive work to develop: Japanese? Argentine? American? British? This executive needs to understand the culture within which he works and how his employees perceive leadership. GLOBE has found that "one size does not fit all". An executive needs to develop bespoke leadership attributes, tailored to the unique culture within which he or she works.

A general description of a leader might be someone who is charismatic and seeks to develop a transformational style of leadership. Charismatic/ transformational leadership is thought to broaden and elevate the interests of followers, generate awareness and acceptance among the followers of the purpose and mission of the group and motivate followers to go beyond their self-interests for the good of the organisation. But different cultural groups may vary in their conceptions of the most important characteristics of charismatic/transformational leadership. In some cultures, one might need to take strong, decisive action in order to be seen as a leader, while in other cultures consultation and a democratic approach may be the preferred approach to exercising effective leadership. GLOBE ask what the leadership behaviors and attributes that are reported to be effective or ineffective across cultures, especially where they are related to charismatic/transformational leadership. Managerial practices and motivational techniques that are legitimate and acceptable in on culture may not be in another.

For example, many attributes associated with charisma are seen as contributing to outstanding leadership, but the term "charisma" invokes ambivalence in several countries. There is concern in some cultures that people tend to lose their balance and perspective as a result of an excessive focus on achievement created by charismatic leaders. Certainly the most notorious example of a charismatic leader is Hitler.

Leaders are expected to have vision, but how this is displayed differs from culture to culture. In China, the influence of Confucian values make people wary of leaders who talk without engaging in specific action. Indian managers, on the other hand, care less about visionaries, preferring bold assertive styles of leadership. Leaders are often thought to be risk- takers, but GLOBE found that risk taking is not universally valued as contributing to outstanding leadership.

Communication skills are also important to the leader, but again, how these skills are perceived differs among and within cultures. What constitutes a good communicator is likely to vary greatly across cultures. American managers are more likely to provide directions to subordinates on a face-to-face basis while Japanese managers are likely to use written memos. In the U.S. subordinates are usually provided negative feedback directly from their supervisors, while in Japan such feedback is usually channeled through a peer of the subordinates. These differences reflect the U.S. individualistic norm of "brute honesty" and the Japanese collectivistic norm of "face-saving".

There are profound differences in the preferred use of language, as well as non-verbal cues. In many cultures, interrupting someone is considered to be impolite, while in most Latin cultures, interrupting conveys that one is interested in what the other person in saying. In Asian cultures the pauses between speakers are often much longer than what we find in the West. Cultural differences are found as well in gestures, intonation, and the use of humor. The GLOBE study found that several attributes reflecting charismatic/transformational leadership are universally endorsed as contributing to outstanding leadership. These attributes include: foresight, a willingness to encourage colleagues and staff, communicativeness, trustworthiness, a dynamic presence, a positive attitude, and being seen as a confidence builder. Certain charismatic attributes are perceived to be culturally contingent. These include enthusiasm, risk-taking, ambition, humility, sincerity, sensitivity, and compassion. Future GLOBE studies will examine the critical issue of whether leaders who are seen to act in accordance with their culturally-endorsed leadership theories are more effective than those who do not act according to culturally imposed expectations. Other questions GLOBE will continue to examine include how labels such as visionary, compassionate, or motivational are interpreted in various cultures. A related question includes that of how and when specific behaviors will reflect such attributes in a given culture.

Paradoxes in leadership abound. Instant communications and easy accessibility may shrink this world, but distinct cultures have always and will always continue to exist throughout the global economy. The most successful businesses will be those that not only understand the nuances that exist among different cultures, but train their executives to lead in ways that demonstrate an understanding of and appreciation for distinct cultures. The global executive's leadership style will need to be protean, changing from situation to situation. Sensitivity to the unique culture within which the executive works may well be the most important leadership attribute in the global economy.

FACTORS AFFECTING USE

Phipps suggests that the individual personality of a leader heavily affects his/her leadership style, specifically with regard to the following components of the Five Factor Model of Personality: openness to experience, conscientiousness, extraversion/introversion, agreeableness, and neuroticism/emotional stability (OCEAN)

Phipps also proposed that all the Big Five dimensions would be positively related to transformational leadership. Openness to experience allows the leader to be more accepting of novel ideas and thus more likely to stimulate the follower intellectually. Conscientious leaders are achievement oriented and thus more likely to motivate their followers to achieve organisational goals. Extraverted and agreeable individuals are more outgoing and pleasant, respectively, and more likely to have successful interpersonal relationships. Thus, they are more likely to influence their followers and to be considerate towards them. Emotionally stable leaders would be better able to influence their followers because their stability would enable them to be better role models to followers and to thoroughly engage them in the goal fulfillment process.

A specific example of cultural background affecting the effectiveness of transformational leadership would be Indian culture, where a nurturant-task style of leadership has been shown to be an effective leadership style. Singh and Bhandarker (1990) demonstrated that effective transformational leaders in India are likes heads of Indian families taking personal interest in the welfare of their followers. Leaders in Indian organisations are therefore more likely to exhibit transformational behaviors if their followers are more self-effacing in approaching the leaders. It is also hypothesized in general that subordinates' being socialized to be less assertive, self-confident, and independent would enhance superiors' exhibition of transformational leadership.

In addition, there is also evidence to suggest that social demographics do not necessarily affect transformational leadership styles.

However, follower characteristics, combined with their perceptions of the leader and their own situation, did appear to moderate the connection between transformational leadership and subordinates' willingness to take charge and be good organisational citizens.For instance, if subordinates in a work group perceive their leader to be prototypical of them, then transformational leadership would have less of an impact on their willingness to engage in organisational citizenship behaviors. Likewise, if subordinates are goal oriented and possess a traditional view of the organisational hierarchy, they tend to be less affected by transformational leadership. Self-motivated employees are less likely to need transformational leaders to prod them into action, while "traditionalists" tend to see positive organisational citizenship as something expected given their roles as followers—not something they need to be "inspired" to do.

Evidence suggests that the above sets of factors act, in essence, as both inhibitors of and substitutes for transformational leadership. As inhibitors, the presence of any of these factors—either independently or especially collectively—could make the presence of a transformational leader "redundant" since, followers' positive behaviour would instead be sparked by their own motivations or perceptions. On the other hand, when these factors are not present (*e.g.*, employees in a work group do not see their leader as "one of us"), then transformational leadership is likely to have a much greater impact on subordinates. In essence, when such "favorable conditions" are not present, managers—and the organisations they work for—should see a better return on investment from transformational leadership.

It was shown that leader continuity enhanced the effect of transformational leadership on role clarity and commitment, indicating that it takes time before transformational leaders actually have an effect on employees. Furthermore, co-worker support enhanced the effect on commitment, reflecting the role of followers in the transformational leadership process. However, there are also factors that would serve to hinder the exhibition of transformational leadership, including the organisational structure, ongoing change, the leaders' working conditions, and the leaders' elevated perceptions of personal power.

EXAMPLES

NELSON MANDELA

Nelson Mandela used transformational leadership principles while working to abolish apartheid and enforce change in South Africa. In 1995, he visited Betsie Verwoerd, the widow of the architect of apartheid Hendrik Verwoerd, at her home in Orania. Orania was an Afrikaner homeland and a striking anachronistic symbol of racial separation, and Mandela's recurring emphasis on forgiveness contributed towards the healing the prejudices of South Africa and as vast influence as a leader. In 2000, he was quoted as saying, "For all people who have found themselves in the position of being in jail and trying to transform society, forgiveness is natural because you have no time to be retaliative.".

He also set an example for others to follow in terms of sacrifice and philanthropy. Schoemaker describes one such instance:

"One such leader received a call from Mandela's office requesting that he accompany the President to the Eastern Cape. This leader was less than enthusiastic and pleaded that he had an appointment around mid-day clashing with Mandela's request. But there was no denying Mandela, so the leader agreed to go—but first consulted with his financial director to set a reasonable limit on the size of the anticipated donation request. They settled on 500,000 Rand, or about $50,000 in those days...upon landing, about 80,000 black school children—all adorned in crisp white shirts—simultaneously bowed to acknowledge the great man's arrival. As they were climbing down from the helicopter, Mandela planted his hand firmly in his guest's back and said, 'Now, I hope you are not going to disappoint me?' The business leader decided in that instance to double the donation...how could he tell a man who sacrificed as much as Mandela that he couldn't afford to be more generous?"

ABRAHAM

There are also numerous examples from the Bible of Abraham, the biblical patriarch, using transformational leadership principles to destroy paganism and spread the roots for Judaism, Christianity, and Islam. He mobilized his small clan and waged war with four powerful kings in order to rescue his nephew Lot, showing the courage to take risks and confidence to carry out visions. He cared a lot about people, often inviting strangers into his home and caring for them, providing food and drink. Abraham also firmly believed in justice for all, and haggled with God to save Sodom and Gomorra from destruction:

Abraham: 'What if there are 50 innocent people in the city? Will you still destroy it?'

God: 'If I find 50 innocent people in Sodom, I will spare the entire area.'

Abraham: 'Suppose there are 45?'

God: 'I will not destroy it if I find 45.'
Abraham: 'What if there are 40?'
God: 'I will not act if there are 40.'" —*"Genesis18:20-33"*

Abraham was also willing to make sacrifices for his beliefs, and the story about God asking him to sacrifice his son Isaac indicated his willingness to make a personal sacrifice for God in Genesis 22. This trial for Abraham may have been God's way of indicating to Abraham that spreading monotheism would require much sacrifice on the part of believers, and transformational leaders must be willing to make sacrifices on behalf of an organisation.

THE TRANSFORMATION OF MANAGERS AND ASSOCIATES

The role every manager must fill in the workplace is leadership. Managers often make the mistake of assuming that because they are the managers, they are also the leaders and that their associates will automatically follow. In reality, position only denotes title, not leadership. Peter Northouse (2001) defines leadership as a process whereby one individual influences a group of individuals to achieve a common goal. To be an effective leader, the manager must influence his associates in a positive way to reach the goals of the organisation. Furthermore, the transformational leadership approach can help managers become exceptional leaders. This paper will explain the transformational leadership approach by discussing its strengths, weaknesses, and steps for application.

TRANSFORMATIONAL LEADERSHIP

To use this approach in the workforce, one must first understand exactly what transformational leadership is. In the simplest terms, transformational leadership is a process that changes and transforms individuals. In other words, transformational leadership is the ability to get people to want to change, to improve, and to be led. It involves assessing associates' motives, satisfying their needs, and valuing them. Therefore, a transformational leader could make the company more successful by valuing its associates.

One such example is Sam Walton, founder of Wal-Mart, who often visited Wal-Mart stores across the country to meet with associates to show his appreciation for what they did for the company. Sam Walton gave "rules for success" in his autobiography, one of which was to appreciate associates with praise.

There are four factors to transformational leadership, (also known as the "four I's"): idealized influence, inspirational motivation, intellectual stimulation, and individual consideration. Each factor will be discussed to help managers use this approach in the workplace.

- *Idealized influence* describes managers who are exemplary role models for associates. Managers with idealized influence can be trusted and respected by associates to make good decisions for the organisation.

- *Inspirational motivation* describes managers who motivate associates to commit to the vision of the organisation. Managers with inspirational motivation encourage team spirit to reach goals of increased revenue and market growth for the organisation.
- *Intellectual Stimulation* describes managers who encourage innovation and creativity through challenging the normal beliefs or views of a group. Managers with intellectual stimulation promote critical thinking and problem solving to make the organisation better.
- *Individual consideration* describes managers who act as coaches and advisors to the associates. Managers with individual consideration encourage associates to reach goals that help both the associates and the organisation.

Effective transformational leadership results in performances that exceed organisational expectations. The "additive" effect of transformational leadership because managers must pull together the components to reach "performance beyond expectations".

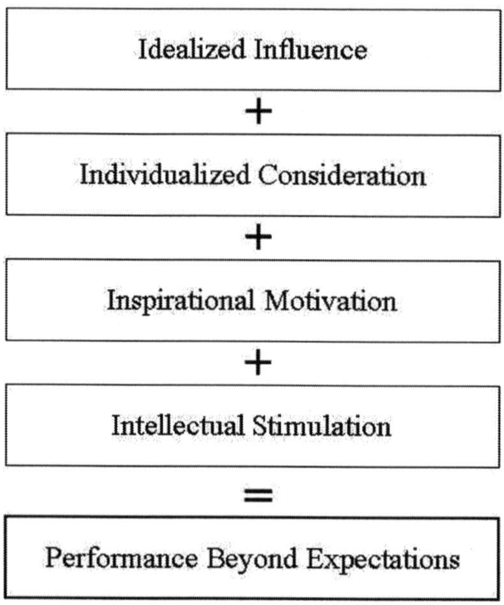

Fig. Additive effect of transformational leadership.

Each of the four components describes characteristics that are valuable to the "transformation" process. When managers are strong role models, encouragers, innovators, and coaches, they are utilising the "four I's" to help "transform" their associates into better, more productive and successful individuals. Northouse (2001) states that in 39 studies of transformational literature, individuals who exhibited transformational leadership were more effective leaders with better work outcomes. This was true for both high- and low-level leaders in the public and private sectors. Therefore, it can be very advantageous for managers to apply the transformational approach in the workplace.

STRENGTHS AND WEAKNESSES OF TRANSFORMATIONAL LEADERSHIP

As with any theory or approach to leadership, strengths and weaknesses become evident. Northouse (2001) identifies the strengths and weaknesses of the transformational leadership approach as follows:

- Strengths are widely researched (using well-known leaders), effectively influence associates on all levels (from one-on-one to the whole organisation), and strongly emphasize associates' needs and values.
- Weaknesses have many components that seem too broad, treat leadership more as a personality trait than as a learned behaviour, and have the potential for abusing power.

APPLYING TRANSFORMATIONAL LEADERSHIP

Because transformational leadership covers a wide range of aspects within leadership, there are no specific steps for a manager to follow. Becoming an effective transformational leader is a process. This means that conscious effort must be made to adopt a transformational style. Understanding the basics of transformational leadership and the four I's can help a manager apply this approach. According to Northouse (2001), a transformational leader has the following qualities:

- empowers followers to do what is best for the organisation;
- is a strong role model with high values;
- listens to all viewpoints to develop a spirit of cooperation;
- creates a vision, using people in the organisation;
- acts as a change agent within the organisation by setting an example of how to initiate and implement change;
- helps the organisation by helping others contribute to the organisation.

Transformational leadership is a vital role for effective managers because leader effectiveness determines the success level of the organisation. According to Hesselbein and Cohen, organisations that take the time to teach leadership are far ahead of the competition. By becoming familiar with the transformational leadership approach and combining the four I's, managers can become effective leaders in the business world.

Transformational leadership can be applied in one-on-one or group situations. Using this approach, the manager (leader) and the associates (followers) are "transformed" to enhance job performance and help the organisation be more productive and successful.

FUTURE

The evolution of transformational leadership in the digital age is tied to the development of organisational leadership in an academic setting. As organisations move from position-based responsibilities to task-based responsibilities, transformational leadership is redefined to continue to develop individual commitment to organisational goals by aligning these goals with the interests of their leadership community. The academic community is a front-runner in this sense of redefining transformational leadership to suit these changes in job definition.

The future of transformational leadership is also related to political globalisation and a more homogenous spectrum of economic systems under which organisations find themselves operating. Cultural and geographical dimensions of transformational leadership become blurred as globalisation renders ethnically specific collectivist and individualistic effects of organisational behaviour obsolete in a more diversified workplace.

The concept of transformational leadership further needs clarification, especially when a leader is declared as a transformational or transactional leader. While discussing Jinnah's leadership style, Yousaf (2015)argued that it is not a number of followers, but the nature of the change that indicates whether a leaders is transformational or transactional.

9

The Empowerment of People and Leadership

EMPOWERING YOUR EMPLOYEES TO EMPOWER THEMSELVES

As a manager or leader, do you let your people assume more responsibility when they are able? Do you know when that is, or do you keep telling yourself that they aren't ready yet?

In my travels from organisation to organisation, I talk with thousands of people every year who want to be treated as "partners" rather than as employees. They want information to flow up as well as down. But, oftentimes, leaders do not want to give up control. We knew a CEO who was the leader of one of the world's largest global organisations. He received feedback that he was too stubborn and opinionated. He learned that he needed to do a better job of letting others to make decisions and to focus less on being right himself. He practiced this simple technique for one year: before speaking, he would take a breath and ask himself, "Is it worth it?" He learned that 50 per cent of the time his comments may have been right on, but they weren't worth it. He quickly began focusing more on empowering others and letting them take ownership and commitment for decisions, and less on his own need to add value.

Your employees understand their jobs. They know their tasks, roles, and functions within the organisation, and it's time for you to let them do what they need to do to get the job done. But there is a critical point that is often missed: It isn't possible for a leader to "empower" someone to be accountable and make good decisions. People have to empower themselves. Your role is to encourage and support the decision-making environment, and to give employees the tools and knowledge they need to make and act upon their own decisions. By doing this, you help your employees reach an empowered state.

The process does take longer — employees will only believe they are empowered when they are left alone to accomplish results over a period of time — but it's effective and worth the time. If a company has a history of shutting down or letting go of initiators, for instance, the leader can't just tell employees, "You are empowered to make decisions."

Part of building an empowering environment is dependent on the leader's ability to run interference on behalf of the team. The leader needs to make sure people are safe doing their jobs. To make sure this happens, an ongoing discussion of the needs, opportunities, tasks, obstacles, projects, what is working and what is not working is absolutely critical to the development and maintenance of a "safe" working environment. You are likely to spend a lot of time in dialogue with other leaders, employees, team members, and peers.

Following are a few things leaders can do to build an environment that empowers people.

1. Give power to those who have demonstrated the capacity to handle the responsibility.
2. Create a favorable environment in which people are encouraged to grow their skills.
3. Don't second-guess others' decisions and ideas unless it's absolutely necessary. This only undermines their confidence and keeps them from sharing future ideas with you.
4. Give people discretion and autonomy over their tasks and resources.

Successful leaders and managers today are willing to exercise their leadership in such a way that their people are empowered to make decisions, share information, and try new things. Most employees (future leaders) see the value in finding empowerment and are willing to take on the responsibilities that come with it. If future leaders have the wisdom to learn from the experience of present leaders, and if present leaders have the wisdom to build an environment that empowers people, both will share in the benefits.

EMPOWERING EMPLOYEES

Having empowered employees is the dream of every leader. All managers want people who show initiative by taking on and completing tasks with little guidance. Of course, the expectation is that these people will perform only in ways consistent with company objectives and values. And there lies the leadership challenge. Often the leadership has not done their part to empower the employees or, worse, has gotten in the way through micro-management.

Not all leaders have selfish intentions or poor skills; many simply haven't had the training, time or focus to create an environment of empowerment. Below are eight tips to help make your company a place where people feel good about stepping up and taking it on.

FOSTER OPEN COMMUNICATION

So many companies are built on top-down communication from management. Employees in this environment feel there is no purpose in taking a stand, since, they have no direct channel and don't feel they'll have an impact. As a leader, you may have clear direction and more experience, but that doesn't invalidate feedback and ideas from people on the front lines. Give employees structured ways to make their thoughts, feelings and observations known easily and regularly. Help them understand that their input is valued even if you decide to go a different way. Make sure you acknowledge them for sharing and reward valuable input that helps the company.

REWARD SELF-IMPROVEMENT

Many leaders complain that employees are stagnant but do little to help them grow. In such cases, somehow management has the idea that promotion and money are sufficient to get people to advance. More often than not, people don't have the resources or knowledge of what to do. Many entrepreneurs are so accustomed to self-improvement that they assume everyone thinks the same way. Budget dollars and time towards management and personal development training. Help employees set a plan for growth and reward them as they advance. They'll be grateful and apply their newly-learned skills as they step up to leadership opportunities.

ENCOURAGE SAFE FAILURE

Many employees, by their very nature, are risk-adverse. That's why they are employees and not entrepreneurs. If they work in an environment where the boss is always correcting them before they have a chance to execute, they will constantly look for approval before taking action or, worse, simply avoid any new or dynamic action. Give employees the opportunity to try new things in a way that doesn't put the company in danger. Create milestone checkpoints or set up laboratory environments where people can test new ideas and learn from the failures as well as the successes. Then your employees will gain understanding and feel comfortable innovating.

PROVIDE PLENTY OF CONTEXT

Most leaders carry lots of information in their brains. Unfortunately, many employees don't get the benefit of all that information, yet they are expected to take action and make good decisions as if they understood every nuance. Great leaders figure out how to extract the important information from their minds and share it in a structured and consistent manner. An employee who clearly understands the core values, purpose and direction of the company can easily make consistent decisions and take appropriate action at any junction. It's on you as the leader to impart your vision. That's how you lead.

CLEARLY DEFINE ROLES

People who don't know what they are supposed to do can't do it very well. Additionally, they need to know their boundaries so they don't step on others' toes or create inefficiency through redundancy. Establish specific roles and responsibilitieswith employees so all are clear and can work together cooperatively.

REQUIRE ACCOUNTABILITY

People need to know when they are meeting expectations and, more importantly, when they are not. No one will maintain accountability if they don't understand the consequences of failure. And if they see others not being held accountable, they will see little need to make the extra effort for success. Be consistent and diligent in your measurement and rewards so employees are motivated to do their best.

SUPPORT THEIR INDEPENDENCE

A leader who is constantly looking over the shoulder of employees is little more than a babysitter. Give your employees reasons and opportunity to stretch out on their own and even lead others. They may stumble, but they'll learn a lot and build the respect of their colleagues while preparing to be great empowering leaders themselves someday.

APPRECIATE THEIR EFFORTS

Yes, it's true that people get paid for the job. But the best employees don't work at your company just for the money. Empowered people need a greater level of satisfaction than simply financial stability. They need to feel that leadership appreciates their contribution and values their participation. Don't be shyabout finding ways to say "thank you" or celebrating the good things your employees do. If they have to ask how they are doing, you are doing your job poorly as a leader.

LEADERSHIP TECHNIQUES TO EMPOWER PEOPLE DURING CHANGE INITIATIVES

Every organisation is affected by change, especially during times of economic volatility. However, project managers tasked with leading change initiatives are all too aware of the alarming failure rates that can occur. The critical missing piece is largely the failure to take into account how change affects an organisation's people. According to a study by PriceWaterhouseCoopers, research shows that nearly 75 percent of all organisational change programmes fail because they don't create the necessary groundswell of support among employees. When organisational leadership employs a three-phase Organisational Change Management Life Cycle methodology and techniques to address the stages of change, change management initiatives stand a much greater chance for success.

Before examining the Organisational Change Management Life Cycle, it's important to consider the three organisational elements that both drive and are affected by change:

- Processes – Business processes, including maps, policies and procedures, and business rules, which are redesigned or realigned for new customers, or provide improved service to existing customers.
- Technology – Driven by process, technology ensures greater organisational efficiency in implementing change.
- People – Those responsible for developing and implementing new processes, and specifying and using new technology.

These elements are closely linked to the three stages of the Change Management Life Cycle: identify the change, engage the people, and implement the change. From the outset of any change management initiative, people must recognize and buy into the need for change. Leaders must recognize that an organisation cannot successfully adopt change unless its people understand and support the reasons for creating the change.

THE CHANGE MANAGEMENT LIFE CYCLE

Phase I: Identify the Change

While it may seem obvious, clearly articulating the proposed change in common, consistent language is the fundamental first step for any change initiative. Leaders need to identify and communicate the need for change so that it is understood and supported by people at all organisational levels. Project leaders should also be aware that there are intellectual, psychological and neurological responses that people have regarding change that can be addressed with the following recommended techniques:

- Get People's Attention – Change distracts and disturbs human beings, so directing their attention in a positive way will help them focus on the proposed change. Introducing the initiative in a setting away from people's daily routines, off-site if possible, will create a shared sense of urgency and ownership in the change.
- Align Their Disturbances – A disturbance is a neurological term for the conflict or gap between a person's current mental map of thinking and the mental map required to operate in a changed state. To align disturbances means to create agreement among the individuals in an organisation so they have a common gap between their current way of thinking and the mental state needed to adopt the change. This will enable them to agree on the direction and organisational response needed for change.

An important technique leaders should use to align disturbances is to create a compelling vision of the future state and continually communicate it. The vision should take into consideration the change need at every organisational level, so that the day-to-day work experience of the staff is described along with high-level change goals. Additional people-related issues leaders should be aware of and address when identifying change opportunities include:

- Potential frustration in performing new tasks
- Clearly defined job responsibilities
- Job descriptions and metrics appropriate to the new process
- Understanding of the end-to-end process
- Organisational culture dynamics that may prevent people from adapting to the changed state

Phase 2: Engage the People

The next step in the change management life cycle is to engage people in the planning of the organisation's response to the change. This concept is the antithesis of a top-down rollout strategy in which a change initiative is delivered to the people expected to implement and adopt the change. Giving them the opportunity for intellectual, emotional and psychological reaction to the proposed change enables them to become accustomed to the idea of change and begin thinking in ways that can identify potential trouble spots and contribute to process improvement. It is critical to their personal stake in the proposed change.

A technique project leaders can use to facilitate people's adoption of a change is to conduct organisation-wide workshops on appropriate change response. These sessions enable people to participate in the dialogue about how a deliverable should be used in the organisation, and contribute to the emergence of an aligned approach for managing and adapting to the change. Aligning reactions and encouraging involvement in the change response typically moves people's behaviour to addressing the problem and creating a direction to facilitate change.

The implementation strategy for change response can then be developed at a high level. The people executing the strategy, as well as those who will be impacted by it, should be included in the strategy development. The strategy needs to be acknowledged by all involved as a flexible plan so that changes can be made once implementation is begun.

Phase 3: Implement the Change

During the final Implementation phase, change strategies developed in the Identify and Engage phases are translated into actions for achieving the proposed future organisational state. If the first two stages were effectively addressed, people will be well prepared to participate in the development and implementation of new processes and technology, and the implementation should essentially be a monitoring activity for leaders. However, most organisations spend the majority of their time in the implementation phase and don't adequately address their people's role in change. In such instances, successful change adoption rarely occurs.

Prototyping is a critical technique to get the change underway incrementally without waiting for a highly detailed, master plan which can potentially stall the change initiative, while allowing flexibility to respond to changing conditions. Prototyping takes into account people's thinking and activities as new processes and technology are deployed. Since, their thoughts and actions are used in developing the change response, it further increases people's ownership in the change initiative.

Techniques leaders should use during implementation include reiterating the change mission through ongoing communications. E-mails, project milestone commemorations, conversations and other channels should be used to remind people why they are expending their hard work on implementing a change.

Organisational leaders should address people-related issues that arise by asking themselves the following questions:

- Does the individual have the ability or desire to work in the new environment?
- Are additional skill sets needed to transition to the new job?
- Are changes to job descriptions needed?
- Are job grades or pay impacted by this change?
- Does the change impact short-term productivity and is additional support needed to ensure business success?

Lastly, leaders should focus on people's performance and satisfaction by questioning the following areas:

- Are change-oriented tasks being accomplished as planned?
- Are energy and enthusiasm present?
- Does alignment still exist among the people?

People First

The urgency of circumstances that precipitate change results frequently in the introduction of new processes and technology which are doomed to failure without the input and buy in of an organisation's people. Leadership that recognizes the importance of making change a personal commitment for all of its people, not just executives and stakeholders, will be more successful at implementing change. Using the Change Management Life Cycle methodology's three phases of Identify, Engage and Implement and related techniques provides organisations with a framework for creating a receptive environment for positive, lasting change.

EMPOWERMENT — HOW TO EMPOWER PEOPLE AND EXTEND YOUR INFLUENCE AS A LEADER

When you empower people, you give your influence to them for the purpose of personal and organisational growth. Successful leaders empower others by delegating power and sharing their influence, position, and power with others.

If you are burnt out, stressed, and tired, you are probably not delegating authority and empowering other people to take charge; you are insecure and afraid of someone taking your job.

Besides helping you as a leader to work with and through people, empowering and investing in people can help them reach their potential.

No matter how much work you can do, no matter how engaging your personality may be, you will not advance far in business if you cannot work through others —John Craig When you decide to empower people, Leadership guru John C. Maxwell said "your goal in the beginning should be to hand over relatively small, simple tasks to the people you wish to empower and progressively increase the responsibility and authority.

Here are 7 foolproof ways to empower people:

EVALUATE THE PEOPLE YOU WANT TO EMPOWER

If you give inexperienced people too much authority too soon, you might be setting them up to fail. If you move too slowly with people who have lots of experience, you can frustrate them. Your job as a leader is to find out what they lack and help them develop it.

MODEL FOR THE PEOPLE YOU ARE WORKING TO EMPOWER

People do what people see. Model the attitude, work ethic, and character you like them to embrace. Take them along with you and include them in your work.

GIVE PERMISSION TO THE PEOPLE YOU ARE WORKING TO EMPOWER

Believe in them, help them to believe in themselves, and show them that you want them to succeed. Let them know you are expecting them to succeed and tell them often that you are confident they are going to make it.

TRANSFER AUTHORITY TO THE PEOPLE YOU ARE WORKING TO EMPOWER

Sharing your workload is delegation, sharing your power and authority is empowerment. Give them opportunity to make decisions, initiate actions, and solve problems.

PUBLICLY SHOW YOUR CONFIDENCE IN THE PEOPLE YOU ARE WORKING TO EMPOWER

When you transfer authority to people, publicly recognize them to let them to let them know you believe that they will succeed. Public recognition also let others know you are backing them up with your authority.

GIVE FEEDBACK TO THE PEOPLE YOU ARE WORKING TO EMPOWER

While it's laudable to publicly recognize and praise the people you are empowering, don't neglect to privately coach them through their mistakes and misjudgments.

RELEASE THE PEOPLE YOU ARE WORKING TO EMPOWER TO CONTINUE ON THEIR OWN

When President Abraham Lincoln appointed General Ulysses S. Grant as commander of the Union armies in 1864, he sent him this message: "I neither ask nor desire to know anything of your plans. Take the responsibility to and act, and call on me for assistance."

EMPOWERING YOUR TEAM

Empowered teams have increased levels of responsibility and authority over the work that they do, giving them the autonomy to plan and manage work, make their own decisions and solve their own problems – responsibilities that are traditionally owned by the team leader.

As someone who leads a team, you'll be used to being the decision-maker, problem-solver, planner, manager and instructor. In short, you're normally the one who's in control. So, empowering others is no doubt very different from what you are used to doing. It means handing over much of this control, along with many associated responsibilities, to your team.

If you're new to empowerment, it's only natural to feel a little anxious about this. You might feel that your role will become redundant. In fact, it's quite the opposite – your team needs you more than ever!

You may have handed over a great deal of control, but you're still ultimately responsible for the work of the team. Just because you've given power to others doesn't mean that you've lost it yourself. You're still the one who defines the goals and boundaries, and your team will still look to you for support, guidance and encouragement. In fact, empowering your team will leave you free to concentrate on new and exciting responsibilities, some of which will include:

DEFINING TEAM GOALS

Your team still need to know what they should be aiming to achieve. Remember, you are the link between your team and the rest of the department/organisation, so your understanding of the wider context in which the team operates will help you define goals that are in alignment with the department/organisation's objectives.

The goals that you set should be results-orientated (*e.g.* maintaining organised office systems) rather than task focussed (*e.g.* opening mail and filing). Results-orientated goals are more helpful than lists of routine tasks as they express only the outcomes that are expected, without dictating how they should be achieved. This gives people the freedom to define their own tasks, as well as a clearer understanding of why they should be doing them.

SETTING BOUNDARIES

People need broad parameters to guide them towards the achievement of their goals. Although empowered teams have a great degree of freedom and autonomy over the way in which they work, they still need guidelines or boundaries to help them understand what is expected of them, so that they can channel their efforts appropriately and work with confidence.

PROVIDING INFORMATION

In traditional teams, team leaders often keep a great deal of information to themselves. However, in an empowered team people can only be fully effective if they have all the information that they need. They must have an idea of the 'bigger picture' to help them understand why they are doing what they are doing, and also their limits and constraints.

You should aim to provide regular feedback to the team on how they are progressing towards their goals so that they can keep themselves on track.

GIVING ADVICE

You're the leader and expert, and people will look to you for advice. Make it easy for your team to approach you to ask questions and seek feedback. Let them know that you're happy to help.

DEVELOPING PEOPLE'S SKILLS THROUGH COACHING

Coaching is an empowering method of development, as it helps people learn for themselves. Coaches help people to learn by challenging their assumptions; encouraging them to explore new ideas and different ways of thinking; setting development tasks for learning; or simply by providing a different perspective. When coaching, you empower the learner by providing them with the tools to learn for themselves.

ENCOURAGING PEOPLE AND BOOSTING THEIR CONFIDENCE

Everyone needs to hear every so often what a good job they're doing, especially people in an empowered team who may be taking on many responsibilities that are completely new to them. Demonstrate your faith in their ability and build their confidence by highlighting and praising their key strengths and achievements. Some of the potential benefits of an empowered way of working are:

- Cost savings – as team members have the autonomy to improve the effectiveness and efficiency of working practices.
- Innovation and continuous improvement – in an environment that encourages ideas, creativity, and the questioning of established wisdom.
- Effective decision-making – the power to make decisions is given to those who need it most to get on with their jobs.
- Commitment – the increased autonomy gives team members a sense

of personal responsibility and therefore more commitment to achieving team goals.

- Motivation – as team members have a clear sense of purpose and ownership of the team goals, opportunities for learning new skills and furthering personal development are increased.
- Increased productivity – as the culture created by empowerment is one of high performance in which team members take on personal responsibility for the achievement of team goals.

Teams are, of course, made up of individuals, so an empowered team will only be successful if the individuals themselves are ready and willing to take on the extra responsibilities that empowerment brings. Power isn't just another thing that you can delegate – it is an entirely individual choice. It will only be accepted if you create a suitable culture for empowerment in the first place.

ORGANISATIONAL EMPOWERMENT

Organisations tackle the uncertainties of today's changing world by drawing out the creative potential of the people who are the organisation. Empowerment means creating an environment where people are equipped and encouraged to make decisions in autonomous ways and to feel that they are in control of the outcomes for which they are responsible. It means opening the door for dissent, avoiding groupthink and encouraging innovation.

To understand some of the complexities of Organisational Empowerment, we will be looking at it from the perspectives of leaders, employees, and organisations. Empowerment involves distributing authority throughout the organisation. The leader's perspective is where it all starts. What does empowerment mean for the CEO and management?

EMPOWERMENT FROM THE LEADER'S PERSPECTIVE

Empowering leaders behave in an empowering manner by (1) influencing through context, (2) creating a culture of inclusion, (3) giving and not taking back control, (4) providing moral and logistical support, (5) communicating a clear mandate, and (6) equipping people for success.

Influence through context implies trust in a higher principle or guiding force and belief in the creative potential of human nature. It is a mater of trusting the process. It is not "giving power," but creating a context where empowerment is released and nurtured. Leaders define the context and standards at every level by giving people freedom to act and innovate, thereby developing leadership and producing proactive employees, giving them a competitive edge.

Create a feeling of inclusion to nurture and empower. Develop an atmosphere of inclusion across all levels, making sure that everyone has a voice and that their voices are heard. Leaders welcome dissent as a source of objectivity and innovation. New ideas must be allowed in the decision-making processes to generate solutions superior to those achieved through the exercise of positional power.

Give up control and do not reclaim it. Expect to go through a phase where managers are faced with ambiguities and a sense that things are out of control. During this uncomfortable phase, one is tempted to tighten the controls. Resist the temptation to tighten control if you want your people to use a proactive approach to problem-solving. Once responsibility is given, do not try to take it back.

Support employee empowerment. Support of superiors is critical. Fear of reprimand or sanctions—because a decision didn't work out—will kill efforts to empower. This is not delegating. Delegating is assigning a task to someone. Empowerment is giving responsibility and the freedom to choose the means of accomplishment. It means the leader moves from "boss" to "coach." However, the objective must be clearly understood. Cesar Guajardo, General Director of Praxair in Mexico, wrote:

I gave people the responsibility and authority to do what they needed to improve performance. I asked them to share large-scale decisions with me. Otherwise, I gave them the authority to make decisions on their own. I encouraged small committees to share ideas and get points of view. I let them learn on their own by making mistakes. At times, I had to support ideas that were not very good at the beginning, but worked just fine.

Articulate the common purpose. Do not mistake empowerment for an absence of direction. The leader needs to create the vision and clarify goals. A lack of clarity about desired outcomes and role expectations is disempowering. Being accountable for specific expectations is better than not knowing where you stand. It is critical for the leader to clearly define the common purpose, goals, and limitations. If not, employees will be hesitant. Pass the ball and let the associate run with it—but run within the ball field. Stay inbounds. Responsibility for and commitment to a clearly articulated mission is essential.

Equip people for success to insure a good chance of success. This involves training, resources, and information. Too often employees are given responsibility for which they are not equipped. This entrapment brings the feeling of being set up. Consider setting up an unallocated resource pool for solving unforeseen problems. Leaders provide their people with all the information they need by making information readily available to people at all levels through more channels.

EMPOWERMENT FROM THE EMPLOYEE'S PERSPECTIVE

To experience empowerment, employees need to develop skills in and practice: (1) open communication, (2) work in teams, (3) critical listening, (4) tolerance of uncertainty, (5) resilience and courage, and (6) accepting responsibility. Open communication is a willingness to put our thoughts on the table; to be exposed to scrutiny; to own up to one's ideas, assumptions, biases and fears; and help others to do the same. Corporate cultures that promote creativity are characterized by direct interaction and openness—a climate where ideas are owned and challenged through honest dialogue. It may not be comfortable but it is a necessary condition of empowerment. Such openness cannot be coerced.

Willingness and know-how for working in teams is essential. It is not just self-empowerment. It is a collective change that comes by learning respect for the contributions of others. Empowerment is not a Win-Lose paradigm where an increase in the power of one results in a decrease in the power of others. In MMC's Team-Building course, participants learn to value the uniqueness of the other players. By discovering and emphasizing the gifts of each individual, the experience of empowerment increases for everyone on the team.

Gain wisdom to be fully empowered. To move from dependence on superiors for decisions, one must move beyond data, information, and knowledge to make appropriate decisions. Data is a collection of categorized numbers. Information is the meaning extracted from data. Knowledge consists of sets of information put in context, and wisdom is merging knowledge with universal principles for application to real-life situations. This requires a higher level of involvement than the old scientific management paradigm that treated employees like machines. In empowered organisations, employees across the board are committed to thinking and acting for success of the organisation, as does top management, but more effectively. Wisdom is the result of thinking about the future, recognising trends and anticipating events or outcomes that may affect the organisation and from interactions with customers, suppliers, and others with whom employees interface directly.

Tolerate uncertainty. Empowerment can be threatening. Expect some employees to resist empowerment. This is especially true when not only the outcomes, but the means and ways have always been clearly defined for them by others. Decisions about how to get things done, when left to the employee, is disquieting for the leader. This uncertainty is a change from working in an established routine where employees adhere to the rules and procedures. Under pressure, employees tend to run to the leader seeking resolution and closure. Leaders who do not understand the dynamics of empowerment, out of misdirected compassion or because it makes them feel more powerful, often succumb to these requests by telling them what to do. This is disempowering and reestablishes dependence. If employees are encouraged to think for themselves, goals and boundaries need to be clearly defined. This establishes guidelines for use of intuition and thinking across departments and disciplines for solutions related to their common purpose. Resilience and courage come from within. The source of confidence is not in others but in one's own inner strength. Empowerment means to be forward thinking enough to live with mistakes and failures without being impaired. Those living with self-doubt will be unlikely to accept the challenge of empowerment because, for them, more responsibility means more chance of failure, and failure threatens their sense of self-worth. Empowerment is very personal. Acceptance of higher levels of responsibility is inherent in an empowering context.

Accept responsibility for outcomes. Empowerment goes beyond delegation, and encompasses the burden of responsibility. Empowerment must be balanced by responsibility. They cannot blame upper management, suppliers, other department heads, or anyone else for failure to produce desired results. This enables them to learn from their mistakes. Empowered employees are willing to have their performance measured by objective written assessments because these are opportunities for feedback and improvement. Part of responsibility happens when you see inappropriate management conduct or receive inappropriate direction. It is important to document all incidents and save them in a safe place.

EMPOWERMENT FROM THE ORGANISATION'S PERSPECTIVE

Empowerment calls for organisations to (1) be more decentralized, (2) to share more information, (3) to have in place a system of contingent rewards, (4) to be team-based, and (5) to align itself with its goals and values.

Decentralization distributes decision-making as close to the action as appropriate. This means giving employees the authority to make timely decisions. Individual empowerment cannot occur within a highly centralized system of control because such systems reserve decision-making power for the few who occupy the center, thus inhibiting individual initiative. People are not motivated to change when they don't have authority to do anything with what they have learned.

Information sharing is empowering. Hoarding knowledge and withholding it is a way to maintain control. Employees need information about the organisation's mission and goals, information needed to meet team objectives, and information about their individual performance. In empowering organisations, information is no longer the property of individuals, but now belongs to the entire group. As information is more openly shared, the organisation will begin to function less on the basis of opinion and bias and more on the basis of facts. Systems must be in place to enable access to both general information about the organisation and also specific information about the performance of their particular department or team.

Contingent rewards are difficult to design. Empowerment works best when a reward system distinguishes between employees based on performance. Empowering organisations reward employees who make decisions that contribute to the accomplishment of the organisation's purpose and goals. Make sure that what is rewarded reflects goals of the organisation. To automatically punish failure inhibits empowerment. It is better to reward employees for attempting new ideas, even ones that fail. Paige Leavitt, of the American Productivity and Quality Center in Houston, explains how they use rewards to encourage empowerment: "We try to foster an atmosphere that has a lot of respect for people who make a contribution. We don't expect success every time a person suggests or tries something, otherwise they won't want to try new things. If you've come up with a good idea and your supervisor sends you a thank-you note or gives you a pat on the back—that does more than anything that we can do in an employee newsletter or a public venue.

Teams develop when individuals move outside themselves and become concerned with the success of all other members. This means that employees become concerned, not only with the success of their immediate responsibility, but also with success of the other members of the team. Then the group becomes a unit where the development of one member increases the power of the team.

Alignment with the common purpose is a must. To empower people in an unaligned organisation can be counterproductive. If people do not share a common vision, and do not share common goals, empowering people will increase organisational stress and make it impossible to maintain coherence and direction. An organisational commitment to empowerment would be foolish if leaders did not share the same visions and goals. Empowered organisations must structure processes, goals, people, and reward systems aligned with each other.

IMPLEMENTING AN EMPOWERMENT PROGRAMME

There is a direct relationship between empowerment and organisational vitality. It is about the probability of change, of keeping up in a changing world. People learn best when they see a relationship between their life and the concepts being taught. Without sensing an organisational commitment to fully implement empowerment, these concepts will be very difficult to implement. Only when people have authorisation to dissent with the leader do new ideas have a chance to appear. Empowerment is the key to organisational vitality

UNDERSTANDING POWER

At the core of the concept of empowerment is the idea of power. The possibility of empowerment depends on two things. First, empowerment requires that power can change. If power cannot change, if it is inherent in positions or people, then empowerment is not possible, nor is empowerment conceivable in any meaningful way. In other words, if power can change, then empowerment is possible. Second, the concept of empowerment depends upon the idea that power can expand. This second point reflects our common experiences of power rather than how we think about power. To clarify these points, we first discuss what we mean by power.

Power is often related to our ability to make others do what we want, regardless of their own wishes or interests. Traditional social science emphasizes power as influence and control, often treating power as a commodity or structure divorced from human action. Conceived in this way, power can be viewed as unchanging or unchangeable. Weber (1946) gives us a key word beyond this limitation by recognising that power exists within the context of a relationship between people or things. Power does not exist in isolation nor is it inherent in individuals. By implication, since, power is created in relationships, power and power relationships can change. Empowerment as a process of change, then, becomes a meaningful concept.

A brief exercise makes the importance of this discussion clear. Quickly, list three words that immediately come to mind when you hear the word power. For most people, words that come to mind when we think about power often revolve around control and domination. Focusing on these aspects of power limit our ability to understand and define empowerment.

The concept of empowerment also depends upon power that can expand, our second stated requirement. Understanding power as zero-sum, as something that you get at my expense, cuts most of us off from power. A zero-sum conception of power means that power will remain in the hands of the powerful unless they give it up. Although this is certainly one way that power can be experienced, it neglects the way power will remain in the hands of the powerful unless they give it up. Although this is certainly one way that power is experienced, it neglects the way power is experienced in most interactions. Another brief exercise highlights the importance of a definition of power that includes expansion. Answer the question; "Have you ever felt powerful?" Was it at someone's expense? Was it with someone else?

Grounded in an understanding that power will be seen and understood differently by people who inhabit various positions in power structures, contemporary research on power has opened new perspectives that reflect aspects of power that are not zero-sum, but are shared. Feminists, members of grassroots organisations, racial and ethnic groups (Nicola-McLaughlin and Chandler, 1984), and even individuals in families bring into focus another aspect of power, one that is characterized by collaboration, sharing and mutuality.

Researchers and practitioners call this aspect of power "relational power", generative power, "integrative power," and "power with".This aspect means that gaining power actually strengthens the power of others rather than diminishing it such as occurs with domination/power. Kreisberg has suggested that power defined as "the capacity to implement" (Kreisberg, 1992:57) is broad enough to allow power to mean domination, authority, influence, and shared power or "power with." It is this definition of power, as a process that occurs in relationships, that gives us the possibility of empowerment.

UNDERSTANDING EMPOWERMENT

Empowerment is a construct shared by many disciplines and arenas: community development, psychology, education, economics, and studies of social movements and organisations, among others. How empowerment is understood varies among these perspectives. In recent empowerment literature, the meaning of the term empowerment is often assumed rather than explained or defined. Rappoport (1984) has noted that it is easy to define empowerment by its absence but difficult to define in action as it takes on different forms in different people and contexts. Even defining the concept is subject to debate. Zimmerman (1984) has stated that asserting a single definition of empowerment may make attempts to achieve it formulaic or prescription-like, contradicting the very concept of empowerment.

A common understanding of empowerment is necessary, however, to allow us to know empowerment when we see it in people with whom we are working, and for programme evaluation. According to Bailey (1992), how we precisely define empowerment within our projects and programmes will depend upon the specific people and context involved.

As a general definition, however, we suggest that empowerment is a multi-dimensional social process that helps people gain control over their own lives. It is a process that fosters power (that is, the capacity to implement) in people, for use in their own lives, their communities, and in their society, by acting on issues that they define as important.

We suggest that three components of our definition are basic to any understanding of empowerment. Empowerment is multi-dimensional, social, and a process. It is multi-dimensional in that it occurs within sociological, psychological, economic, and other dimensions. Empowerment also occurs at various levels, such as individual, group, and community. Empowerment, by definition, is a social process, since, it occurs in relationship to others. Empowerment is a process that is similar to a path or journey, one that develops as we work through it. Other aspects of empowerment may vary according to the specific context and people involved, but these remain constant. In addition, one important implication of this definition of empowerment is that the individual and community are fundamentally connected.

INTERCONNECTION OF INDIVIDUALS AND COMMUNITY

Wilson (1996) pointed out that recently, more researchers, organizers, politicians and employers recognize that individual change is a prerequisite for community and social change and empowerment (Speer and Hughey, 1995; Florin and Wandersman, 1990; Chavis and Wandersman, 1990). This does not mean that we can point the finger at those with less access to power, telling them that they must change to become more like "us" in order to be powerful/ successful. Rather, individual change becomes a bridge to community connectedness and social change. To create change we must change individually to enable us to become partners in solving the complex issues facing us. In collaborations based on mutual respect, diverse perspectives, and a developing vision, people work towards creative and realistic solutions. This synthesis of individual and collective change (Wilson, 1996; Florin and Wandersman, 1990; Speer and Hughey, 1995) is our understanding of an empowerment process. We see this inclusive individual and collective understanding of empowerment as crucial in programmes with empowerment as a goal. It is in the critical transition, or interconnection, between the individual and the communal, or social, that programmes such as ours, People Empowering People, can be invaluable for people and communities.

EMPOWERMENT AND PEP

The People Empowering People (PEP) programme uses the definition of empowerment to connect research, theory, and practice. The Connecticut PEP programme builds on theory of critical adult education developed by Friere (1970), Horton (1989), and others. PEP focuses on the strengths of people, providing opportunities and resources for people to gain experiences and skills while they also gain control over their lives.

Underlying this process is mutual respect between participants, facilitators, advisory committee members, and others involved in the programme. PEP opens to participants the recognition of their own values and beliefs, and encourages expression of their own issues as they define them. The focus is on the connection between individual action and community action, encouraging individual change through training sessions and discussions, and supporting community action through participants' efforts to change their communities. While we cannot give people power and we cannot make them "empowered," we can provide the opportunities, resources and support that they need to become involved themselves.

In conclusion, we see empowerment as a multi-dimensional social process that helps people gain control over their own lives. It is a process that fosters power in people for use in their own lives, their communities, and in their society by acting on issues that they define as important. In PEP as in Extension we strive to teach people skills and knowledge that will motivate them to take steps to improve their own lives — to be empowered.

LEADERSHIP AND EMPOWERMENT

I was pleased and honored to have had the opportunity to participate in the "New Leadership For A New Era" Conference. I see leadership as an important component in the disability movement. Leadership is a pathway towards empowerment. I will explore some critical ingredients that I believe are necessary to help in the formation of good leaders and leadership. This article is intended to highlight a few "nuts and bolts" about leadership that may be useful to persons with disabilities, their families, and organisations advocating for such individuals.

WHAT IS A LEADER?

A leader is an individual who guides other people or organisations in a certain direction or on a charted course. A leader directs the operations or activities of a group of people. Leadership is critical in any organisation, because without leadership, organisations and people tend to go astray. Now, more than ever, leadership abilities are essential skills that the disability community must nurture and fully utilize. The Americans with Disabilities Act {ADA} opens up opportunities for persons with disabilities to exercise the empowerment they are now afforded. Civil rights organisations serving people from minority groups, women, and other protected classes have been able to make significant strides because they have had persons within their ranks that were able to lead and advocate. It is essential that people with disabilities have persons within their ranks who can effectively project the new empowerment embodied in ADA.

WHY BE A LEADER AND AN ADVOCATE WITHIN THE DISABILITY COMMUNITY?

It is important that persons from the disability community become leaders. Currently, there are too few individuals within the disability community who have taken on the mantle of leadership and it is critical that an increasing number of persons with disabilities take on leadership roles. With ADA, leaders are needed now more than ever to guarantee that the law is fully implemented. Leaders are continually needed to keep persons with disabilities informed and organized. Leaders must also advocate for the empowerment, rights, and privileges of persons with disabilities. Existing leaders and advocates are role models for other persons with disabilities. Being a leader can be both challenging and satisfying.

In addition, I would like to point out that there is a dearth of leaders within minority communities. We need leadership badly. Therefore, those of us who have gained some measure of success must work hard to assist others. Many minority individuals with disabilities lack the essential skills to advocate for themselves and we must work to correct that problem. Persons of colour must be provided opportunities to demonstrate their leadership skills and they must take advantage of all opportunities to do so. For instance, the collaborative arrangement between the Howard University Research and Training Center (HURTC) and the President's Committee on Employment of People with Disabilities (PCEPD) has been a major stepping stone towards developing multicultural leaders with disabilities. The PCEPD Disability and Employment Concerns (DEC) Standing Committee's Leadership 2000 project and Howard

University's Bridges To Leadership 2000 project have greatly assisted in the empowerment of minority persons with disabilities.

WHAT DOES LEADERSHIP ENTAIL?

Leadership entails being a responsible, strong-willed, and strong-minded person. Leadership must show strength and yet be willing to compromise when necessary. Having good interpersonal and human relation skills is essential. Leaders must be able to persuade other people to rally for causes when necessary. Good leadership requires that persons be well informed about issues that impact on them and their constituents. Being a good leader also requires working in the trenches along with comrades. Good leaders must be motivators, negotiators, and consensus builders. Good leaders must always be concerned about the welfare of comrades. Effective leaders must always be able to communicate with comrades, government, the private sector, and political leaders.

Leaders must be knowledgeable about laws like ADA, and be politically astute as well. They should have the ability to effectively lobby for the rights of people with disabilities. Leaders within the disability community must be able to communicate with persons who have various disabilities. A leader must also possess diplomatic and advocacy skills.

CAN I BE A LEADER AND A FOLLOWER?

One of the most frequent questions raised by persons with disabilities is, "Can I be a Leader?" Yes, you can be a leader and a follower, often at the same time. Too often, leaders make the critical mistake of not wanting to be followers. Good leaders are also good listeners. A good listener pays attention to the concerns of others, and a sensitive leader remains attuned to the needs of his/her constituents. Leaders emerge from the ranks of followers and often continue as followers of others. Every great leader must fall in line with others and work in the background. Every great leader has sought and acted upon advice from followers and has merged the roles of following and leading. Within the disability community, we must both lead and follow in order to become completely empowered and fully implement the ADA for all American citizens with disabilities. We cannot afford to be fragmented on the basis of our roles. Leaders at all levels must work together in a coordinated, cooperative effort just as we did in the campaign for the passage of the ADA.

DO YOU NEED A LARGE FOLLOWING TO BE CONSIDERED A LEADER?

Contrary to what most people think, you do not need a large following to be a leader. Oftentimes, leaders that have small followings are quite effective. For instance, in the political arena, the precinct leaders and ward captains are extremely valuable because they help provide the glue that keeps the larger organisation intact.

In order to make ADA effective for all persons with disabilities, leaders of large and small groups must work together. Persons with disabilities in every hamlet, village, town, county, city, and state will need dedicated leadership to work for the full implementation of ADA and the empowerment of their peers. Sharing the media spotlight is not a prerequisite for being a good leader. Not all leaders will receive the recognition that they believe is due them.

Just as there is a place for leaders of large constituents, there is also a place for leaders of small groups. It is imperative for existing leaders to create and develop new leaders within the disability community so that they work for the full implementation of ADA and the struggle for empowerment of such persons.

HOW AND WHERE ARE LEADERS FOUND?

1. Leaders within the disability community may be found in:
- a) Churches and in local and national church organisations
- b) Schools and colleges
- c) Community organisations such as Kiwanis, Lions, etc.
- d) Independent Living Centers
- e) Rehabilitation agencies
- f) Federal, state, and local government
- g) Advocacy groups

2. Leaders within the disability community may be recruited by:
- Other persons with disabilities
- Community people
- Friends and family
- Pastors, officers, and members of churches
- Teachers
- Human service professionals
- Legislators and other government officials

HOW CAN I BECOME INVOLVED AND UTILIZE MY LEADERSHIP SKILLS?

You might ask yourself, "How can I get involved and use my leadership skills?" You can and should get involved to advocate for yourself and others. Here are a few suggested ways of getting involved:

1. Become involved in local community activities (*e.g.* neighborhood associations, citizens groups, public interest groups, consumer groups, etc.);
2. Volunteer for PTA's, school boards, civic library boards and other organisations to put the views of persons with disabilities views into accessibility plans;

3. Attend local community hearings and public meetings and speak out;
4. Attend Private Industry Council (PIC) meetings;
5. Join local organisations such as the Junior Chamber of Commerce, Kiwanis Club, Lions Club, local professional organisations, etc.;
6. Attend legislative sessions at local, state, and national levels. For example, attend city council meetings, county council meetings, state legislative sessions, and national legislative sessions (United States House of Representatives and The United States Senate). Participate, to the extent possible, in the legislative process;
7. Attend and participate, to the extent possible, in the administrative process at the local, state, and national levels (*e.g.* housing and zoning appeals, transportation authority hearings and meetings);
8. Lobby local, state, and national governmental bodies and officials to introduce and promote the passage of legislation that will be beneficial to persons with disabilities;
9. Become active in local, regional, and national religious bodies and social organisations and advocate for change;
10. Join local disability groups and actively participate in them (*e.g.* organisations for persons with hearing and visual impairments, persons with various disabilities such as Cerebral Palsy, Multiple Sclerosis, Polio, etc., and local independent living centers). Initiate new ideas for change that will be advantageous to persons with disabilities. Organize groups and organisations, if necessary;
11. Seek appointments to serve on local private, state, and national governmental boards and councils (*e.g.* school boards, neighborhood advisory councils, advisory boards for persons with disabilities, industrial boards and commissions, zoning boards, transportation committees, etc.);
12. Persons with disabilities should exercise their rights to vote in local state and national elections;
13. Seek elective offices if you desire to do so; and
14. Write letters to editors of newspapers, magazines, and television and radio stations concerning issues relating to persons with disabilities.

The aforementioned are only a few suggestions of how you can become involved. You should think of as many ways as possible to become involved and attempt to effectuate change for the empowerment and betterment of people with disabilities.

THE LEADERSHIP RESPONSIBILITIES OF PEOPLE OF COLOUR

With Impairments in the 21st Century

Initially, I had been asked to present a paper which would basically outline ways in which one might prepare professionals of colour with impairments for leadership in the next century. Immediately I considered the task to be misdirected for our discussion here today, in so far as I have always known people of colour and individuals with impairments in leadership roles in this country. I am hopeful that the recent legislation for persons with impairments will allow for an increase in professional opportunities and economic empowerment. However, my optimism is somewhat tempered by the enormous challenges facing all of us in this century.

In light of the fact that America has become more culturally and racially diverse, non-white professionals will have a greater responsibility in their role in providing culturally relevant services. This type of professional often enters settings that have addressed technological and environmental barriers without having devoted the necessary time and attention to the human barriers. Our fundamental task should be that of preparing the workplace and institutions to receive this type of professional with dignity and human respect.

More often than not, businesses and institutions tend to view communication training as unnecessary for sensitizing employees for this on-going process. Training tends to consist of explaining the "Americans with Disabilities Act" and defining "reasonable accommodations" for persons with impairments and how the Act impacts upon one's life. Reserved parking spaces are designated and ramps built, yet co-workers are not schooled on various medical conditions and communication techniques used to solicit information respectfully when they have questions and concerns. Non-White professionals with impairments are expected to teach, handle, and address everyday interpersonal conflicts of colleagues while defending their self-esteem and worth from the assaults of ignorance, fear, and avoidant behaviors.

As we approach the 21st century, people with impairment conditions, in ever increasing numbers, will become role models for us all. Communities that previously practiced overt discrimination, must work through anxieties that necessitate their need to create "outcast" groups of people with impairments. Legislation has been passed stating that "these people" are your equals. The Americans with Disabilities Act is a catalyst for positive social change and the beginning of a very difficult and painful process for many. If handled properly, this civil rights ruling will benefit the entire country. Professionals, role-models, and leaders with impairments have a critical role in this process. However, we must all be in support of changing community attitudes, so that people of colour with impairments can celebrate their self-worth, and receiving communities can reap the benefits of their contributions.

In closing, I cannot stress enough the task before us and the importance of having professionals with impairments being an integral part of the process. Unfortunately, receiving communities remain emotionally and attitudinally ill-prepared to accept many leaders and professionals with impairments. This reality became painfully apparent to the public when Magic Johnson announced that several players refused to play basketball with him despite his professional history, talents, and abilities as an athlete. They were afraid of becoming infected when there was community support for Magic Johnson's decision to play again. Magic, therefore, decided to withdraw from the challenge. However, there are others who will not. There will continue to be similar confrontations at the workplace, regardless of the type of impairment conditions, unless we all stand vigil in protection of our human rights, and unless we all learn appropriate interpersonal skills, while elevating our knowledge base as informed citizens in this country. I leave you with the recommendation that communication training of employees be implemented with equal fervour as your environmental and technological considerations. Companies and institutions across this country are preparing their workforce for multicultural diversity in the 21st Century. Non-white professionals with impairments are part of the plurality and deserve your diligence in the area of communication sensitivity if any of us is to benefit from America's gesture of people empowerment.

ENTREPRENEURIAL LEADERSHIP

Entrepreneurial leadership is organising a group of people to achieve a common goal using proactive entrepreneurial behaviour by optimising risk, innovating to take advantage of opportunities, taking personal responsibility and managing change within a dynamic environment for the benefit of the organisation.

Entrepreneurial leadership is effectively using the skills associated with successful individual entrepreneurs and applying those within the environment of the larger organisation. This especially means within an organisation where those skills have been lost and replaced with a "corporate" mindset that focuses on process, systems and risk minimisation rather than entrepreneurial behaviour.

DEFINITIONS AND THEORIES

Various more detailed definitions of entrepreneurial leadership have also emerged...

The best leaders empower their employees to act on their vision for the organisation. The entrepreneurial leader executes through inspiration and aligns relationships to achieve common goals. An entrepreneurial leader will proactively identify opportunities to gain advantage through creativity, innovation and market understanding and then hold themselves responsible for delivering what customers need via the effective management of risk to optimise outcomes for both the organisation and the customer.

SOCIAL ENTREPRENEURSHIP

The concept of the social entrepreneur has emerged recently to define individuals who work to achieve community or social benefits, not just a profit motive. This is not the same thing as a social enterprise – although they may often be found helping to set up these sorts of organisations. A social entrepreneur recognizes a social problem and usesentrepreneurial principles to organize, create and manage a venture to achieve social change (a social venture). While a business entrepreneur typically measures performance in profit and return, a social entrepreneur focuses on creating social capital.

ATTRIBUTES OF AN ENTREPRENEURIAL LEADER

The entrepreneurial leader will work within a formalised organisational structure, but use the approaches normally expected of an entrepreneur to identify opportunities to gain advantage. They also have the ability to then manage change to deliver that advantage. Key to this is the effective management of risk rather than the minimisation of risk often sought within corporate environments. The entrepreneurial leader must have the ability to learn fast and within environments of ambiguity and change, while providing clarity and coherence for those around them.

The entrepreneurial leader takes responsibility for their actions and those actions must be more proactive than reactive. They think about achieving organisational outcomes in an innovative way and working with a diverse group of people and resources to achieve these goals.

NOTABLE EXAMPLES

Perhaps the best known and most widely considered example of an entrepreneurial leader is Steve Jobs, but there are many real life examples in the world of business and other industries, such as Bill Gates, Mark Zuckerberg and Richard Branson.

HISTORY

The search for the characteristics or traits of leaders has been ongoing for centuries. History's greatest philosophical writings from Plato's *Republic* to Plutarch's *Lives* have explored the question "What qualities distinguish an individual as a leader?". Underlying this search was the early recognition of the importance of leadership and the assumption that leadership is rooted in the characteristics that certain individuals possess. This idea that leadership is based on individual attributes is known as the "trait theory of leadership".

The concept of entrepreneurial leadership was introduced in 2000 by McGrath and MacMillan who suggested that in dynamic markets where there is increased uncertainty and competitive pressure a new type of leader is required. They described this as the "entrepreneurial leader". These fast changing markets or situations give those with an "entrepreneurial" approach the ability to exploit opportunities to gain advantage for their organisation faster than others.

A number of organisations have sought to develop the concept of entrepreneurial leadership within the business world. A good example is UBS, the global bank, which in the period 2002 to 2006 proactively developed entrepreneurial leadership amongst its top 500 leaders. The success of this was demonstrated by improvements in individual, team and financial performance, the project becoming a key element in the Harvard Business School Case study, "UBS Aligning the Integrated firm". The bank was subsequently awarded the title Best Company for Leaders (Europe) 2005. The implementation of this project over a multi divisional bank spread globally was complex and took number of years. This is reviewed in a case study by Chris Roebuck, Visiting Professor of Transformational Leadership at Cass Business School in London. Roebuck was one of the leaders of the team who implemented entrepreneurial leadership in UBS.

The principles of entrepreneurial leadership can be applied to a number of sectors and to a wide variety of organisations. The success of this approach has confirmed the compatibility of entrepreneurial leadership to the majority of organisations seeking to improve client/customer service and overall performance.

Prof Chris Roebuck notes that in recent examples of applying entrepreneurial leadership to organisations, the link to employee engagement has increasingly become as a key success factor. This has also allowed development of the concept of entrepreneurial support functions, such as Entrepreneurial HR and Entrepreneurial IT, to support the customer or client facing parts of organisations.

Entrepreneurial Leadership is not so much a style of leadership as a focus of leadership and employees' efforts on specific actions that either maximise the effectiveness of service delivery currently or seek to improve it in the future.

STYLES OF LEADERSHIP

Leadership style refers to a leader's behaviour. It is the result of the philosophy, personality, and experience of the leader. Rhetoric specialists have also developed models for understanding leadership (Robert Hariman, *Political Style*, Philippe-Joseph Salazar, *L'Hyperpolitique. Technologies politiques De La Domination*).

PARTICIPATIVE OR DEMOCRATIC STYLE

The democratic leadership style favors decision-making by the group. Such a leader gives instructions after consulting the group. They can win the cooperation of their group and can motivate them effectively and positively. The decisions of the democratic leader are not unilateral as with the autocrat because they arise from consultation with the group members and participation by them.

AUTOCRATIC OR AUTHORITARIAN STYLE

Under the autocratic leadership style, all decision-making powers are centralized in the leader, as with dictators.

Leaders do not entertain any suggestions or initiatives from subordinates. The autocratic management has been successful as it provides strong motivation to the manager. It permits quick decision-making, as only one person decides for the whole group and keeps each decision to him/herself until he/she feels it needs to be shared with the rest of the group.

10

The Power of Vision in Leadership

Many inexperienced leaders fail to sufficiently convey a vision to the subordinates they lead. If you are not skilled in telling everyone which direction to head you'll have confusion. Worse yet, you'll have a situation where people start creating their own direction. For some leaders their deficiency comes not from a lack of communication but from not having a vision themselves.

Vision is what determines what an organisation is going to try to accomplish. Without a clear vision the organisation will be pulled in many different directions. Some of these directions will cancel each other out, so even though much work will be done, very little is actually accomplished.

It is much easier to lead if you have a clear idea of what you want to achieve and your ideas are good. Even if you don't have a tremendous amount of skill as a leader, having a clear vision can help you through your shortcomings. People want to follow someone with a plan. By having a clear vision of what you want to accomplish, you will attract followers and people who want to align themselves with your vision. Individuals realize that on of the cornerstones of success is a clear vision. For this reason they want to align themselves with someone who articulates a vision—they want to join in the success.

In fact a poor leader with a great vision, will achieve more than a great leader with an ill-conceived plan. Success covers a huge number of failures. If you are successful, people will tend to forget many mistakes you make as a leader. If you are ineffective people are less likely to overlook your deficiencies in vision. People want to follow someone who will lead them to success. If you appear to be able to do this, people will want to follow you. If you have a track record of success, people will want to follow you. If you have a track record of failure, people will want to distance themselves from you in order to avoid your failures in the future.

If you are pushing people towards shared success, they will tend to stick with you because they are succeeding. In some cases they may even start mimicking some of your poor leadership habits thinking they are part of the reason for your success. Many people mistake success for good leadership skills. That is because people want to follow people with whom they can be successful.

Obviously good leadership skills are very important. It is much better to lead with a solid vision and skillful leadership expertise. Just make sure that as you develop your leadership skills, you don't overlook the skills that will let you develop a vision that makes it worth it for followers to follow you.

THE KEY ELEMENTS OF VISION

If the vision is to achieve all that I maintain it can do, it must be famed carefully and with considerable detail. How much detail? In working with corporations, I have tended to emphasize six elements. And, although the terminology may reflect this corporate origin, these elements are, perhaps surprisingly, quite transferable to the sphere of education.

The following examples illustrate the sort of questions that a college or university might seek to ask and answer in the course of developing such a detailed vision statement:

Scale. Although there may not be any intrinsic value in growth per se, it obviously makes a considerable difference—to strategy, organisation structure, financing, and so on—whether the institution chooses to double in size or to remain about the same size. So "How big do we want to be?" is a valid question.

Scope. What should be the future mix of undergraduate, graduate, and postgraduate education? What role should research play in defining the character of the institution? To what extent should we be in the field of continuing education?

Competitive Focus. On what basis will we seek to compete for students? For faculty? For research funding? How should we differentiate ourselves from other similar institutions?

Product and Market Focus. This further defines the future scope: What disciplines should we emphasize? Will we seek to cover a broad front, or be a niche player? How broadly should we define our market (the area from which we draw our student body)—regionally? nationally? globally?

Image and Relationships. How do we want others to see us? What image do we want to project? How should we manage our relationships with external stakeholders?

Organisation and Culture. How should we structure our organisation? To what extent do we want to build strategic alliance with other institutions? What values should dictate our organisational behaviour?

K-12 school leaders can ask similar questions. In particular, private elementary and secondary schools, which face at least a quasi-competitive environment, should be able to adapt this vision structure to their specific needs, substituting (in the Scope and Product Focus segments) questions concerning the range of levels to be included (K–12? 7–12? K–6?) and the desired emphases in curriculum. For public schools, typically the vision is more likely to be systemwide than specific to a particular school. Overall size is a factor more of demographics than of choice, although choices remain as to the size of individual schools within the system, and—absent any pronounced spread of the school voucher system—questions about competitive focus are less relevant.

Twenty-five years ago, I chaired a citizens' commission to develop long-range goals for the Westport, Connecticut, school system. We didn't call what we produced a vision, but in retrospect we might well have done so—and our work would have benefited from the more structured approach I have outlined here. However, our final report did lay out a detailed vision of an elementary and secondary school system that was to be but one part of lifelong learning and based on three core values we called the three "I's"—*Individualization* (of curriculum choices and the pace of learning); *Innovation* (the encouragement of new methodologies, interdisciplinary studies); and *Integration* (this was, after all, the Civil Rights era).

The level of detail I have specified here is at least a target. Not every vision statement will include all the elements, but the aim should be to move in this direction. When we read or hear the vision statement, we should have a clear picture of what we want the organisation to become, a sense of purpose and direction that will guide our everyday actions and decisions. The statement need not be lengthy; a single page will do. More important than length is depth and originality—the vision must go beyond trite generalities to sound some basic truths about what this particular organisation can achieve.

Is vision the product of one individual's thinking? Or is it the result of a group process?

The history of education in this country is replete with examples of university presidents whose vision cast a long shadow, not only over their own institutions, but over the whole field of education—James Conant of Harvard, Robert Hutchins of Chicago, Nicholas James Butler of Columbia. In the field of business, the names of Jack Welch of General Electric; Jan Carlzon, formerly of SAS; the late Sam Walton; and Akio Morita of Sony stand out in the current field of executives. In all these cases, the vision sprang from the insight and inspiration of individuals.

The current climate of educational institutions requires a less hierarchical and more consensual approach than these examples would suggest, in line with the earlier comment about the difference between corporate and collegial organisations. This is not, however, to deny the role of leadership in the process. Indeed, it will usually be the leader's insight, drive, persuasiveness, and, yes, charisma that will start the process, guide it past the dangers of meaningless compromise, drive it to a successful conclusion, and then use the "bully pulpit" of the leader's office to communicate the final vision.

However it originates, the vision must be a shared vision. The purpose of the vision, after all, is to stimulate action and achieve results, not to have an impressive piece of prose. If a vision is to shape the future and drive action, then the leader—and others in executive positions—must communicate it broadly, consistently, and continuously, until it becomes an integral part of the organisation's culture. General Electric's Welch, for example, takes every public and corporate opportunity, in speeches, management meetings, articles, and interviews, to drive his message home. It is not simply a matter of an initial announcement, but a constant drumbeat of emphasis—words backed up by action.

The power of vision derives from its ability to capture the hearts and minds of an organisation's members by setting forth a goal that is both feasible and uplifting. It can reinforce the empowerment that most organisations today seek to promote. It focuses thought and action, providing both the readiness and the aim—as in "ready, aim, fire"—for strategic and tactical decisions, helping to ensure consistency in decision making. It is the star by which the organisation steers.

THE POWER OF HAVING A VISION FOR YOUR LIFE

Imagine what it would mean if you had perfect clarity on your life's purpose, the kind of clarity that propels you forward in life. Imagine the impact you could have on the lives of those around you, in your community and the world at large.

What I'm talking about involves more than just having an extraordinary marriage and being a great spouse and parent, which I'm not minimizing at all. But I'm talking about more than just raising your kids on a solid spiritual foundation, but being the kind of parent whose kids truly become your best friends as they develop into adulthood. As you're raising your kids I want you to think about creating the kind of memories that last a lifetime. Spend time together building that bond and savoring every wonderful moment together because this is your life.

In creating those memories see if you can form a vision of what your true purpose is in this life. Having a vision about one's life purpose is one of the most powerful things we can have. A vision gives us four critical things that can make all the difference in our lives and the lives of others.

A Vision gives us passion – When we know why we're here, when we're emotionally connected to what we're doing, we come alive, we have a goal. We can see our destiny before us. It gives us the drive and energy to do everything it takes to achieve it. We live and dream about reaching our goal, and everything becomes part of the journey.

Living in anticipation of your future as you envision it and working constantly to achieve it causes everything else to vibrate with your energy as you move towards your future.

A Vision provides motivation – Every mundane task we do to fulfill our vision begins to take shape and we find meaning that spurs us on to the next step in the process. People with a vision are motivated and this is one of the true powers of having a clear vision, clarity as to your purpose in life.

Looking back on my own life, I was a pretty average student in college. But when I set my sights on flight school, when I formed this vision, this dream of pinning those golden wings on my uniform, and becoming a fighter pilot, flying off aircraft carriers, well this was the most exciting and most powerful feeling I'd ever had. This was my vision, the picture I played over and over again in my mind.

The following two years that it took me to get through my training was the hardest time in my life up 'till then. But I was determined to do whatever it took. I hung onto my vision. I didn't care what I had to do or to go through, it was all propelling me forward towards my vision of becoming a fighter pilot in the U.S. Navy. I had clarity of purpose and that motivation served me very well, to the point where I was able to finally achieve all my dreams.

If you take a minute to look at the trajectory of your life now, you'll see that there are really three directions you are pointing towards:

- A place so exciting you can't wait to get there and it defines everything you are doing in your life.
- An average place, or maybe you don't even know the destination and you have no idea where your life is heading.
- The trajectory of your life is going sideways, or maybe in reverse. You are aware on some level that this is not the direction you want to be headed in right now.

A vision forms our priorities – You can now prioritize your values, understand your strengths, the gifts that God has given you so that you can pull all of them together and harness them in such a way that you can change the trajectory of your life towards something that totally excites you and gives you passion.

One of the observations I've had in working with people with a clear vision is that they are not easily distracted. When you know where you're headed and you know why you're doing what you're doing then everything is important. Everything on your calendar, every meeting you have scheduled, every activity that you have planned is purposeful. Everything is essential and it all serves to move you forward.

Vision gives us purpose – Our vision becomes our purpose in life. Think back to a Monday morning when you couldn't wait to get out of bed because there was so much going on in your life that was propelling you forward that you felt this purpose pulling you into your future, the one you had visualized.

When you marry your clarity of vision to your purpose you have the link between your current reality, where you are now, and this future that God has put in your heart to manifest for yourself. Your vision and your purpose are unique to you. God has placed them in your heart.

It will be different than everyone else's around you. And it makes me think of the verse from Ephesians 2:10, "For we are his workmanship, created in Christ Jesus for good works, which God prepared beforehand so that we would walk in them". Now think about that! We are his workmanship!

If we could just shift our perceptions of ourselves and see ourselves from God's perspective, that he created us with purpose. Before the world was even formed, before we were even on this Earth, God created us with gifts and talents and strengths so that we could lead lives that are significant and be effective in this world. We are meant to form extraordinary relationships, to have an impact on everyone and everything we touch.

COMPELLING VISIONS

Compelling visions that move people to action, change their behaviors, focus on key priorities, and follow the pathway that the leader lays out, have three attributes that can be summarized under the broad headings ofcontent, context and credibility. Beyond that, they are developed as part of a collaborative process that engages key stakeholders.

THE CONTENT OF VISIONS

Compelling visions are not just slogans. For example, consider General Electric's "We bring good things to life" or "Imagination at Work", Nikon's "Our Aspirations — Meeting needs. Exceeding expectations", "Honda's "How we see things" or Coca-Cola's "It's the real thing." These may all have worked well as advertising slogans or signature lines, but they didn't lay out with any degree of clarity what the leadership of these organisations wishes them to become in the future. Toronto-Dominion Bank's vision, "To be the Better Bank," is more goal-oriented, while Manulife Financial's is more specific, stating boldly that its vision "...is to be the most professional life insurance company in the world: providing the very best financial protection and investment management services tailored to customers in every market where we do business." These vision statements give a better sense of where those companies are heading. But, since, they are targeted to multiple stakeholders, they also lack the specificity that some of those stakeholders would like to see.

The content or substance of a leader's vision must appeal to would-be followers as well as the leader. This appeal generally rests on the belief of followers-to-be that the leader can deliver something that they want and need – the feeling that their leader serves their needs and that they can achieve through their leader. They might assume this servant-leader role for altruistic reasons, without care for her or his own needs, or on the other hand, to satisfy their own needs through satisfying the desires of their followers.

Effective leaders are good at understanding the wide variety of physical, economic, psycho-social, and emotional needs that people have, and in their ability to tailor a "vision" so that it promises to satisfy unmet needs. The person who doesn't have a job, can't pay the rent, has a family to support and has other basic needs may be attracted to any vision that seems to promise material rewards and security. Someone who has savings, a secure pension or is near retirement age may not care too much about getting paid more, but may put a high value on the social satisfaction that they get from doing their job – the quality of interaction that they have with clients, suppliers, co-workers, and so on. Someone who has a high need for achievement may be attracted to an audacious vision; someone who has a high need for security may reject that same vision in favour of one that promises security and stability. Charismatic or transformational leaders can get followers to transcend their narrow, personal "economic" interests and embrace the leader's mission, whereas transactional leaders operate on a more material plane. Both types have to develop a content-rich vision to motivate people to follow them.

For any leader, the challenge is to figure out what will "turn people on," at least those people who will be essential for achieving the vision. The problems arise when very different, sometimes totally contradictory, things turn on the people who need to be motivated to follow. A CEO or executive team may be turned on by profit growth, especially when they have substantial stock options that vest when certain profitability targets are met.

The union leader may see these profitability targets being achieved only through plant closures, loss of jobs and consequent reduction in union membership. Little surprise, then, that the union leader does not enthusiastically embrace the leadership vision. For the vision of profitable growth to be embraced by both union leaders and management, each has to see a payoff somewhere in the content of that vision. It is not essential that everyone agrees with every aspect of a vision, only that they find something in that vision which resonates with them.

Even within management teams, there may be a lack of buy-in to certain corporate visions. A risk-averse CEO who has a substantial portion of his personal wealth tied up in in-the-money options may embrace a vision that emphasizes slow and steady domestic growth. On the other hand, the head of the international division may be focused on the higher-risk strategy of entering emerging markets.

The problem with many enterprise-level visions is that they have to be crafted to appeal to multiple stakeholders or, at a minimum, so as not to create conflict among any interests that have some countervailing power. This is a high hurdle for visionaries to overcome. One vision has to appeal to shareholders, managerial and non-managerial employees, partners, customers, governments, supply-chain participants, and community activists. Such "enterprise" visions, as they are referred to, often lack the focus or an edge. Indeed, many corporations are vague about their visions, at least in public, preferring instead to focus on their broader "missions," often stated in socially progressive, non-threatening ways. Who can argue with British Petroleum's "Beyond Petroleum" in an environmentally-conscious world or Archer-Daniel-Midland's "To unlock the potential of nature to improve the quality of life"?

VISION AND THE NECESSITY FOR CONTEXT

If visions are to motivate, especially employees, it's essential that employees find the vision meaningful in the context of their work. A vision for an HR department may well be "to create the best employment brand of any company in our industry," or for a risk management department of a bank to embrace "the highest risk-adjusted return in our industry," or for the marketing department of a food processing company to "have 50 percent of sales in products that are less than five years old that match the lifestyles of busy people today." This means that there may be several visions within a company. All need to be aligned with the company's overall mission, though each would have a particular meaning for a selected constituency in the enterprise. Each person should have a line of sight to the firm's higher-level organisational mission and vision, and be able to see how they can contribute to its fulfillment by realising their own visions. This means that everyone with a leadership role in an enterprise, from a team leader to department manager to business unit manager, to functional leader and CEO, must be involved in "the visioning thing." It's not just one, over-arching vision from on high that does it.

Individuals' salient wants and needs are dynamic, and vary by circumstances, time and place. Desperate people, experiencing material or psychological threats to their immediate wellbeing, are primed to respond to a leader who promises the hope of delivering them from their current situations.

We see this most evidently in the socio-political context. Martin Luther King drew on a deep vein of anger and frustration in the civil rights community and mobilized Afro-Americans to action. Barack Obama called for an era of change for an American population frustrated and angry with the Bush administration. Margaret Thatcher roused the British from their welfare-state torpor in the 1970s and got that country moving again, although there are still many people who would say it was in the wrong direction.

But we also see the ability of a vision to mobilize in a corporate context. Jack Welch used the powerful vision of "being number one or number two in each market we are in" to focus a number of the small, powerful business units in the conglomerate-like General Electric. He subsequently used powerful visions such as "the largest small company on earth, smart, agile, nimble" to bust the silo mentality and excessive bureaucracy that characterized the GE that he had inherited from his predecessors. The contexts for these visions were situations in which employees felt constrained, restricted and dissatisfied with the way the company operated. As well, shareholders were unhappy with results that were negatively influenced by the slow, resource-wasteful practices of the "old" GE, suppliers who found the company hard to deal with, customers who were unhappy with product and service reliability and quality, and even unions and employees that saw the only real security in the face of free trade and Japanese competition was in superior performance.

A business leader in a turnaround situation may be able to articulate a vision that compels people to act, whereas that same vision, articulated a year earlier or later, before the enterprise has run into trouble or after it has started a recovery, may well fall on deaf ears. One who seeks to build a long-lasting institution by making long-term investments may attract few people to that vision when the stock price is low; however, such a course of action may stimulate interest when the organisation is performing well. One whose vision focuses on innovation and creativity may stimulate followers to action when the basics are working well, though he or she may fail to do so when the fundamentals of the business need fixing. There are times when there are several competing visions and a leader must consider the relative power of his or her vision to move people who may be torn between competing, attractive alternatives.

Time and circumstances may compel a shift of a particular vision. As the economic slowdown of early 2008 merged with the global banking meltdown of the second half of the year, most companies had to re-think their goals in light of what was achievable over a specific time frame. As competitors succeed in reducing a market leader's advantage,, that leader may have to adjust the vision. Michael Dell discovered this when Hewlett-Packard, under the leadership of Mark Hurd, achieved supply-chain economics comparable to Dell's. Dell found that the shift to notebook computers required potential buyers to have a tactile experience. This persuaded Dell to re-embrace the retail distribution channel that it had abandoned many years previously, when it switched to the Dell Direct business model.

While flexibility is required to deal with dramatically changed circumstances, constant vision changing inevitably creates confusion and consternation, a lack of faith that the leadership knows where they are heading. Vision drift is a constant danger and the "vision-du-jour" phenomenon is to be avoided at all costs.

The President and CEO of TD Bank Financial Group, Ed Clark, continues to focus on creating a truly North American powerhouse in the face of an economic slowdown, a continued focus that has some critics calling for a time-out from the pursuit of this goal. But Clark is determined and very conscious of the fact that any perceived weakening of resolve could derail the achievement of a worthwhile, long-term aspiration for the Bank. This is not some innate stubbornness, but rather the resolve of a leader for whom the creation of an enduring institution is a higher-order imperative.

CREDIBILITY: OF VISION AND VISIONARY

There are those who just have dreams and those whose dreams will inspire others to follow them. The difference may have more to do with the credibility of the visionary rather than with the content of the vision.

The leader with a good track record, who is known for having achieved what they set out to do in the past, who "knows the business" and is recognized as an expert by those they are seeking to influence, is more likely to inspire a following than one who lacks such credentials, other things being equal. Such a leader has personal credibility which, when allied with the right content and context may provide powerful transformational leadership. Such was the case with Lou Gerstner, a former, highly successful CEO of RJR Nabisco, who was hired to turn a moribund IBM around and transform it from a product-focused company in to one that had a blend of products and services. He had an impressive track record at American Express and, importantly, was not steeped the culture of IBM, a culture that had spawned a great company in the period 1950 – 1990, but was in danger of strangling it in the much faster-moving, high-technology environment of the 1990's.

But such personal credibility may not outweigh a vision that lacks substantive appeal and is credible in its own right. Has this been done before? When and where? By whom? With what resources? A vision may be appealing and the visionary may have some degree of personal credibility, but if the vision seems too fantastic, too implausible, it will not be seen as compelling, an absolute must for any successful leadership vision. When Mike Zafirovski came to Nortel Networks from Motorola, he came with high personal credibility. However, the company was in so much trouble, faced such serious financial problems, and had an innovation deficit compounded by the need to limit R&D expenditures that personal credibility could not carry the day. Individuals that might have made it possible for Nortel to succeed had defected to competitors, where they saw the resources required to be a leader in the telecommunications field. Those that remained at Nortel discovered that they did not have the resource base to compete effectively against the Cisco's and Alcatel-Lucent's of this world.

Then sometimes, we see a newcomer who, armed with words but without a history of deeds, and who may lack a degree of evidence-based credibility, can nevertheless still be persuasive. In Barack Obama's presidential campaign, we saw a leader whose oratory, command of language and personal presence in a context where people were desperate for new leadership — but one who carried a very thin resume – elected to the most powerful office on earth. This charismatic leader may inspire a following based on little except their "magnetic" force, a force that is magnified and distributed through the mass media. This charisma may exist independently of their other leadership attributes or may substantially add to them. One thinks of a Steve Jobs at Apple,

Warrèn Buffet of Berkshire Hathaway, or Herb Kelleher of Southwest Airlines, as examples of charismatic leaders who have founded or resurrected businesses.

COLLABORATION: WHOSE VISION IS IT, ANYWAY?

Throughout history there have been individuals who have seen something that others did not see, who were able to articulate that "something" and build followers, and manage those followers through the many changes called for by the vision. Bill Gates and Bill Allen did this with Microsoft, Steve Jobs and Steve Wozniak did it at Apple; in earlier generations there was Thomas Edison, David Sarnoff and Timothy Eaton to name just a few. But there have been many failures as well; prophets who could not change the minds of others, false messiahs, CEO's who promised the world and failed to deliver, team leaders who could not get the support of their teams and eventually were either deposed or who left under their own steam.

Several acolytes of Jack Welch failed to deliver for their organisations when they sought to "import" elements of the GE culture to their new organisations. Bob Nardelli failed to deliver at Home Depot, and Jim McNerney did not lead 3M to greater performance. Both of the organisations they joined had strong cultures and, while neither of them had sterling performance records in the years immediately before their arrival, they were not organisations that recognized that they were in trouble and in need of a savior. The visions that Nardelli and McNerney tried to impose on their new organisations were rejected by employees and failed to deliver business results that were satisfactory to shareholders.

For any new leader, the challenge is to create a vision that reflects the wants, needs and aspirations of those who will be tasked with achieving it. Such visions are borne from the dissatisfaction that people have with the current situation and their perception that there could be something better. The leader may have an important role in generating this dissatisfaction and in postulating a better way, but he or she will do so with great sensitivity to the way that people view the past and present. The challenge is to envision rather than to have a vision, and this is best done by engaging people in the process of developing that vision and giving them a meaningful opportunity to shape the product of this engagement. Commitment to it will develop only from this empowerment; mere involvement in a process will not result in commitment. The truly compelling vision has content, context and credibility; the process of developing it is collaborative. When people can say "That's my vision" or at least lay claim to having influenced it, it's an indication that the task of execution has started well.

This need for collaboration when framing a vision requires what Jack Welch called "aggressive-patience" on the part of a leader. While challenging the status quo, leaders must respect those who have contributed to success in the past and seek their involvement and engagement in developing the way forward. This takes time and some process skills. Leaders must approach the visioning process with an open mind, not an empty mind, one that is receptive to the concerns and inputs of those who will have a stake in the emerging vision and on whom the achievement of that vision depends. If this takes some time, if people find it necessary to develop a new vision in a gradual, iterative way, then this must be viewed as an investment in developing commitment.

STRATEGIC VISION

Vision is a widely used term, but not well understood. Perhaps leaders don't understand what vision is, or why it is important. One strategic leader is quoted as saying, "I've come to believe that we need a vision to guide us, but I can't seem to get my hands on what 'vision' is. I've heard lots of terms like mission, purpose, values, and strategic intent, but no-one has given me a satisfactory way of looking at vision that will help me sort out this morass of words. It's really frustrating!". To understand vision, clarify what the term means.

DEFINING VISION

One definition of vision comes from Burt Nanus, a well-known expert on the subject. Nanus defines a vision as a realistic, credible, attractive future for [an] organisation. Let's disect this definition:

- Realistic: A vision must be based in reality to be meaningful for an organisation. For example, if you're developing a vision for a computer software company that has carved out a small niche in the market developing instructional software and has a 1.5 percent share of the computer software market, a vision to overtake Microsoft and dominate the software market is not realistic!
- Credible: A vision must be believable to be relevant. To whom must a vision be credible? Most importantly, to the employees or members of the organisation. If the members of the organisation do not find the vision credible, it will not be meaningful or serve a useful purpose. One of the purposes of a vision is to inspire those in the organisation to achieve a level of excellence, and to provide purpose and direction for the work of those employees. A vision which is not credible will accomplish neither of these ends.
- Attractive: If a vision is going to inspire and motivate those in the organisation, it must be attractive. People must want to be part of this future that's envisioned for the organisation.
- Future: A vision is not in the present, it is in the future. In this respect, the image of the leader gazing off into the distance to formulate a vision may not be a bad one. A vision is not where you

are now, it's where you want to be in the future. (If you reach or attain a vision, and it's no longer in the future, but in the present, is it still a vision?)

Nanus goes on to say that the right vision for an organisation, one that is a *realistic, credible, attractive future for that organisation*, can accomplish a number of things for the organisation:

- It attracts commitment and energizes people. This is one of the primary reasons for having a vision for an organisation: its motivational effect. When people can see that the organisation is committed to a vision-and that entails more than just having a vision statement-it generates enthusiasm about the course the organisation intends to follow, and increases the commitment of people to work towards achieving that vision.
- It creates meaning in workers' lives. A vision allows people to feel like they are part of a greater whole, and hence provides meaning for their work. The right vision will mean something to everyone in the organisation if they can see how what they do contributes to that vision. Consider the difference between the hotel service worker who can only say, "I make beds and clean bathrooms," to the one who can also say, "I'm part of a team committed to becoming the worldwide leader in providing quality service to our hotel guests." The work is the same, but the context and meaning of the work is different.
- It establishes a standard of excellence. A vision serves a very important function in establishing a standard of excellence. In fact, a good vision is all about excellence. Tom Peters, the author of *In Search of Excellence*, talks about going into an organisation where a number of problems existed. When he attempted to get the organisation's leadership to address the problems, he got the defensive response, "But we're no worse than anyone else!" Peters cites this sarcastically as a great vision for an organisation: "Acme Widgets: We're No Worse Than Anyone Else!" A vision so characterized by lack of a striving for excellence would not motivate or excite anyone about that organisation. The standard of excellence also can serve as a continuing goal and stimulate quality improvement programmes, as well as providing a measure of the worth of the organisation.
- It bridges the present and the future. The right vision takes the organisation out of the present, and focuses it on the future. It's easy to get caught up in the crises of the day, and to lose sight of where you were heading. A good vision can orient you on the future, and provide positive direction. The vision alone isn't enough to move you

from the present to the future, however. That's where a strategic plan, discussed later in the chapter, comes in. A vision is the desired future state for the organisation; the strategic plan is how to get from where you are now to where you want to be in the future.

Another definition of vision comes from Oren Harari: "Vision should describe a set of ideals and priorities, a picture of the future, a sense of what makes the company special and unique, a core set of principles that the company stands for, and a broad set of compelling criteria that will help define organisational success." Are there any differences between Nanus's and Harari's definitions of vision? What are the similarities? Do these definitions help clarify the concept of vision and bring it into focus?

An additional framework for examining vision is put forward by Collins and Porras. They conceptualize vision as having two major components: a Guiding Philosophy, and a Tangible Image. They define the guiding philosophy as "a system of fundamental motivating assumptions, principles, values and tenets." The guiding philosophy stems from the organisation's core beliefs and values and its purpose.

CORE BELIEFS AND VALUES

Just as they underlie organisational culture, beliefs and values are a critical part of guiding philosophy and therefore vision. One CEO expressed the importance of core values and beliefs this way:

I firmly believe that any organisation, in order to survive and achieve success, must have a sound set of beliefs on whichit premises all its policies and actions. Next, I believe that the most important single factor in corporate success is faithful adherence to those beliefs. And, finally, I believe [the organisation] must be willing to change everything about itself except those beliefs as it moves through corporate life.

Core values and beliefs can relate to different constituents such as customers, employees, and shareholders, to the organisation's goals, to ethical conduct, or to the organisation's management and leadership philosophy. Baxter Health care Corporation has articulated three *Shared Values: Respect for their Employees, Responsiveness to their Customers, and Results for their Shareholders*, skillfully linking their core values to their key constituencies and also saying something about what is important to the organisation. The key, however, is whether these are not only stated but also operating values.

PURPOSE

The second part of guiding philosophy is purpose-why the organisation exists, what needs it fills. Collins and Porras believe a good purpose statement should be "broad, fundamental, inspirational, and enduring." Consider this purpose statement: "The purpose of the United States Naval Academy at

Annapolis, MD, is to prepare midshipmen to become professional officers in the naval service." Or this purpose statement from Apple Computer: "To make a contribution to the world by making tools for the mind that advance humankind." How do these statements of purpose stack up?

Whether individual, team, organisation or nation, a sense of purpose and direction is essential to commitment. A shared sense of purpose is the glue that binds people together in common cause, often linking each individual's goals with the organisation's goals. Properly formulated, a shared sense of purpose provides understanding of the need for coordinated collective effort — for subordinating individual interest to the larger objective that can be achieved only by the collective effort. When it is long range in nature, it is the basis for detailed planning for the allocation of resources. When it is noble and inspiring, it gives dignity and respect to those participating in the effort. And, when it promises a better future, it gives hope to all who seek it.

The second major component of vision is tangible image. This is composed of a mission and a vivid description. Mission is "a clear and compelling goal that serves to unify an organisation's effort. An effective mission must stretch and challenge the organisation, yet be achievable" (Collins and Porras). There are four ways of approaching developing a mission statement: targeting, common enemy, role model, and transformation. Targeting means developing your mission statement around a clear, definable goal. An example is the mission Merck Pharmaceuticals set in 1979: To establish Merck as the preeminent drug-maker worldwide in the 1980s.

The common enemy approach is to focus the mission on overtaking or dominating a rival. Athletic shoe, automobile, and telecommuncations companies are all examples of areas where competition with rivals dominates company missions. Role model missions take an exemplar in another industry, and benchmark off that exemplar. For example, a mission "To be the Microsoft of retail sales companies" employs the role modeling technique. Finally, the internal transformation approach mission tends to focus on the internal remaking, restructuring, or rebirth of an organisation. One example of a transformational mission might be the Army's recent efforts to transform itself into a newer, leaner Army positioned for the 21st century.

This may be a good point to address the confusion over the use of the terms purpose, mission and vision. Collins and Porras view purpose and mission as components of vision. Others, such as Nanus, differentiate between mission and vision. Nanus states, "A vision is not a mission. To state that an organisation has a mission is to state its purpose, not its direction." Further complicating the semantics, different organisations may have mission statements, vision statements, purpose statements, or all three. To take one example, Quorum Health Group, Inc. a hospital management company, differentiates between its mission and vision this way:

MISSION STATEMENT

Quorum Health Group, Inc., is a hospital company committed to meeting the needs of clients as an owner, manager, consultant or partner through innovative services that enhance the delivery of quality health care.

VISION STATEMENT

Quorum Health Group, Inc., will be valued for its expertise in hospital management and its ability to positively impact the delivery of quality health care.

What are the differences between these two statements? Note that the mission is oriented in the present, while the vision is oriented in the future ("QHG will be valued..."). The mission states what QHG does in relatively concrete terms (meet the needs of clients by providing services that enhance the delivery of quality health care), while the vision states what it wants to do in more idealistic terms (be valued for its expertise and its ability to positively impact the delivery of quality health care).

One final example may illustrate how confused mission and vision can become. The Coca-Cola Company in 1994 published a booklet entitled "Our Mission and Our Commitment." In that booklet, the company defines their mission as follows:

We exist to *create value for our share owners* on a long term basis by building a business that enhances The Coca-Cola Company's trademarks. This also is our ultimate *commitment*. As the world's largest beverage company, we refresh that world. We do this by developing superior soft drinks, both carbonated and non-carbonated, and profitable non-alcoholic beverage systems that create value for our Company, our bottling partners, and our customers.

Does this sound like a mission, a vision, or a combination of both?

In Collins and Porras's framework for vision, their last element is a vivid description or picture of the end state that completion of the mission represents. They view this as essential to bringing the mission to life. A vivid description gives the mission the ability to inspire and motivate. Look back at the Coca-Cola Company mission shown above. Does it paint a vivid description of completion of the mission, or would The Coca-Cola Company have to amplify the mission statement?

To put this all together, Collins and Porras present the following framework:

core beliefs and values + purpose = guiding philosophy
mission + vivid description = tangible image
guiding philosophy + tangible image = vision

Note that, as opposed to Nanus, Collins and Porras do not focus on a vision statement, but on a vision as consisting of elements shown above. It's worth exploring the properties of a good vision. Nanus has several guidelines for creating a realistic, credible, attractive future for an organisation:

PROPERTIES OF A GOOD VISION

- A good vision is a mental model of a future state. It involves thinking about the future, and modeling possible future states. A vision doesn't exist in the present, and it may or may not be reached in the future. Nanus describes it like this: "A vision portrays a fictitious world that cannot be observed or verified in advance and that, in fact, *may never become reality*" (emphasis added). However, if it is a good mental model, it shows the way to identify goals and how to plan to achieve them.
- A good vision is idealistic. How can a vision be realistic and idealistic at the same time? One way of reconciling these apparently contradictory properties of a vision is that the vision is realistic enough so that people believe it is achievable, but idealistic enough so that it cannot be achieved without stretching. If it is too easily achievable, it will not set a standard of excellence, nor will it motivate people to want to work towards it. On the other hand, if it is too idealistic, it may be perceived as beyond the reach of those in the organisation, and discourage motivation. A realistic vision for that software company might be to maintain their current market share and produce instructional software that meets quality standards. Realistic, yes; but inspiring? No. A realistic yet also idealistic vision might be: *To become the industry leader in the development of state-of-the-art instructional software products, known for the quality and the innovativeness of their design.*
- A good vision is appropriate for the organisation and for the times. A vision must be consistent with the organisation's values and culture, and its place in its environment. It must also be realistic. For example, in a time of downsizing and consolidation in an industry, a very ambitious, expansionistic vision would not be appropriate. An organisation with a history of being conservative, and a culture encouraging conformity rather than risk taking, would not find an innovative vision appropriate. The computer software company mentioned above, with a history of producing high quality instructional software, would not find a vision to become the industry leader in video games or virtual reality software an appropriate one.
- A good vision sets standards of excellence and reflects high ideals. Generally, the vision proposed above for the software company does reflect measurable standards of excellence and a high level of aspiration. The actual measure could be the external reputation of the company, as assessed by having users evaluate the company and its products.
- A good vision clarifies purpose and direction. In defining that "realistic,

credible, attractive future for an organisation," a vision provides the rationale for both the mission and the goals the organisation should pursue. This creates meaning in workers' lives by clarifying purpose, and making clear what the organisation wants to achieve. For people in the organisation, a good vision should answer the question, "Why do I go to work?" With a good vision, the answer to that question should not only be, "To earn a paycheck," but also, "To help build that attractive future for the organisation and achieve a higher standard of excellence."

- A good vision inspires enthusiasm and encourages commitment. An inspiring vision can help people in an organisation get excited about what they're doing, and increase their commitment to the organisation. The computer industry is an excellent example of one characterized by organisations with good visions. A recent article reported that it is not unusual for people to work 80 hour weeks, and for people to be at work at any hour of the day or night. Some firms had to find ways to make employees go home, not ways to make them come to work! What accounts for this incredible work ethic? It is having a sense of working organisations that are building the future in a rapidly evolving and unconstrained field, where an individual's work makes a difference, and where everyone shares a vision for the future.
- A good vision is well articulated and easily understood. In order to motivate individuals, and clearly point towards the future, a vision must be articulated so people understand it. Most often, this will be in the form of a vision statement. There are dangers in being too terse, or too long-winded. A vision must be more than a slogan or a "bumper sticker." Slogans such as Ford Motor Company's "Quality Is Job One" are good marketing tools, but the slogan doesn't capture all the essential elements of a vision. On the other hand, a long document that expounds an organisation's philosophy and lays out its strategic plan is too complex to be a vision statement. The key is to strike a balance.
- A good vision reflects the uniqueness of the organisation, its distinctive competence, what it stands for, and what it is able to achieve. This is where the leaders of an organisation need to ask themselves, "What is the one thing we do better than anyone else? What is it that sets us apart from others in our area of business?" A good example of a visioning process refocusing a company on its core competencies is Sears. A few years ago, Sears had expanded into areas far afield from its original business as a retailer. Among other things, Sears began offering financial services at their stores. Poor

performance led Sears to realize that they could not compete with financial services companies whose core business was in that area, so they dropped that service and eliminated other aspects of their business not related to retailing. Interestingly, Sears' primary competitor is Wal-Mart, an organisation with a very clear and compelling vision. Sam Walton found a niche in providing one stop shopping for people in rural areas, and overwhelmed "Mom and Pop" stores with volume buying and discounting. Wal-Mart is very clear about their vision, and has focused on specific areas where they can be the industry leader. The key is finding what it is that your organisation does best. Focus your vision there.

- A good vision is ambitious. It must not be commonplace. It must be truly extraordinary. This property gets back to the idea of a vision that causes people and the organisation to stretch. A good vision pushes the organisation to a higher standard of excellence, challenging its members to try and achieve a level of performance they haven't achieved before. Inspiring, motivating, compelling visions are not about maintaining the status quo.

DEVELOPING A VISION

At this point you should know what a good vision consists of, and recognize a vision statement when you see one. But how does a strategic leader go about developing a vision for an organisation? Nanus also offers a few words of advice to someone formulating a vision for an organisation:

- Learn everything you can about the organisation. There is no substitute for a thorough understanding of the organisation as a foundation for your vision.
- Bring the organisation's major constituencies into the visioning process. This is one of Nanus's imperatives: don't try to do it alone. If you're going to get others to buy into your vision, if it's going to be a wholly shared vision, involvement of at least the key people in the organisation is essential. "Constituencies," refer to people both inside and outside the organisation who can have a major impact on the organisation, or who can be impacted by it. Another term to refer to constituencies is "stakeholders"- those who have a stake in the organisation.
- Keep an open mind as you explore the options for a new vision. Don't be constrained in your thinking by the organisation's current direction - it may be right, but it may not.
- Encourage input from your colleagues and subordinates. Another injunction about not trying to do it alone: those down in the organisation often know it best and have a wealth of untapped ideas. Talk with them!

- Understand and appreciate the existing vision. Provide continuity if possible, and don't throw out good ideas because you didn't originate them. In his book about visionary leadership, Nanus describes a seven-step process for formulating a vision:

1. Understand the organisation. To formulate a vision for an organisation, you first must understand it. Essential questions to be answered include what its mission and purpose are, what value it provides to society, what the character of the industry is, what institutional framework the organisation operates in, what the organisation's position is within that framework, what it takes for the organisation to succeed, who the critical stakeholders are, both inside and outside the organisation, and what their interests and expectations are.

2. Conduct a vision audit. This step involves assessing the current direction and momentum of the organisation. Key questions to be answered include: Does the organisation have a clearly stated vision? What is the organisation's current direction? Do the key leaders of the organisation know where the organisation is headed and agree on the direction? Do the organisation's structures, processes, personnel, incentives, and information systems support the current direction?

3. Target the vision. This step involves starting to narrow in on a vision. Key questions: What are the boundaries or constraints to the vision? What must the vision accomplish? What critical issues must be addressed in the vision?

4. Set the vision context. This is where you look to the future, and where the process of formulating a vision gets difficult. Your vision is a desirable future for the organisation. To craft that vision you first must think about what the organisation's future environment might look like. This doesn't mean you need to predict the future, only to make some informed estimates about what future environments might look like. First, categorize future developments in the environment which might affect your vision. Second, list your expectations for the future in each category. Third, determine which of these expectations is most likely to occur. And fourth, assign a probability of occurrence to each expectation.

5. Develop future scenarios. This step follows directly from the fourth step. Having determined, as best you can, those expectations most likely to occur, and those with the most impact on your vision, combine those expectations into a few brief scenarios to include the range of possible futures you anticipate. The scenarios should represent, in the aggregate, the alternative "futures" the organisation is likely to operate within.

6. Generate alternative visions. Just as there are several alternative futures for the environment, there are several directions the organisation might take in the future. The purpose of this step is to generate visions reflecting those different directions. Do not evaluate your possible visions at this point, but use a relatively unconstrained approach.

7. Choose the final vision. Here's the decision point where you select the best possible vision for your organisation. To do this, first look at the properties of a good vision, and what it takes for a vision to succeed, including consistency with the organisation's culture and values. Next, compare the visions you've generated with the alternative scenarios, and determine which of the possible visions will apply to the broadest range of scenarios. The final vision should be the one which best meets the criteria of a good vision, is compatible with the organisation's culture and values, and applies to a broad range of alternative scenarios (possible futures).

IMPLEMENTING THE VISION

Now that you have a vision statement for your organisation, are you done? Formulating the vision is only the first step; implementing the vision is much harder, but must follow if the vision is going to have any effect on the organisation. The three critical tasks of the strategic leader are formulating the vision, communicating it, and implementing it. Some organisations think that developing the vision is all that is necessary. If they have not planned for implementing that vision, development of the vision has been wasted effort. Even worse, a stated vision which is not implemented may have adverse effects within the organisation because it initially creates expectations that lead to cynicism when those expectations are not met.

Before implementing the vision, the leader needs to communicate the vision to all the organisation's stakeholders, particularly those inside the organisation. The vision needs to be well articulated so that it can be easily understood. And, if the vision is to inspire enthusiasm and encourage commitment, it must be communicated to all the members of the organisation.

How do you communicate a vision to a large and diverse organisation? The key is to communicate the vision through multiple means. Some techniques used by organisations to communicate the vision include disseminating the vision in written form; preparing audiovisual shows outlining and explaining the vision; and presenting an explanation of the vision in speeches, interviews or press releases by the organisation's leaders. An organisation's leaders also may publicly "sign up" for the vision. You've got to "walk your talk." For the vision to have credibility, leaders must not only say they believe in the vision; they must demonstrate that they do through their decisions and their actions.

Once you've communicated your vision, how do you go about implementing it? This is where strategic planning comes in. To describe the relationship between strategic visioning and strategic planning in very simple terms, visioning can be considered as establishing where you want the organisation to be in the future; strategic planning determines how to get there from where you are now. Strategic planning links the present to the future, and shows how you intend to move towards your vision. One process of strategic planning is to first develop goals to help you achieve your vision, then develop actions that will enable the organisation to reach these goals.

THE POWER OF CONVERSATIONAL LEADERSHIP

Communication is always a challenge, especially in multinational corporations. Boris Groysberg and Michael Slind discuss why it makes sense to adopt the principles of face-to-face conversation in organisational communication.

When a company is small, communication among employees is as simple as rolling a desk chair around the room to talk to the president, the admin, or the chief engineer. But as a company grows, communication becomes more difficult. And strategic direction can suffer as a result, even if those at the top assume otherwise.

"Having communication that goes bottom-up is just as important as having communication that goes top-down."

"In many cases you have an executive team that's so sure about company strategy, but then you go inside the organisation and find that nobody else has a clue," says Harvard Business School Professor Boris Groysberg. "Nobody knows what strategic conversations are actually unfolding."

For that reason, many CEOs are reconsidering the classic command-and-control structure in which a few people are sending all the directives from the top of the corporate hierarchy. Instead, they are adopting a conversational approach. In their new book, Talk, Inc.: How Trusted Leaders Use Conversation to Power Their Organisations, Groysberg and communication professional Michael Slind show how several global companies are adopting principles of face-to-face conversation, and why this approach positively affects a company's bottom line.

"In many ways the book is not about communication as much as it is about performance," Groysberg says. "In an economic environment where there is so much uncertainty, the senior management of a company might not know where the company should be going in three years. But your frontline customer-facing people might. Having communication that goes bottom-up is just as important as having communication that goes top-down."

To try to suss out best practices for communication, the authors interviewed communications directors and CEOs at more than 100 companies. "We were struck by how often that word 'conversation' kept popping up," Slind says. "CEOs, especially, expressed an aspiration to promote a conversation in their organisation. They talked about wanting everyone to be on board with the conversation about what they want to do with the company."

Borne of those interviews, the book advocates an approach called "organisational conversation," which applies to all processes a company uses to circulate information across the organisation, rather than just from the top down. “It’s about creating a culture in which the communication function becomes something that more and more resembles the way that two friends would talk,” Slind says.

THE PROPERTIES OF A GOOD ORGANISATIONAL CONVERSATION

The book divides good organisational conversation into four alliterative elements—intimacy, interactivity, inclusion, and intentionality—each of which applies to a particular attribute of an organisation. “Intimacy is about leadership,” Groysberg explains. “Interactivity is about channels. Inclusion is about content. And intentionality is about goals, vision, and the strategy of getting things done.”

INTIMACY: The authors note that intimacy need not require physical proximity, which would be impossible in a multinational company where employees are separated by thousands of miles. Rather, it requires emotional or mental intimacy. “It’s about trust, it’s about being authentic, it’s about communicating your vision but also at the same time listening to what employees have to say,” Groysberg says.

Talk, Inc. highlights the case of the Indian company Hindustan Petroleum Corporation Ltd., which at the turn of the twenty-first century launched an effort to develop a new vision statement. Rather than keeping the effort confined to the C-suite, Hindustan held an extensive series of “vision workshops” where employees at all levels of the company were invited to share their thoughts.

A typical vision workshop included about 20 people and lasted three days. HPCL is a Fortune Global500 company employing more than 11,000 people, so it took years to complete the workshops. But by the end of the process, “almost every person felt that the company vision was his or her own vision,” Groysberg says.

INTERACTIVITY: Once some intimacy is established, it’s important to keep the conversation flowing. “It’s not just that one person is both talking and listening, it means that there is a real sort of back and forth where the act of listening actually changes what you think and say,” Slind explains. “As your company gets larger, that gets more difficult. But one of the ways to do it is by using technology.”

The book provides a quick overview of the social technology that helps global corporate communication mimic personal conversation: internal blogs (in which leaders share their thoughts and employees have a chance to comment), wikis (which enable collaboration on corporate databases), online communities (which help far-flung employees find like-minded colleagues), Twitter (which lets employees broadcast information widely, both internally and externally), networks such as Facebook and LinkedIn (which enable information sharing among a particular group), video sharing, and web-enabled video chat (which help to mimic in-person communication).

Global computer networking giant Cisco Systems, for example, uses its own TelePresence videoconferencing technology to simulate in-person meetings among its ranks—more than 6,200 executives and some 72,000 employees in total. "You really forget that you're speaking across a fibre-optic cable," says Slind, who has observed videoconferences at the San Jose, California-based company. "You feel like you're sitting across from this person."

Slind hastens to add that technology is only as effective as those deploying it. "Interactivity isn't just about technology," he says. "It's equally important to build an interactive culture."

INCLUSION: In organisational conversation, inclusion means giving employees a chance to help tell a company's story. Ceding a measure of control over communication to employees comes with the obvious risk of uncontrolled messaging, but the authors report that the rewards of inclusion often outweigh the risks. A traditional command-and-control company will filter a bunch of top-down messages through the communications department. But the book recommends a more organic approach. Sales teams can share success stories from the field via public video blogs, which journalists and customers may consider more authentic and more useful than slick marketing material. Furthermore, besides meeting with sales teams, customers might have a chance to meet with the no-nonsense engineers who actually created the technology.

Talk, Inc. discusses a project at EMC, a Hopkinton, Massachusetts-based storage networking company with more than 40,000 employees. In 2009, the company employees produced a book about the lives of working mothers at the company, gathering personal essays by 97 women at EMC (and one essay by a man). "It bubbled up organically," Groysberg says. "And in that way the message they created was more compelling than a marketing campaign. It's helping the company to recruit women, which creates a great competitive advantage. And internally, it has served to engage employees by letting them become content creators. That's an example of being inclusive and allowing people to have voice. And what we find is that that fundamentally will drive engagement. And engagement will drive more effort. And effort will drive individual performance, and subsequently that will drive organisational performance."

INTENTIONALITY: While the goal of organisational conversation is to draw on the characteristics of a talk between friends, it must always have an agenda—and a leader must always have a goal in mind. Otherwise it might take the form of talk just for the sake of talking. The goal may be to ensure that all the employees understand the company's competitive strategy, or it may be to ask every employee to help shape that strategy. But there must be a goal, and the leader should use conversation to achieve that goal.

"Even if you can't control everything anymore you still are the leader," Slind says. "You still have responsibility for setting the tone and setting the direction. And that's what intentionality is about. As you're planning a conversation, you need to make sure that it's in alignment with your company's strategic goals. And if it's done well, the power of communication can support those goals."

THE CONTENT OF LEADERSHIP

Leadership is always ABOUT something: values, strategy, politics, markets or technology; it has content. It advocates a better way on a particular issue. But the role of content is obscured by our obsession with the character of the person in charge.

Style thus looms much larger than content. Because those in charge have vast power over us, we naturally need to trust them. But this has the disastrous effect of obscuring the leadership of front-line employees with great content but limited interpersonal skills. They are all content and no style.

To fully engage key knowledge workers and generate faster innovation, we need to see how they can show leadership with compelling content even if they lack the style required to be positional leaders.

Exploring how groups lead other groups highlights the place of content. Businesses lead their competitors in a market, sports teams lead their leagues and countries lead other countries by example on the economy, green policies or social issues, among other issues. Similarly, in a single organisation, high performing divisions or teams show leadership to their colleagues. Demonstrating "best practice" is a form of group leadership. Because we persist in concentrating on individuals in charge of groups, we ignore the leadership shown by groups to other groups. In fact, so fixated are we on the individual in charge that we regard group leadership as odd or irrelevant. But we can learn a lot about leadership by examining how groups lead other groups.

Much of group leadership is shown by example, but not exclusively. Greenpeace might show leadership through vocal influence by, for instance, persuading Japan to stop hunting whales. But companies and sports teams lead their competitors by example only. They never use intentional influence because they aim to win, not to take others with them. They show leadership BY winning, not by trying to persuade others to follow them. Indeed, through patents and subterfuge, they strive to prevent competitors from following too closely. Even high performing company divisions may resent losing the limelight by sharing best practice with lower performing peers.

Groups lead by WHAT they are doing, by getting somewhere first or performing at a higher level than others. Apple, for instance, leads with products that consumers find more appealing than competitor offerings. Here, content is surely king!

Group leadership illustrates the core of what it means to lead: to show the way, which is often best achieved by going somewhere first. Companies lead by being first to develop a new product or process. GE had a leadership impact on other businesses with processes like workout.

Conversely, CEOs can't go anywhere without the help of their groups. CEOs are like ship captains because they need a crew to run the ship. A ship captain can't lead the way by going somewhere first because the ship can't move without the crew. Thus, the crew doesn't follow the captain; they travel to the destination together. But, you object, the crew follows the captain's orders. Not really. "Following" in this context is just shorthand for saying that the crew obeys the captain's orders. That is, you can't literally "follow" an order. You can execute it or ignore it, but you can only follow a person who is going somewhere ahead of you.

The key point here is that we recognize an essential connection between leading and following but we overlook the fact that we can only literally follow someone who goes somewhere first and that group leadership illustrates this principle better than does the person in charge. Leading by example thus captures the real essence of leadership and shows why content is more important than we realize.

THE PLACE OF CONTENT AND STYLE

Leadership is never totally content-free, just a matter of style or hype. Conversely, compelling content alone is rarely sufficient. Businesses like Apple lead, not just through attractive WHATS, but also with appealing HOWS: packaging and marketing. The relative power of content depends on how engaging it is on its own, whether it can sell itself, or whether people need persuading to buy it.

Our receptivity to new ideas ranges from stubborn resistance through neutral to an insatiable drive to be a first adapter of everything new. Some people will never agree to permit abortion, for example, while others are ultra quick to jump on the latest bandwagon whenever any new technology arrives.

Trying to lead others to give up their stance on abortion is nearly impossible. Wherever an issue involves deeply entrenched human values, leaders need to have the oratorical brilliance of a Martin Luther King. In this case, style is at least as vital as content.

In technical domains, however, content comes into its own, especially if prospective followers are opportunists. Naturally, we admire leaders who tackle value-laden topics as Martin Luther King did because he had to risk his life to challenge the status quo. Still, a product developer who promotes a new product also challenges the status quo even though the risk is low because the content, let's assume, virtually sells itself.

The point here is that, it is in technical domains where front-line innovators can show leadership. It is not that influencing skills or emotional intelligence do not apply in this context, but rather that it is POSSIBLE to show leadership without such wherever content is compelling or where a hard, factual case is enough to get followers on board. Such employees may have a leadership impact, bottom-up, even if they lack the character and other qualities necessary to be a positional leader.

CONTENT AND THE MEANING OF LEADERSHIP

Leadership between groups is not about individuals in charge, let alone their style or character. Groups lead other groups by going somewhere new first or being better than their competitors. Group leadership not only demonstrates the role of content, it tells us something vitally important about the meaning of leadership.

Leadership is shown by one group to another by outsiders. It does not entail a joint effort between leader and led to pursue a shared goal. Such leadership simply shows the way for others where those who are led literally follow the leader.

Martin Luther King was also an outsider relative to the general population and the government. The only difference between his leadership and that of a group is that he promoted a better way while groups lead by example.

Similarly, when front line knowledge workers convince senior management to adopt a new product, they are outsiders to the senior management team. Such leadership doesn't mean employees taking charge of senior management, even informally. So, there are two forms of outsider leadership: that shown by groups to other groups and that shown by individual outsiders who challenge the status quo.

Now, we have two choices:

1. We can say that we need two concepts of leadership, one to cover individuals in charge of groups and one to account for outsider leadership.
2. We can adopt one concept of leadership but define it so as to cover both cases.

The first option is messy, but because we ignore outsider leadership we fool ourselves into believing that being in charge of others is all there is to leadership. But, taking the second option, we can define leadership broadly as showing the way for others, either by example or by the explicit promotion of a new direction, a better way. CEOs show leadership when they advocate a new vision, but only then because most of the time, they operate as managers.

Benefits of a Broader Definition of Leadership

1. A general concept of leadership covers a much wider range of situations, including leadership shown by CEOs and that shown by groups: businesses, sports teams, countries or high performing units within single organisations.

2. We gain an account of leadership shown by outsiders such as Martin Luther King and front line innovators who show leadership bottom-up.
3. By portraying innovative knowledge workers as leaders, we can better engage them and motivate them to innovate more.
4. We gain clarity about the relative roles of leadership and management, thus allowing a sharper focus on what it takes to succeed in executive positions.
5. Management upgraded resumes its rightful partnership with leadership instead of being relegated to a minor, negative role.

IMPLICATIONS OF LEADERSHIP REDEFINED

The major implication of defining leadership as showing the way for others is that most of what executives do needs to be reframed as management, suitably upgraded. Specifically, leadership itself can't make decisions for anyone or get work done through people. Outsiders can only lead by influencing others to behave differently; they have no power to decide anything. An outsider can't implement anything either, so this must be the province of management. If we want a definition of leadership that covers outsiders, then we must exclude the making of decisions for followers, thus leadership can only influence.

ENCOURAGING YOUNG, ASPIRING LEADERS

Developing young leaders by focusing on style puts the proverbial cart before the horse, especially for innovation-driven businesses where content is king.

Inspiring leaders are passionate about something. Indeed, it is arguable that passion outweighs all other leadership traits. Without passion, how can anyone hope to lead, even with all the character and emotional intelligence in the world? Form without substance is empty.

Aspiring leaders should be encouraged to find ideas that they feel passionate about first and foremost. With passion and compelling content, all employees can show leadership on a particular issue immediately without having to wait to be promoted to a leadership role or first acquiring better influencing skills.

Putting the cart before the horse means telling young employees that they need to develop interpersonal skills or character before they can lead. Daniel Goleman said that maturity was another word for emotional intelligence, meaning that young people must grow up before they can be leaders. How empowering is that?

Why Content is King

Content comes to the fore when leadership is dynamic, when providing direction is more important than merely dominating the group. The chief of a primitive tribe, for example, strives to maintain a static position of power over the group. A chief is regarded as a leader even if the tribe is going nowhere and nothing is being achieved through them.

Conversely, leadership in modern business is dynamic; it is totally goal-oriented. Vision rises to prominence because dynamic groups are constantly on the move, seeking a better way. They aggressively pursue their chosen destination, determined to get there ahead of others.

In dynamic contexts, direction is central to leadership. Regardless of what other qualities leaders possess or lack, the ability to provide direction in a complex, fast changing context is what matters most.

Why Content Will Eclipse Form

Despite the rising importance of content, we insist on retaining our primitive role-based image of leadership. We want one individual to take charge, someone we can look up to, who can protect us, give meaning to our lives AND provide direction in fast-changing times. But, so great is our obsession with form: the character of the person we want to take charge, that we downplay content.

Our need for one person to look up to, however natural, distorts the meaning of leadership, which we will only fully understand when we can separate our needs from the true function of leadership: to provide direction.

As the world becomes ever more knowledge-driven and as evidence-based decision-making becomes more valued, content will eclipse form or style. This is liberating because it means that all employees can show some leadership on a local, small-scale issue, as a one-off effort, even if they have no talent or interest in positional leadership.

LEADERSHIP DEVELOPMENT PROGRAMME SUPPORTS A DISTRICT'S VISION

Lay leaders are clearly key to the strength and growth of our congregations and our movement. But, what makes a lay leader strong? What helps a lay leader grow? And, what is unique about the leader's role in the context of a Unitarian Universalist congregation?

In 2009, Northern New England (NNE) district executive Mary Higgins brought these questions to a team of professional and lay religious leaders. The district had recently expanded into a merger of two smaller UUA districts, and Higgins felt the time was opportune to shape a vision for leadership.

"We had been hearing from people in our congregations that they lacked a bank of leadership inside a congregation to call on when venerable leaders needed to rotate off," Higgins recalls. The team she gathered worked to develop a vision for district-wide leadership development and create training to prepare emerging leaders grounded in our faith.

DEEPER THEMES IN UU LAY LEADERSHIP

From the start, the Leadership Visioning Team acknowledged that in a Unitarian Universalist context, leadership can be more than a technical skill set, even more than the time, willingness, and temperament to step up. In Unitarian Universalism, leadership has the potential to be a spiritual practice.

"Many of us serve as leaders in other capacities," says Mary Heafy, a member of the Keene Unitarian Universalist (UU) Church in Keene, NH, as well as the Northern New England (NNE) visioning team who serves professionally as executive director of a non-profit agency and is a former congregational board president. "But, there is something much deeper about assuming leadership in a UU congregation. How could we help lay leaders access that deeper experience?"

The Leadership Visioning Team crafted a vision statement that lifts up the deeper themes in lay leadership. For example, the statement includes an affirmation that conflict is an integral part of change which we can use to grow our movement.

CHOOSING A CURRICULUM: HARVEST THE POWER

The team considered writing a leadership training programme for NNE to actualize their vision. Yet, they decided first to explore the newly published Tapestry of Faith programme, Harvest the Power, online, and perhaps avoid "re-inventing the wheel." The 12-workshop programme for leadership development in congregations is appropriate for new as well as experienced leaders. It provides a framework and vocabulary for leadership in the congregational context, raising themes such as the difference between "management" and "leadership," issues of mattering and marginality in a congregational community. It gives participants practices to keep their leadership experience spiritually dynamic, and tools to keep focused on the congregation's faith mission and purpose. For example, Harvest the Power guides participants to remain mindful of the leadership question "Are we doing right things? Or are we doing things right?"

The NNE team gave Harvest the Power a comprehensive review, and then chose the programme to provide UU faith-based leadership training. To cover a district that spans New England's three largest states, the team decided to train a core group of lay leaders from around the district who could, in turn, facilitate Harvest the Power in local geographical clusters. The team invited congregational ministers and board presidents to recommend emerging or experienced leaders to become Harvest the Power facilitators. The facilitators would need to participate in a full weekend and commit to facilitating a cluster group.

The Leadership Visioning Team fanned out to promote the programme. "The message was that this initiative would be a transformational experience that would grow participants personally, grow their spirituality, and give them a framework to look at leadership," Heafy recalls. "It's not 'Management 101;' it's more than leadership skills such as 'How do you build an agenda, take good notes, ask someone else to serve?' That was the greatest challenge—helping people consider leadership in a more visionary way, as a spiritual practice, something different from skill-building."

TRAINING THE TRAINERS

Twenty-three lay leaders completed an April 2010 weekend workshop at Crawford Notch, New Hampshire, led by Harvest the Power co-author Gail Forsyth-Vail, director of adult programmes for the UUA. "In a train-the-trainer model, you do not experience every part of a curriculum," notes Heafy. "They had to work very hard at experiencing portions of it and learning the theory behind it."

In 2010, the trained facilitators, each supported with participation by an NNE Leadership Visioning Team member, launched four cluster groups—in Vermont, Southern New Hampshire/Vermont, the New Hampshire seacoast, and Bangor, Maine. Each cluster was asked to do all 12 workshops of Harvest the Power to maintain consistency across the pilot programme. However, the facilitators were encouraged to adapt each workshop to suit their comfort with the material, their teaching style, and their group's meeting schedule. (Each Harvest the Power workshop is configured as a set of core and alternate activities which facilitators select and tailor for their group. As part of the UUA Tapestry of Faith family of faith development programmes, the entire curriculum is online, so it is easy for individual facilitators to browse, download, and adapt.)

Leadership Visioning Team members supported the facilitators by attending the pilot clusters, and thus were positioned to observe the programme in action. "In each group, it was thrilling to see the self-discovery and the learning that occurred between sessions," says Heafy. "One amazing thing about Harvest the Power is the conceptual language it gives people to apply to their work life, their volunteer work, and their lives outside of the congregation.

"Over and over again, I found that although participants recruited from congregations did not know each other well, because of the topics and concepts, the weekend created deep and meaningful relationships. In one group, three facilitators who had never before had experiences beyond their local congregations forged a lifelong connection as they experienced leadership together. There were hard moments. 'Gee, it's low registration, should we move forward or not?' and 'Gee, you did not cover what I thought you would. What should we do now?' This opened their eyes, and mine, about us as a movement."

One cluster had several participants from a congregation which was grappling with a congregational issue. When an activity called for small groups to discuss a hypothetical situation, a participant suggested it would be useful to apply the model to the real issue. "The facilitators agreed to have this group work as a local team, and the participants thought it was invaluable," Heafy says.

REFLECTIONS AND NEXT STEPS

At the congregational year's end, 100 lay leaders across the NNE district "had been fueled by Harvest the Power," according to Heafy. The Leadership Visioning Team looks forward to rolling out the second phase of their vision by supporting additional, local cluster Harvest the Power programmes, and by using Internet tools to connect "alumni" across the district.

When the facilitators met to celebrate the completion of the cluster trainings and to reflect together, their comments revealed the programme had begun to meet the Leadership Visioning Team's goals:

- A facilitator noted, "Connections developed that influenced [participants'] work in their respective congregations. They were holding up a mirror to each other."
- Another said, "This experience got me back in touch with [my] own capacity for leadership and the blocks to it."
- A third said, "Interconnectedness is one of the things that fuels my spirituality—[the] ability to impart something important and get something important back, faith in the goodness (or at least the neutrality) of the universe. [Harvest the Power] is a good product, just trust it—and let it happen."

Heafy notes that the Harvest the Power programme exposed her to concepts she uses in her professional role as president and CEO of the non-profit Alliance for Resource Management, as well as her congregational and district leadership roles. "All aspects of service can have spiritual dimensions," she says—"finance," for example, invites a spiritual practice of stewarding shared resources.

Heafy recalls that, as a new leader in the late 1990s, she felt overwhelmed by all she believed she was expected to know. From Harvest the Power, she has gained useful, concrete guidance to make service in a congregation not an obligation but a way to nurture the spirit while giving back to the community. "My home congregation had grappled with leadership as a spiritual practice, but I did not have a framework for doing that," she says. "If we really care about each other and about our faith, we are going to develop our leaders from the first spark we see in them. It is the opposite of spiritual generosity to push people into leadership, and then wonder why they do not understanding everything, and why they drift away."

"My dream for this," says Higgins, "is that people are equipped and feel competent when their congregation asks them to serve. That they feel confident they have the basic grounding in our faith. That they feel they can say 'yes' to a job that does not necessarily offer on-the-ground training.

"Our leaders need to understand how this works, how our faith transforms lives at every level, that leadership is a spiritual journey."

VISION AND CHRISTIAN LEADERSHIP

WHAT IS VISION?

Vision has always been considered an important component in leadership, both in Christian and secular circles. The term usually refers to the ability leaders have to form a plan for the future and to get others excited about their plan. Often, leaders have less a plan, but more of a simple picture of a possible future, and let people sort out the action steps towards that more general picture.

In the Bible, the word vision is more often used as an encounter with God where he imparts special revelation, often intuitively, in dreams, or "in dark sayings." Sometimes visions can be theophanies, where God speaks directly to the visionary. We don't necessarily see a direct connection between visions and leadership explicitly taught in Scripture, but we do see a general correlation—most of the main leaders in biblical times were recipients of visions. Others received visions too, but were not leaders (like Isaiah and Jeremiah). But notice that Paul's qualifications for elders and deacons say nothing about needing to have visions.

Recently, Christian literature has been referring more than ever to vision as the key to effective leadership. However, these books appear to be drawing as much from the new fascination with vision found in secular business literature as from the Bible. I think Christians should read this literature, but must also carefully ask themselves how much of the material comes from the Bible, from common sense, from pragmatics, or from New Age concepts of imaging or visionizing. This last stream is based on the belief that because of the mind's latent power, merely picturing a result may cause it to become real.

If we combine the biblical notion of a vision with the common sense idea of leaders selling people on their directions, we can imagine a hybrid notion of leadership vision. That is, leadership vision is a picture of a better future for a group or individual, informed by the principles of Scripture, and possibly supplemented by direct communication from God. In other words, we can always know in general what God wants for the church because the Bible tells us God's will. On the other hand, God will often supply a special spin on that direction based on local conditions and personalities. Leaders seek out these supplemental insights during times of prayer and reflection.

While I would argue that vision is a useful tool for leaders, I do not see any warrant in Scripture for saying leaders have to be visionaries. We see that key leaders like Moses, Abraham, Paul, David, and Peter all received visions. However, as noted above, when Paul discusses the requirements for leaders, he includes no mention of visions, and focuses on character instead. Probably high-level leaders or pioneering leaders are usually visionaries, but others can lead as well. Non-visionary leaders often work together with visionary leaders. They lead by their example and by persuasion, usually in accord with someone else's vision, and this makes team leadership feasible. Interestingly, the emphasis on vision as the key to leadership in today's leadership literature often leads those same authors to reject the concept of team leadership in favour of the single leader. I think the ability to sell a vision (here in the simple sense of a picture of a possible future) is part of all leading, whether the vision is my own or another's.

HOW DO LEADERS GET VISION?

In my experience, leaders do not have direct control over whether they have vision. Notice that the Bible gives no guidance on how to receive a vision. Instead, visions from God appear to be gifts given at his discretion. A sense of vision for the future seems to come to leaders most often in the context of their Bible study, their prayer, and their reflection about a group or individual. It seems that God stimulates the leader's imagination at certain times to see a desirable future. This often happens during times of prayer, but also could happen, for instance, while listening to another person teach. Sometimes such pictures may come unexpectedly at strange times, and even during sleep.

Leaders should definitely ask God to give them a vision for any individual with whom they work, not to mention for their group. It may be that we already know where our group should head, but lack excitement about that goal. We could call this a lack of vision. Therefore, we are often seeking not just information, but a sense of urgency and passion about goals we already know are right. And this sense of excitement often results from imagining the future as it might develop if people follow God's will, or if they fail to do so. This suggests leaders need both a positive and a negative vision of the future.

To deliver this inner sense of excitement God can use a number of stimuli besides the Bible and prayer. As a leader, you may want to expose yourself to some of these, but always with a critical perspective.

Visiting other churches or ministries. These often have ideas that are new and may become part of your vision. At other times, being in the presence of another model of ministry will stimulate us to a sense of vision that has nothing to do with the way that group does things. In other words, the mere presence of different approaches seems to stimulate a creative part of our own mind, even though our conclusions may be antithetical to the conclusions reached by the group we are visiting. Indeed, seeing another group may serve to remind us why we do things the other way. Always beware of imitating other ministries. Take the time to discover whether their approach is compatible with your own, and remember that groups tend to recount their own ministries in ways that are idealized and stripped of ugliness. Church History. Like other contemporary churches, church history is never authoritative. We may take parts and pieces from different movements in church history while deploring other parts. Many of the best ideas have been around at other times in history, and seeing how God has used such ideas can stir us with excitement and a thirst to try our own hand. Watch for author bias, left out material, and problems that accompanied various movements. Correlate independent sources in order to check on the accuracy of any account. Don't forget to include the New Testament church in your study, and try to assess other movements in light of the example God gave us in the Bible.

Christian or secular biographies. The stories of great men and women are known to fire our imagination and desire to emulate them or avoid their errors. These biographies (especially the ones about missionaries and Christian leaders) are often inaccurate and idealized. It is impossible, for instance, to know how much lust, anxiety, egotism, or bitterness was in the heart of a great missionary, so these parts are left out to one extent or another. Some biographies make it seem like these Christians never did anything but pray and witness. Nevertheless, these books are fun to read and stimulating. Be careful not to go too far in comparing yourself with the idealized biographical characters, becoming defeated as a result.

Hanging around other visionaries. Known visionaries are an important resource to the church. We may not agree with them or want to go the same direction, but we may still find that just listening to them jogs our own mind and spirit in a positive way. Whether these are leaders of other churches, or other home churches, look for opportunities to hang around with a known visionary once in awhile. Again, be sure you aren't just aping a ministry approach that is not compatible with the foundation you have already laid with personnel in your group, or with conditions in your own field of ministry.

Doing a strength and weakness assessment or a force-field analysis of your own group. Doing the hard work of assessing our present state is often the occasion for God to stimulate a new vision for the future. We often suffer from a sense of confusion about where we are at the moment, and I find that such confusion effectively stifles new vision. Only when we are confident that we have a relatively good grip on the present, will we trust our impressions about the future. Strive for realism in this assessment, leaning against any personal tendencies you may have to be overly optimistic or negative. I like doing this in a small group of trusted colleagues.

For group vision, spend time with lost people in your field of ministry. As we hang around lost people, we are better able to empathize and imagine what they would find appealing or at least palatable. Some of our best ideas for fishing come while we are standing in the stream. Christian leaders who rarely hang out with non-Christians and in sinful situations often come up with corny visions that turn off the lost. While at a bar or rock concert, pray to God, "How can we reach these people?"

Go over a journal or other historical materials (including pictures) of your own ministry. I find that reviewing earlier periods in my ministry often causes me to "recapture" some aspect of vision that has slipped away. Pictures of former associates and groups can take you back to a spirit and tone you may have forgotten. Jesus calls on the Ephesians to "remember the former things and repent and do the deeds you did at first." (Rev. 2:5) Some authors warn against trying to relive the past, and we can see why that is never possible. But we can reacquire ethos and pathos from the past if we adapt our methods to present conditions.

After you begin to feel a sense of vision, the next step is to verify it. Spend time praying about it and reading supporting materials, including anything the Bible has to say on the subject. As you reflect over a period of time, God will tend to weaken or strengthen your conviction. Beware of thinking that others can tell you whether your vision is of God. By being a visionary, you are moving out ahead of others. They may resist change or risk, preferring the status quo. Of course a theological or ethical critique from others is perfectly valid to the extent it is based on solid biblical grounds.

THE VISION OF PARENT LEADERS

Any time people engage in an important, responsible undertaking for others' welfare—whether a business, a job, government affairs, or a family—there's a need for clear, competent leadership. The more serious the challenge, the greater the need for someone to direct everyone's efforts in an inspiring, encouraging way towards the ultimate goal.

The real mission for parents is to raise their children towards responsible adulthood. All the dynamics of family life lead to this: what kind of men and women the children will grow to be. No challenge is more important than this, and so great parents emerge in family life as real leaders.

How do they do this? How do fathers and mothers lead their children effectively? To form a picture of parental leadership, let's look at the characteristics of leaders and see how parents fit the profile of leadership in family life.

LEADERS ARE MOVED BY A DISTANT VISION, AND THEY THUS WIN PEOPLE'S RESPECT.

Here's a broad statement that you'll probably agree with: In business and professional life and in affairs of state, our most respected leaders are those who look farthest towards the future and foresee oncoming perils and opportunities. Respected leadership and strategic foresight go hand in hand. The farther and clearer the vision, the greater the respect.

It seems that this dynamic works in successful families, too. Parents—all kinds of men and women with different temperaments—succeed in family life through their confident leadership. Successful parents base their confidence in knowing they have this sacred mission to carry out with their children. They see themselves *raising adults, not children*. They have been called by God to carry out a job, and that holy task is this: to lead their children—with daily sacrificial effort—to grow into confident, responsible, considerate, generous men and women who are committed to live by Christian principles all their lives, no matter what the cost. Being conscious of this mysterious and sacred mission, holding it always before their eyes, is what turns these parents into great men and women themselves, real heroes to their children, and makes their family life together a great, rollicking, beautiful adventure.

Effective parent leaders look at their children and picture them 20 years from now, as grown men and women with job and family responsibilities of their own. They seem to understand a truth of life: Children will tend to grow *up* to our expectations or *down* to them. So, these parent leaders set high ideals for their children's later lives. They think of their children's future along these lines—

- The children will have excellent judgement, especially in the choice of a spouse and the upbringing of their own children.
- They will center their lives in a stable, permanent, happy marriage—raising a great family like the one they grew up in.
- They will succeed in their careers, whatever these may be—doing work they enjoy, putting their powers up against problems for the welfare of others.
- They'll be able to support their families comfortably but not luxuriously, for a life of excess, they know, may destroy their children (the parents' grandchildren).
- They will be generous to friends and those in need.
- They will never live as quitters, slackers, whiners, or cowards—nor will they let their own children live this way.
- They will be nobody's fool or pushover. They will not be swayed by charlatans. They will know malarkey when they see it.
- When they've done wrong, they'll face the truth and apologize. They will not let their pride stand in the way of truth and justice, especially in family life.
- They will be esteemed by all who know them for their honesty, integrity, hard work, generosity, religious commitment, and good humor.
- They will remain close to their brothers and sisters for life, giving and receiving encouragement and support.
- They will live by their parents' principles. They'll have a conscience

for life—the voice of their parents' lessons of right and wrong—and they'll pass these lessons on to their own children.

- Their whole lives will be moved by love—the willingness to endure and overcome anything for the welfare and happiness of others, starting with their family.

ALL LEADERS UNDERSTAND, AND SHUN, THE LAMENTABLE CONSEQUENCES OF NEGLECT.

Consider this: Public monuments are never set up to honor someone who *intended* to do something.

Leaders act. Though they spend time in study and planning, they mostly act. For leaders, study and planning are a ramp-up for action, not a substitute for it.

Moreover, real leaders never let indecision lead to inaction. When confronted with several tough choices of action, they do not shrink back. They brace themselves, choose what they judge as the best way forward, and then set to work as best they can.

Sometimes great leadership means just this: doing the best you can with what you have. If you're climbing a mountain, you sometimes have to backtrack or surmount obstacles or thrash your way through tangled shortcuts—but as long as you keep moving upward, you'll reach the summit. The one thing you don't do is quit. Neglect—to do nothing—is the worst mistake of all.

Parent leaders, too, understand the consequences of neglect. They know they have a job to do—a change to effect—in the minds and hearts of their growing children. And they draw courage to act from foreseeing what awful things could happen to their kids if that job remains undone, if their children retain the flaws and selfishness of childhood into adult life. For instance....

- If our children remain self-centered—"Me first!"—they will neglect or mistreat others, and their marriages and careers will fly apart. If their marriages break up, we would lose our grandchildren, or our grandchildren would grow up in a fatherless home.
- If they have no conscience, they will have no inner force to resist temptation. They could cave in to peer-pressures and meet with disasters: drugs, alcohol abuse, recreational sex, trouble with the law.
- If they never learn to say "please" and "thank you" on their own, without prompting, they will remain as self-centered ingrates. They will neglect or mistreat their spouses and think the world owes them a living.
- If they do not respect their parents' authority, they will have trouble with all other rightful authority: teachers, employers, the law, God Himself.
- If they receive no life-directing guidance from their parents in

childhood, they may desperately need guidance later from parent-substitutes: marriage counselors, physicians, mental-health professionals, even cult gurus.

- If they see life as mostly play, they will treat the automobile as a toy. If they cannot control their tempers, they will fly headlong into "road rage" and treat the car as a weapon. Either way, they could kill or cripple themselves and others.
- If they form no principled framework for assessing people's character, they may marry jerks.
- If they cannot manage their own affairs, they cannot take care of others.
- If they do not keep their promises, they cannot keep commitments—not to spouse, nor children, nor employers.
- If they never learn to set and meet goals, they cannot set and meet ideals.
- If they form a habit of lying, they will someday get fired.
- If they never learn to balance healthy work and play, their lives could shuttle between drudgery and debauchery. If they never learn to be confident producers, they will live as lifelong adolescent consumers.
- If they remain lazy and sloppy in work, they'll get shoved aside by their competition.
- If they see work as "hassle" to be shunned, they will have wobbly, precarious careers—or will see work as adolescents see it: just a source of "spending money."
- If they always expect to have their way, their adult lives will be ravaged by rage and frustration—and their marriages will implode.
- If they sulk and bear grudges, they will muddle through life as smoldering, self-pitying "victims"—and never amount to anything.
- If they remain as egocentric children, they may shun having children of their own.
- If they do not stand for something, they will fall for anything.

Bibliography

A.K. Banerjee: *Art of Leadership*, Lotus Press, 2004.

Angela Wadia: *Broadcast Management in India : Major Guidelines and Policy Frameworks*, Kanishka, Publication, Delhi, 2007.

Arvind Virmani: *Accelerating Growth and Poverty Reduction: A Policy Framework for Indias Development*, Academic Foundation, 2004.

Asit K. Biswas, R. Rangachari and M.M. Sainju: *Ganges-Brahmaputra-Meghna Region : A Framework for Sustainable Development*, The University Press Limited, 2001.

B.L. Gupta: *Competency Framework for Human Resources Management*, Concept, Publication, Delhi, 2011.

Bartosz Porebski: *Building PHP Applications With Symfony Cakephp and Zend Framework*, Wiley India, 2011.

Carolyn Chambers Clark: *Creative Nursing Leadership and Management*, Jones and Bartlett Learning, 2010.

Hrishikes Bhattacharya: *Banking Strategy Credit Appraisal and Lending Decisions : A Risk Return Framework*, Oxford University Press, 2011.

J B Lal: *Economic Tools and Institutional Framework for Forest Development Planning*, International Book, 2005.

Jan L. Carmichael: *Leadership and Management Development*, Chris Collins, Peter Emsell and Jon Haydon, Oxford University Press, 2011.

Jeff Gold: *Gower Handbook of Leadership and Management Development*, Richard Thorpe and Alan Mumford, Gower Publishing Ltd, 2013.

Jogendra Mehta: *Art of Leadership*, Yking Books, 2011.

K. Ravichandran and S. Nakkiran: *Cooperative Entrepreneurship in Action: A Conceptual Framework*, Studera Press, 2015.

Lisa S. Price: *Feminist Frameworks : Building Theory on Violence Against Women*, Aakar Books, 2009.

Nihar Nayak: *Cooperative Security Framework for South Asia*, Pentagon Press, 2013.

Noorjehan N. Ganihar: *Fundamentals of Educational Management : Structural Framework and Monitoring Mechanism*, Global Vision Publication, 2012.

P B Rathod: *Framework of Public Policy : The Discipline and Its Dimensions*, Commonwealth, 2005.

Pawan Kumar Oberoi: *Business Regulatory Framework*, Global Vision, 2011.

Pradeep M Tulachan and Juhani Maki-Hokkonen: *Community Empowerment in Livestock Resource Planning : A Suggested Participatory Policy Framework*, International Centre for Integrated Mountain Development, 2002.

Pradeep S. Chauhan: *Asian Economic and Financial Integration in Global Framework*, New Century, 2009.

Radharaman Agarwal: *Team Leadership and Management*, Oxford Book Company, 2011.

Rakesh Jalal: *Analysing Banking Risk : A Framework*, Cyber Tech Publications, 2012.

Reidar Dale: *Evaluation Frameworks for Development Programmes and Projects,* Sage, Publication, Delhi, 2000.

S Sundar and S K Sarkar: *Framework for Infrastructure Regulation*, TERI Press, 2000.

S.K. Singh: *Leadership and Management Development*, Pearl Books, 2010.

Stefano Mostarda: *Entity Framework 4 In Action*, Marco De Sanctis and Daniele Bochicchio, Dreamtech Press, 2011.

V.C. Pandey: *Framework for ICTs and Teacher Education*, Isha Books, 2005.

Index